THE RADICAL PROBE

MICHAEL W. MILES

THE RADICAL PROBE

The Logic of Student Rebellion

ATHENEUM   *New York*   1971

FOR MY FATHER AND MOTHER

COPYRIGHT © 1971 BY MICHAEL W. MILES
ALL RIGHTS RESERVED
LIBRARY OF CONGRESS CATALOG CARD NUMBER 76–139320
PUBLISHED SIMULTANEOUSLY IN CANADA BY
MC CLELLAND AND STEWART LTD.
MANUFACTURED IN THE UNITED STATES OF AMERICA BY
H. WOLFF, NEW YORK
DESIGNED BY KATHLEEN CAREY
FIRST EDITION

PREFACE

There are in the United States several political and cultural movements having to do with "the young": the New Left, the student movement, the youth culture, and the youth wing of the black liberation movement. All of these are distinguishable, but they overlap and interact in a kaleidoscopic manner. The result is an actual confusion in social manifestation that is reflected in an even greater degree of analytical confusion among spokesmen, publicists, politicians, investigative committees, editorial writers, and the paranoid middle of the intelligentsia.

The focus of this essay is student rebellion; therefore the reform wing of the student movement is mentioned only in passing. As political impact is the criterion for consideration, the cultural movement is regarded only from the point of view of its political influence. The heart of the essay deals with the black and white student movements which are led by the black left and the New Left. These movements are also the heart of the youth movement and the whole of its potential for lasting significance. Student rebellion disrupts the institutions for higher education which are crucial installations of the "knowledge industry." The knowledge industry is the most dynamic sector of modern capitalism, and the rebellion of students is, ultimately, a product of the application of industrial methods to education, culture, science, and other fields of knowledge. This thesis accounts, in my opinion, for the international scope of the contemporary student movement which has appeared in every country undergoing this stage of industrialization. Before our own era, student movements were typically a phenomenon of pre-industrial societies. Rebellion in these advanced sectors, organized by the left, presages a new revolutionary opposition in the industrial West that can not only go beyond the social integration of the post-war era but transcend the scheme of politics which opened with World War I and the Bolshevik Revolution. This is a momentous possibility, particularly for that politically depressed area, the United States of America.

The purpose of this essay is to explain the origins of the student movement, the dynamics of rebellion and reaction, the revolutionary nationalism of black students, the industrialization of education. It is not a polemic against student rebels; it is not a sentimental tract. But in the age of mass education and mass communication, more than ever, explanations and counter-explanations of social phenomena are a part of the political process they attempt to describe; and that includes this book.

I would like to thank a number of friends who have helped me in the writing of this book—Christopher Jones, Richard Hathaway, John Alexander, and Francis and Ellen Voigt. Special thanks to Donnie.

East Ryegate, Vermont
August 1970

CONTENTS

THE RADICAL PROBE

*. . . a sudden burst of sunshine seemed to
illumine the Statue of Liberty, so that he saw
it in a new light, although he had sighted it long
before. The arm with the sword rose up as if
newly stretched aloft, and round the figure blew
the free winds of heaven.*

Franz Kafka   AMERIKA

1 THE DYNAMICS
OF STUDENT REBELLION

THE OFFICIAL THEORY of the dynamics of student rebellion—elite manipulation—runs like this: A *hard core* of
student radicals decides to move against the university. Since
they are revolutionary nihilists, these hard-core radicals de-
spise reforms in university policy or structure, but use these
issues as *pretexts* to mobilize student *moderates,* who are
young idealists genuinely concerned about such matters (and
therefore should be listened to and not alienated by faculty
and administration). The objective of the hard core is to *destroy the university* as a form of sabotage of the American
democratic system. They proceed to seize a building or perform some other irresponsible act of force, managing to gain
a naïve following which is a *small minority* of the total student population. The point of the initial act of force is to
provoke a repression—police intervention at the request of
the administration—which will immediately mobilize against

the authorities a large number of liberals and moderates who were previously uncommitted. Acting according to plan and still in effective control of events, the hard core calls a strike against the university on the basis of the police action; the strike disrupts classes and sometimes closes down the university for a time, while at the same time *radicalizing* a large number of students.

Although this explanation of the political dynamics of student revolt purports to be a neutral description of events, any description of what happens carries with it an implicit explanation—and a value judgment—of the event. The thrust of this account is to discredit students for a "democratic society" as a manipulative elite which employs undemocratic tactics and has undemocratic objectives. The constant reiteration of the phrase "hard core" places the explanation in the school of faculty/administration criticism that perceives the student left as neo-totalitarian. The intent is to recall to the academic and public minds the image of Communist practice in the 1930s and to convince both that they are witnessing a reprise of the Red Decade. In any case of student revolt, the practitioners of the elite-manipulation theory will ferret out those radicals who take the hardest line and attribute to them the controlling role in events. If this is momentarily implausible, it is argued that the dynamics of events ultimately favors left authoritarians. This hypothesis is maintained by analogy to the French and Russian revolutions, although student rebellion hardly constitutes social revolution.

In some of its formulations, the elite-manipulation explanation of campus rebellion is simple conspiracy theory. In its hearings on "campus unrest" in 1969, the U.S. Senate's Government Operations Committee devoted its deliberations to the concepts of "hard-core revolutionaries" and "outside agitators." Senator Karl Mundt (R—North Dakota), a McCarthyite politician in the early 1950s, was determined to discover a "master plan." Like-minded colleagues in the Congress wrote anti-riot provisions, applicable to student demonstrations, into the Civil Rights Act of 1968, and these provisions depend upon an outside-agitators rationale for their operation. Commending the use of anti-riot legislation against student rebellion to the Detroit Bar Association at its May Day "Annual Law Day Dinner" in 1969, U.S. Attorney-General John Mitchell observed: "We have substantial information confirming the widely accepted belief that several major university disturbances have been incited by members of a small core of professional militants who make it their tragic occupation to convert peaceable student dissatisfaction into violence and confrontation." [1]

The outside-agitators theory is not confined to the official right. As president of San Francisco State College during the 1968–69 strike organized by black and "Third World" (Oriental and Latin) students, S. I. Hayakawa, who styled himself a law-and-order liberal, made common cause with Governor Ronald Reagan's hard line against student demonstrations, and was forthwith apotheosized by the California right. When an interviewer from *U.S. News and World Report* asked, "Dr. Hayakawa, is a conspiracy developing to disrupt higher education in America?" Hayakawa replied, "That seems to be the case. Certain familiar faces appear and reappear. . . ." As evidence, Hayakawa cited a phone call from the police chief of Chico, California, who asserted that in demonstrations at Chico State College he had arrested some of the same people who were demonstrating at San Francisco State.

Just how far out outside agitators can be has been indicated by an address to school superintendents in 1969 by Adolph Berle, Jr. An emeritus law professor of Columbia University and an advisor to Democratic presidents, including Franklin D. Roosevelt as Asssistant Secretary of State, Berle is best known for his authorship, with Gardiner Means, of the thesis of the "seperation of ownership and control" within the modern corporation. "Forces of student unrest," he said,

[1] *Vital Speeches*, June 1, 1969, p. 499.

"probably originated in the political and propaganda warfare set up by the Chinese Communist Government six or eight years ago—an aftermath of the Korean War—before its quarrel with the Soviet Union became active." [2] Liberals of internationalist persuasion seem particularly inclined to take the broad view of outside student agitation. After a 1969 tour of Latin America for the Nixon Administration, where he was welcomed by riots, Nelson Rockefeller called the fact-finding trip a "tremendous success," and attributed the demonstrations against him to "highly organized militant forces in many cases directed from outside this hemisphere." Pressed for evidence, Rockefeller cited a twenty-two-year-old Swiss student, "one of the leaders in the uprising in France," who had come to Latin America with "specific instructions to organize student riots." [3]

It would be unfair—in the extreme—to attribute the crude theory of outside agitation to university administrations themselves. They have another explanation: inside agitation. In its "Declaration on Campus Unrest," the American Council on Education, an umbrella organization of higher educational associations, noted: "On the undisturbed campuses and among the majority of orderly students, however, there are widely shared discontents which extremists are at times able to manipulate to destructive ends." Written by officials of California, Harvard, Michigan, Minnesota, and Wisconsin universities and the Carnegie and Ford foundations, the statement denounced student leftists as a "minute group of destroyers" and stated, "Students and faculty are increasingly aware of the true nature of this group and are moving to deal with its destructive tactics." [4]

The inside agitators, according to Berkeley Chancellor Roger W. Heyns in a *Newsweek* interview, want to "seize control of the university or destroy it, one or the other. I

[2] *The New York Times,* July 17, 1969.
[3] *Newsweek,* June 16, 1969.
[4] "Declaration on Campus Unrest," American Council on Education, press release, April 4–5, 1969.

don't think they much care. They're using the race issue as a good cover for it." In the case of the Third World Liberation Front's demands in the winter of 1969 for open admissions for non-white students and an autonomous ethnic-studies program, Heyns offered his judgment that the minute group of destroyers consisted of ten or twelve people out of a student population of 27,500. These were the "hard-core people who were trying to create another Columbia."

As for the original Columbia, the administration there also favored an inside-agitators explanation (Truman: "nihilist hard core of 35"). It suffered an embarrassment when its own impartial fact-finding Cox Commission rejected the "view that ascribes the April and May disturbances primarily to a conspiracy of student revolutionaries." As the radical movement has grown in influence, however, there have been new noises from the realm of commissions. In a public statement at the time of the student uprisings of spring 1969, the National Commission on the Causes and Prevention of Violence declared: "A small but determined minority, however, aims not at reform but at the destruction of existing institutions. These are the nihilists." These nihilists, the Commission explained, are the "agent that converts constructive student concern into mindless mob hysteria." [5]

Although simple conspiracy theory of the outside/inside-agitator variety will do for political purposes, it clearly will not serve as academic analysis. It grossly overstates the influence of the "hard core"; it seriously understates the volatility of political events; it is utterly confused about the nature of radical politics. An academically respectable theory of elite manipulation has to purge itself of the demonological qualities of pure conspiracy theory while preserving the essence. In his account of the Columbia uprising, Daniel Bell, a Columbia sociologist, is careful to do justice to the inchoate quality of the student rebellion: "Clearly, neither Rudd nor any of the SDS leaders had a specific tactical plan. . . ." Thanks

[5] *The New York Times*, June 9, 1969.

largely to the militant tactics of the black students who took
Hamilton Hall and the hard-line response of the administration which called in the police, the Students for a Democratic
Society found themselves leading a major campus revolt
which had emerged out of "unplanned and often accidental
events." Bell adapts the conceptual framework of his *Marx-
ian Socialism in the United States* to explain the degree of
student support for the building occupations and the subsequent strike. Once the first two buildings had been occupied
by a small group of students, there was a "contagion of excitement"—in fact, a "classic illustration of the contagion
phenomenon of mass that Gustave LeBon described so
graphically in *Psychologie des Foules* in 1895"—which led to
the seizure of other buildings and the flow of other students
into the wake of the leaders. Since the enormity of the commitment in action could hardly be justified by the relatively
minor questions which were the ostensible purpose of the insurrection, non-radical students who had acted on impulse—
the majority of the students in the buildings—had to ration-
alize their actions after the fact. Because only a radical world
view could justify the magnitude of the act, these students—
"most of them liberal, moderate, and pacifist, and not members of SDS"—underwent out of necessity a "conversion experience" to the extremist way of seeing things. When the
police bust came with its regrettable violence, liberals and
moderates outside the buildings were mobilized in support of
a student strike. The administration blundered into this tactic because it, like the radical converts, was traumatized by
the radical challenge to its legitimacy. According to Bell, the
Kirk-Truman administration failed to understand the political situation in two respects: (1) by not distinguishing between the "hard-core SDS members" and their good-hearted
followers, and (2) by playing into SDS's hands with police
force. There was a group, Bell continues, which understood
the situation. This was the Ad Hoc Faculty Group, the "third
force," which stepped forward with a policy of tactical con-

cessions to split the SDS leadership from its following, and which steadfastly opposed police intervention for reasons of political strategy and liberal principle. Truly *ad hoc*, with no mandate from the general faculty, the AHFG was guided by a steering committee consisting of "individuals who were politically liberal in orientation, who had studied radical movements, and who had some experience in the study of 'comparative politics.'" [6]

Just as the outside-agitator and conspiracy theories, Bell's theory of radical conversion employs the basic vocabulary of elite manipulation—hard core, nihilists, destruction of the university, pretexts, moderates, provocation, repression, radicalization. The point of the explanation, like every variety of elite-manipulation theory, is to deny the presence of a radical *movement* in the universities; the thrust of the theory is to refute the evidence of the senses. In the case of Columbia, more than 500 undergraduates were arrested in the police bust, and the clear implication was that for 10 percent of the students of the college—at a minimum—the university administration had lost its ruling legitimations. These students no longer recognized the authority of the university, although they might concede its power to retaliate. But for elite-manipulation theorists, the analytical problem is to dissolve the radical movement. The procedure is to unpeel layer after layer of the movement and as each is unpeeled to categorize it as something other than radical—"moderates," "liberals," "pacifists"—until what is left is the "hard core," that irreducibly bad seed which is totally indigestible. This treatment is accorded not only to those students of ambiguous political affiliation who have remained outside the buildings and perhaps supported a subsequent boycott of classes, but to those students whom common-sense logic would consider of a rather nonconformist bent—those who seize university buildings, reconstitute them as student communes, and fly red-and-

[6] Daniel Bell, "Columbia and the New Left," *The Public Interest,* Fall, 1968, pp. 61–102.

black flags. Liberal analysts perceive within the occupied buildings and the disruptive demonstrations themselves only a few *real* radicals. Their quest is for the hard-core professionals, the revolutionary cadres, the sinister organization. In this enterprise they succeeded in finding, before its disintegration, the Students for a Democratic Society. At this point, the analysts are faced with the difficulty of explaining how transparently subversive organizations could mobilize large numbers of students on hundreds of campuses. So in drawing up their "contingency plans" (the Eisenhower Commission's phrase), university administrators and the experts at the Orwell Institute are forced to pose some queer questions: How radical are the moderates? How large is the small minority? How soft is the hard core? How real are the false issues?

An alternative to the elite-manipulation explanation is the "radical probe" analysis of the dynamics of student rebellion. The distinction between these theories is politically important because the student left acquires legitimacy as it acquires student support and loses legitimacy as it loses support. These gains and losses are registered not only in action but in later interpretations which may aim either to legislate or to repeal the radical movement after the fact through the designation of various forms of support as "radical," "liberal," or "moderate." The disagreement between elite-manipulation and radical-probe theories turns on the use of political language.

One source of confusion is the use of the words "moderate" and "militant." These are relative terms. There are "moderate" and "militant" wings of every political formation, including those of the revolutionary left. If there are moderate and militant positions on a tactical question in a radical demonstration, it is possible to transform verbally the tactical moderates into substantive moderates. In such an analysis, it may appear that liberal Republicanism has taken a turn to the left. In this book, "radical" will mean opposition to corporate capitalism as a system, while "liberal" will mean support for social change within the established social order, and "moderate" the equivocal center position between liberal support for change and conservative opposition to it. Like "moderate," "liberal" is a slippery word because there is a direct-action liberalism which approves the use of radical means for reformist ends, while official liberalism may shade into a high conservativism opposed to reform even by legal means. Still, the mainstream of liberalism, including student liberalism, continues to disassociate itself from illegal tactics and favors reform within the established order by legal means.

The beginning of an alternative explanation to the elite-manipulation theory is a reconstitution of the phenomenon in order to see what is there: not a hard core, but a movement. A "radical probe" analysis has to grant the elite role of radical activists in student rebellion, but places this elite function in the context of a mass movement. In this view, the dynamics of a social movement is decisive and not the operations of a restricted elite, while the relationship between the "elite" and the "masses" is not of radicals to moderates, but of radical activists to a radical constituency. The objective of this radical movement is furthermore not "destruction" but socialist revolution, and ultimately the construction of a "socialist university in a socialist society," while its issues are not pretexts but real criticisms which are related to the larger objective of a socialist order. Since these objectives are revolutionary, the movement's tactics of direct action are an effort of rational adjustment of means to ends, and not the expression of an urge to destruction. In these several respects, the radical-probe analysis substitutes new categories for those of the elite-manipulation explanation. This analysis does *not* imply, however, that the existence of a radical mass movement—with social justifications as well as social causes—necessarily results in a democratic movement that transcends political manipulation.

Without question, the precipitating act for a student rebellion has been carried out by a limited number of activists, often SDS members, who have been few in number compared to the later level of participation. This initial act is the radical probe, the key act in the strategy of "confrontation politics." This act—the occupation of a building, a disruptive demonstration, or whatever—is what the authorities call an act of force or even an act of violence. The probe itself has not generally been violent in fact. The probe courts violence, however, because violence is a possible result of the political process which follows. But this result is always problematic. What is not in question is the *test*—of the will and real constituency of the authorities, of the commitments and values of the local community. To succeed, the test must raise issues, both real and symbolic, which are of crucial concern to the community and which the authorities have not raised and will not raise themselves. An initial probe which is also an act of violence against persons is usually a prescription for failure, since the potential constituency will probably repudiate the act. This potential constituency often does not materialize in any case because the issues do not strike home, the tactics are disapproved as premature or inappropriate, the personalities of the activists are not respected, or whatever. In other cases, the potential constituency does support the probe in force, and a rebellion may result.

These activists are the proverbial hard core. The implication of the hard-core notion is that the activists constitute an organizational cadre. This supposition is false. The activists themselves are part of a large, rather amorphous movement—the "New Left." By and large, the New Left has recruited most of its members from the universities and found its only radical constituency to date on these same campuses, although it is not only a student movement and does not operate solely on the campuses. Student rebellion represents a temporary merger of two forces: the New Left movement and a student population of which a significant proportion is consciously radical but not necessarily activist.

From its founding in 1962 to its disintegration in 1969, the Students for a Democratic Society was the most significant organizational expression of the New Left. It was never an organized cadre, however, and its efforts to transform itself into a revoutionary cadre simply resulted in its disintegration into its component parts. Instead of a hard core, SDS turned out to consist of a Revolutionary Youth Movement (which soon split into the Weathermen and RYM II); the Progressive Labor Party, a Maoist splinter of the Communist Party, U.S.A.; and a smaller number of anarchists, libertarians, and independent radicals. The former two groups were quite definitely Marxist, but the Marxism itself came in several varieties: Maoism, orthodox Marxism-Leninism, neo-Marxism, and Pop Leninism. SDS, then, was not a "hard core" and its factional components were often reflected in its campus chapters. Nor was SDS the New Left. Trotskyist groups— namely, the Independent Socialist Club and the Young Socialist Alliance—have wielded influence within the New Left movement, while draft resistance groups, such as The Resistance, and anti-war organizations have probably wielded considerably more. There have also been a multitude of *ad hoc* groups devoted to particular questions, such as women's liberation, poverty organizing, and the like. Finally, the black student left, although remaining aloof from white leftists, has nonetheless wielded enormous influence over the New Left's evolution on campus. The black student left, too, has disparately expressed itself in Black Student Unions, Third World Liberation Fronts, Afro-American Societies, and so on. Though the activists may play an elite role in campus political action, they are a circulating elite which moves in and out of active politics and never comprises a definite personnel. The New Left lives a fugitive organizational existence. Although the drift to Marxism-Leninism has been undeniable, the New Left has failed to develop the characteristic Marxist-Leninist organization, the vanguard party, and thus continues to operate as an amorphous movement unified only by two general principles: (1) an opposition to corporate capitalism, and (2) a commitment to direct-action tactics.

These realities were reflected at Columbia. SDS did call the initial demonstrations in April 1968, which were designed to break a ban on indoor demonstrations and thus challenge the administration's authority. This probe did not involve, however, a plan to occupy any building indefinitely. The "hard-core" SDS leadership was divided into two factions: the "action faction" committed to *ad hoc* militant action and led by Mark Rudd, newly elected SDS chairman, and the "praxis axis," devoted to more considered educational tactics and led by the former leadership. This division was further complicated by the incipient Progressive Labor faction. While SDS could claim not more than 50 members, 500 people actually appeared for the demonstration. Among these were members of The Resistance group on campus and of the Citizenship Council, an organization which had challenged the right of the university to construct a gym on public park land.

The dynamics of student revolt naturally involve political accident and popular spontaneity not originating with the radical leadership. The Columbia demonstrators found themselves occupying Low Library after a series of incidents in which neither Rudd nor the SDS leadership provided much guidance. It was the Students' Afro-American Society which took the first decisive move of occupying Hamilton Hall and evicting the white leftists, who almost randomly occupied Low Library. The initial Low Library occupation was not carried out simply by "hard-core SDS members," as Bell claims, but by some 250 people, only 50 of whom at most could have been SDS members. This group later took over a second building, Mathematics Hall, but architecture students and social-science graduate students, having no connection with SDS, also spontaneously occupied two more buildings, Avery Hall and Fayerweather Hall. In the end, almost a thousand people were occupying five buildings.

A minimum of 10 percent of Columbia undergraduates—those who entered the buildings—can be regarded as radicals.

During the radical action, several student service organizations conducted an opinion survey of over 5,000 students outside the buildings. In the poll, the results of which were similar to a later after-the-fact survey by Columbia's Bureau of Applied Social Research, 25 percent of the students outside the buildings supported the *tactics* of SDS and the SAS (Students' Afro-American Society). Minimally, these active sympathizers with the revolt were left-liberals and were the group most probably "radicalized" by the seizure of buildings, police repression, and a class boycott. A still larger percentage of students, 40 percent, favored only a class boycott, a less militant but still an immoderate tactic. These students were liberals, perhaps, but hardly moderates. On the issues themselves—an end to university construction of the gym and to its relationship to the Institute for Defense Analyses—65 percent of students polled were in favor. Thus, an additional 25 percent of the undergraduate body which opposed the tactics still favored the issues. These students came closest to a traditional liberal position, although their sensitivity to military power and racial injustice placed them in a "New Politics" position. An actually moderate position would presumably have involved a *compromise* on the issues, while conservatism would have entailed support of the administration. By the questions asked in the poll, there was no way to distinguish these positions among the remaining 35 percent of undergraduate students.[7]

Surveys of the Free Speech Movement in Berkeley yield similar results. That question was complicated by the fact that the conflict was fought over a liberal issue (on-campus political advocacy as a category of free speech) at a stage of the student movement when direct-action tactics were employed for liberal, civil-rights causes. There were approximately 1,000 active participants in the FSM—somewhat less than 4 percent of the total student enrollment, but almost

[7] Jerry L. Avorn *et al.*, *Up Against the Ivy Wall* (New York, 1968), p. 163.

twice that percentage of the undergraduate population. One third of Berkeley's students supported both the tactics and goals of the movement. Another 30 percent favored only the goals, while 22 percent opposed both the tactics and the goals of the movement. A separate survey of the participants in a militant FSM demonstration indicated that somewhat more than one third of the activists subscribed, even in 1964, to socialist politics.[8]

The radical student movement, then, is a minority, but it is not a "small minority" even in advance of any particular student rebellion. Any "conversion experience" once the issue is joined is impotent to persuade people to join a militant demonstration or cross the threshold into an occupied building; radical convictions are required to face the substantial risks, both short- and long-range.

It is instructive to compare New Left tactics with Communist practice of the 1930s. When the Communist Party wished to bring reform-minded individuals into the left opposition, it was common practice to set up "front groups" which purported to be reformist organizations in which revolutionary politics played no part. This is not the style of "the Movement" (as the New Left describes itself), which broadcasts its radical and/or revolutionary politics in the most explicit terms. The element of deception—"duping the innocents"—is absent. It would require extraordinary naïveté for students to join a building occupation or a disruptive demonstration without understanding that the ultimate issue is the legitimacy of the authorities, when all the while red and black flags are flying, radical literature is being cranked out in reams, and the local establishment is being denounced in countless harangues. The implications of the commitment are transparently clear.

There is little positive evidence for the "conversion" thesis

[8] Robert H. Somers, "The Mainsprings of the Rebellion," and Glenn Lyonns, "The Police Car Demonstration," in S. M. Lipset and Sheldon S. Wolin, eds., *The Berkeley Student Revolt* (New York, 1965), pp. 530–59 and 519–30.

of Bell and others. In his study of young radicals in the "Vietnam Summer" project of 1967, Kenneth Keniston found: "Missing as well in this group are those precipitate conversions that suggest a sudden re-ordering of the personality, accompanied by the suppression of what was previously dominant." [9] The absence of evidence for radical-conversion theories, the substantial personal risks of militant demonstrations, and the clearly left-wing auspices of these actions all indicate that a large majority of the participants in militant actions are radicals.

The evidence suggests that 10 percent at a minimum of the student population at elite universities may be aligned with, if not continuously active in, the radical movement in advance of any particular "contagion of excitement." The Katz-Sanford survey estimates 15 percent at a highly activated campus. This percentage can be reduced by drowning the movement in the total student population of America, including Catholic colleges, military academies, vocational/technical schools, denominational colleges, and so on. But even 2 percent of the total constitutes the formidable number of 150,000 radical constituents. This procedure also ignores the social dynamics of the situation, which are more likely to emanate outward from the elite universities than the other way around; the method constitutes a sociological freeze on a historical process. If the Columbia and Berkeley surveys are any indication, another 25 percent of the student population at the elite universities does not oppose direct action on principle and composes a potential constituency for radicalism. Some 28 percent of all students, according to a Gallup poll, have already demonstrated for some cause or another. In a survey undertaken for *Fortune*—which, like the *Wall Street Journal*, can usually be relied upon for a certain cool realism—Daniel Yankelovich Inc. discovered the most disquieting statistical profile yet. According to the Yankelovich firm, 3.3 percent of *all* college youth considered them-

[9] Kenneth Keniston, *Young Radicals* (New York, 1968), p. 112.

selves "revolutionaries," while another 9.5 percent were self-described "radical dissidents" and 39.3 percent were "reformers." The results of all such opinion surveys are, of course, inconclusive. They assume that the respondents understand the political meaning of these terms and are willing to act on them. Nonetheless, these results dispose of the 2-percent-nihilist hypothesis.[10]

If its active sympathizers are included, the radical movement can mobilize under favorable conditions 35 percent of the students on the campuses of the elite universities—and some non-elite universities as well—in the United States. This is a radical plurality for most practical purposes. Since 30 percent or more of the undergraduates also support the radical causes but not its tactics, they are effectively neutralized politically, and can only be mobilized against the radicals by an astute administration. Of the remaining 35 percent or so, a good half are moderates and can be counted on to support the administration only in the manner of moderates—namely, moderately. In adverse circumstances, a university administration may thus be left with the unequivocal support of only the conservative students, or 15 percent or so of the student body. These percentages are, of course, only rough estimates which reflect the experience of several universities and also represent the radical movement at high tide.

Only the student conservatives who oppose both the ends and the means of the radicals support the administration forthrightly. Within the ranks of student conservatives, there is a small student right which is willing to take action. In every student rebellion, there appears some avatar of counter-revolt—the Students for Law and Order on Campus during the FSM, the Majority Coalition at Columbia in 1968, the Young Americans for Freedom charging into the lines of the left demonstrators at Wisconsin in 1969. According to the sociological surveys, student rightists are typically of Republican and Protestant parentage, whose child-rearing is authori-

[10] *Fortune,* June 1969, pp. 73–4.

tarian and achievement-oriented. In college, they are concentrated in the business, technical, and professional curricula.[11] The true stomping grounds of the student right are in the South and West outside the major universities, but in periods of student revolt at the major institutions, student rightists, particularly athletes and fraternity men, have been the activists in small counter-revolts. Philip Luce, who moved from the Maoism of Progressive Labor to the All-American variety of rightism without apparant psychological disorientation, has recommended that the right organize in fraternities, athletic teams, church organizations, and the like. But the efforts of the student right to mobilize the Silent Majority have been futile, since in the universities this majority is on the other side.

The elite-manipulation theory begins to take on relevance only after a student rebellion is under way and the mobilized forces of the student left and the administration confront each other. It is after the student left has developed a visible constituency that it may be expected to create popular democratic forms, and that its failures in this regard are most evident. The student communes at Columbia were an effort in this direction, but functioned at the mercy of the steering committee which controlled the flow of information into the buildings and interpreted the course of events outside. In the composition of the steering committee, SDS was heavily represented and a manipulation controversy arose over the steering committee's failure to circulate to the other buildings a proposal, originating in Fayerweather Hall, which went against the policy of SDS. The Fayerweather proposals suggested that a demand for equal punishment of all occupants should be substituted for the amnesty demand, on the grounds that equal punishment would prevent selective reprisals against the leadership and clarify the radical commit-

[11] See the discussion of the survey literature by Seymour Martin Lipset and Philip G. Atlbach, "Student Politics and Higher Education in the United States," in S. M. Lipset, ed., *Student Politics* (New York, 1967), pp. 199–253.

ment to social justice. In his account, Bell regards this episode as the crucial instance of the hard core manipulating the
moderates. Since the Ad Hoc Faculty Group had proposed
equal punishment as the basis for a negotiated settlement,
Bell portrays the Fayerweather proposal as an effort by the
moderates to achieve a negotiated settlement, which is sabo-
taged by the hard-core SDS, intent on repression. However,
the Fayerweather representative who argued the proposal to
the steering committee was herself an SDS member. The
proposal was offered by Fayerweather not in the spirit of
compromise but because the demand for amnesty was considered a plea for mercy and thus absurd on radical principles.
The Fayerweather rebels believed that the administration
would reject the equal-punishment principle in any case, and
also favored the addition of several new demands to the original six. These demands, including one for student/faculty
control of the university, raised the political ante considerably
and would have placed a compromise even further out of
reach. The case of SDS manipulation is genuine, but it signi-
fied a conflict between two policies, both of which were radical, and not a case of the moderate masses trying to come to
terms.

Since compromise is not the soul of radical politics, there is
always the large possibility that negotiations will fail and the
police will intervene. It is at *this* point of police intervention
—and official violence—rather than in the radical demonstrations themselves, that the traditional liberals and moderates
are brought into the affair. Wary of radical tactics and the
leftist formulation of the issues, the moderates and doubting
liberals swing into support on the issues of police violence
and due process in discipline arising from revolt. During the
period of the class boycotts and other broad-based protests
after the police bust, new organizations have often appeared
to represent the student liberals and moderates. The Students for a Restructured University was such an organization
during the Columbia strike. The "Mem Church Group" at

Harvard and the Barton Hall Assembly at Cornell appeared during the radical demonstrations themselves.

This brief schematizaton of student revolt, taking Columbia as a test case, has established three main propositions: (1) that the "hard core" is a fiction; (2) that the student movement has the characteristically volatile and inchoate quality of a mass social movement; and (3) that the New Leftists have a *radical* constituency in the universities as well as influence on the liberal and moderate students. A corollary of this analysis is that the radical issues have substantial validity and cannot be regarded simply as "pretexts." These issues, which will be taken up in detail in Chapter III, center on two main aspects of university functioning: the universities' relationships with the military/industrial complex (and thus with the Vietnam War and "U.S. imperialism"), and the universities' "institutional racism" reflected in its curriculum, admissions, and real-estate and investment policies.

Unfortunately, none of these characteristics of the radical student movement—characteristics which it shares with most significant radical social movements in history—requires that it be democratic either in action or in result. This outline of student revolt also applies mainly to the earlier stages of radical action at an institution, when the antagonists are the student left and the university administration and faculty. At a later stage, the student left has tended to lose touch with its constituency, not to say reality, while state authorities have entered the contest with massive police force (see section 2 of this chapter, and Chapter V). These factors have resulted in a volatile combination of inactive demoralization and availability for instant mobilization, usually against the national authorities in off-campus demonstrations or in on-campus uprisings against the "over-reaction" of state forces. The University of California at Berkeley, the main center of protest from 1964 to 1968, reached this stage by 1967. Other institutions have lately reached—or have still to reach—this same situation, since the student movement became a national phenomenon only in the 1967–68 school year, when over 100 colleges and universities experienced protests. The movement leaped to a new level of significance in 1968–69, when over 500 institutions experienced disruptive protests. In 1969–70, protests were just as numerous, spreading to many colleges, community colleges, and universities which had never had student protest.

The increasing use of state police and National Guard during 1969–70 increased the probability of violent confrontations and protests. In 1969, left terrorists also entered the lists with bombings and arsons. Their actions on and off the campus were essentially spectacular protests and had little effect on the mobilization of mass action. Mass political action and paramilitary operations are different political species; the essentially non-violent "radical probe" of this essay, which sometimes results in violent developments on either side, is characteristic of *successful* mobilizations of the student masses. The lonely infatuation of the New Left with terrorism is a separate subject.

I. THE RESPONSE: THE OLIVE BRANCH
AND THE ARROWS

The administrative response to the radical probe is a species of "political realism." This realism is reductionist. In their analysis of the student movement, university administrations employ, as we have seen, some variation of the elite-manipulation theory, the thrust of which is to dissolve the student movement before the eyes. Their response follows logically from the analysis: (1) identify the hard core, isolate it, and eliminate it; and (2) identify the responsible elements of student opposition, channel them, assimilate them (by substantial reforms, if necessary). Virtually all the variations in administrative response result from tactical differences within this formula. There are large discrepancies in the per-

ception of the "hard core" and "responsible dissent"; there
are disagreements over the level of reform necessary to channel opposition. But all are agreed on the necessity for this
general strategy.

The basic elements of administrative analysis, rhetoric, and
response have changed not at all since the Free Speech
Movement of 1964. Clark Kerr's strategy was a classic exercise. In their response, administrations employ a democratic
rhetoric, although universities are non-democratic bureaucratic organizations. They also employ an open society rationale, although the openness of most institutions of higher education consists more in the variety of cultural entertainments
than in actual political rights and due process for students.
Although, as chancellor of the Berkeley campus, Clark Kerr
won the Alexander Meiklejohn academic-freedom award for
his defense of faculty in the loyalty-oath controversy of the
early 1950s, one of his first acts upon assuming the presidency
of the university system in 1959 was to restrict student political rights. The Kerr Directives required that student governments be under the authority of the campus chancellor and
that student organizations have faculty sponsors. They also
forbade both student government and student organizations
to take positions on off-campus issues, or to have purposes
"incompatible" with the objectives of the university.

Nonetheless, Kerr told the university community in 1964
that the "university, which has always stood for democratic
principles, including observance of the law, expects faculty,
staff, and students to carry on the orderly processes of the
university and to reject what has become an FSM attempt at
anarchy" [12] In his defense of university policy Kerr noted
that the university employed "wide consultation" in its effort
to evolve "constructive solutions." There were, he asserted,
"channels of communication" which the Free Speech Movement had ignored. "When patience and tolerance and rea-

[12] "Statement by President Clark Kerr," in Lipset and Wolin, p.
245.

sonableness and decency have been tried," Kerr explained, "yet democratic processes continue to be forsaken by the FSM in favor of anarchy, then the process of law enforcement takes over. This nation is devoted to freedom under law, not to anarchy under a willful minority, whether that minority be radical students in the north or white supremacists in the south. The ends of neither group justify the means they employ." [13]

In the 1969 student rebellions, the limits of the discussion of student rebellion in the national press were defined by the question: How are we to "deal with" them? Conservatives and reactionaries were in favor, naturally, of cracking down. In California, Max Rafferty, Superintendent of Public Instruction and unsuccessful Republican candidate for the U.S. Senate in 1968, was in favor of "cleaning out" the hippies, the subversives, and their ultra-liberal, soft-on-Communism professors. The liberals thought that a hasty conclusion. True, there were some subversive elements in the universities, but ill-considered action might be counter-productive. Repressive measures might actually increase the level of student rebellion by driving liberal students into the camp of the radicals. It was especially necessary not to reduce indiscriminately the level of public support for higher education, since national prosperity was related to the welfare of the universities.

In his new role of syndicated columnist, Hubert Humphrey sounded the liberal trumpet: "The time has come for men and women who prize civil liberties and academic freedom to take a public stand against the coalition of destruction that is terrorizing American classrooms and campuses. It is time to act." The "coalition of destruction," Humphrey explained, was the anti-intellectual right and the student left. "Because of the excesses of a hard-core minority of recalcitrant radicals," the former Vice-President noted, "the entire structure of federal, state, and private financial support to in-

[13] *Ibid.*, p. 247.

stitutions of higher learning is now imperiled." But in these times of trouble it was necessary to steer between the "clear need for discipline and the grave dangers of mindless repression." Otherwise, there was the danger of increasing tensions, damaging university autonomy, and reducing the level of funding. For this reason, the universities should handle their own problems and discipline and, when necessary, make use of local police forces and court injunctions. Humphrey's remarks were not simply negative: "We must not close our ears to what the present generation of students is saying." "Constructive reform" was of the essence. And not only that: "I strongly urge the creation of a national commission on the problems and promises of higher education. . . ." [14]

Within this context, there was much discussion in the press in 1968–69 of how various university administrators were doing. First, there was the hard line. Its most famous exponent was S. I. Hayakawa at San Francisco State, who shot the works: mobile police force, dismissals, and tough rhetoric. Hayakawa became a political hero; however, he also managed to mobilize a large percentage of the college faculty and even the San Francisco labor unions for the student opposition. In a settlement, he and the trustees of the state college system conceded—verbally, at least—to the student rebels much of what they wanted: a black-studies department and the promise of an ethnic-studies school. Official policy evaluation: a media triumph, a mixed success in fact. At Columbia the previous spring, Grayson Kirk called in the police but only after several days' delay while negotiations were undertaken. During the delay, student opposition seemed to grow, and the indefinitely postponed police bust came, finally, as a great shock. Policy evaluation: a failure, since the delay in the use of force seemed to legitimatize the radicals. At Harvard, Nathan Pusey avoided Kirk's error and called in the police immediately. Yet a large part of the university still

[14] Hubert H. Humphrey, "Repression's Gaining Speed," *Nashville Tennessean*, May 18, 1969.

went on strike against him. Policy evaluation: mixed results; a subject for further research. At Notre Dame, Father Theodore Hesburgh became a national figure after his policy statement that the university would give rules violators "fifteen minutes of meditation" before it suspended them. Results: difficult to evaluate; there was never any student revolt at Notre Dame.

Empirically, the soft line was actually the more successful strategy. Kirk's acting successor at Columbia, Andrew W. Cordier, an experienced diplomat, practiced an open-door policy by which he would see anyone, consult with anyone, understand the views of anyone. The '69 spring offensive of SDS did not catch on. When black students at Brandeis University took a building to demand a black-studies program, Morris Abram did not call in the police and after a few days negotiated them out. James Perkins at Cornell was a tragic case. He was able to negotiate black students out of buildings without resorting to police force and without substantive concessions. However, in a shot seen round the nation, black students were photographed marching out with rifles in paramilitary fashion. For Perkins: an actual success, a media failure (and vice versa for the blacks). Edward Levi at the University of Chicago also scored against the radicals by avoiding the radicalizing police bust, leaving discipline to the faculty, and mobilizing moderate opinion against the occupation. Later, the university expelled 42 students and suspended 81— a record for a white university.

The University of Chicago case clarifies the essence of the soft line. It is really a Fabian strategy. The point is to avoid a direct engagement (especially the radicalizing police bust), wait until the radicals are over-extended, their supply lines long and their troops demobilized, and then throw them out. In a *U.S. News & World Report* interview, Seymour Martin Lipset, a leading political sociologist of the end-of-ideology school and a Berkeley faculty refugee, noted with approval the University of Chicago expedient and Berkeley's "extremely tough rules which rolled the political tide there way back beyond where it was before 1964."

The favored instrument for "rolling back" the student movement is now the court injunction. The rationale of its use is to set the radical movement against the court system, while the university steps aside with virtue intact. The university does not bear responsibility for police intervention; the penalties for contempt of court are more severe than the minor misdemeanor charges arising from a conventional campus bust; the radical students must directly flout the public weal. The beauty of the "ex parte temporary restraining order" is that it is granted initially without a hearing solely on the affidavits of the plaintiff, who claims "irreparable injury" without adequate legal remedy. By the time the defendants are able to make their case at the return-date hearing some five days to two weeks after the granting of the injunction, the student movement has—if all goes well—been demobilized. In this intervening period, the defendants may on the grounds of "incitement" even be restricted in their Constitutional rights of speech and assembly. If the defendant students disobey the injunction, they are subject to contempt charges in which there is no jury trial, little limit to a judge's discretionary power to punish, and a narrow scope of appeal.

In its essence, the court injunction is a *summary* process to replace the normal forms of civil and criminal relief. An ideal instrument of reactionary policy, it was a notorious method of repression in the history of the labor movement. In 1969, it was used to good effect at Columbia, City University of New York, Dartmouth, San Francisco State, and Stanford, among others. From the point of view of the authorities, the danger of the injunction is that it, too, will prove "counterproductive." The resort to a court order is a nice demonstration of the radical thesis of interlocked university and political directorates.[15]

[15] See Frank J. Donner, "The Injunction on Campus," *The Nation*, June 9, 1969, pp. 718–20.

In their menu of repression and reform, administrators serve up little of the latter. Reform has followed political strategy rather than social vision; there was little evidence of the restructure schemes, the ethnic-studies programs, the elimination of classified research, the disengagement from military research spin-offs before the impact of radical action in the late '6os. Universally, reform has either been a direct response to radical challenge or an *anticipatory* response to the prospect of it. The race goes to the quick and nimble administration. Yale developed an early prototype of a black-studies department; Princeton, Fisk, and Vanderbilt developed plans for student representation on their boards of trustees. Harvard was a little slow to produce policies governing ethnic studies and university housing and real-estate policies, and so was caught by a student revolt before it could put up a finished posture of progress.

The reforms are generally tokens. Classified research, for instance, represented only 4 percent of military research at universities even before it began to be phased out. The elimination of academic status for ROTC and legal disengagement from military research institutes do not necessarily affect the system, which may still depend on the personnel and resources of the university. The ethnic-studies programs are more substantive (although the universities are adamant about retaining control), and reflect the official consensus that the blacks are only militant reformists whose "black rage" can be channeled by the right reforms, properly administered.

Repression and reform are, above all, not mutually exclusive alternatives. They are the defining limits of a range of policy choices. McGeorge Bundy has referred to this strategy as "The End of Either/Or" in its international dimension: "Over and over [President Kennedy] insisted on the double assertion of policies which stood in surface contradiction with each other: resistance to tyranny and relentless pursuit of accommodation; reinforcement of defense and new leadership for disarmament; counter-insurgency and the Peace Corps; openings to the left but no closed doors to the reasonable right; an Alliance for Progress and unremitting opposition to Castro; in sum, the olive branch and the arrows." [16] Before becoming Special Assistant for Foreign Affairs to the Kennedy and Johnson administrations and President of the Ford Foundation, Bundy was a Harvard dean.

Another internationalist, Andrew Cordier, illustrated the meaning of this conception in his tenure as Acting President of Columbia University after its student rebellion. Cordier explained his policy to a Senate investigatory committee "under two headings": (1) the "steps that were taken to contain and terminate disruption and to establish a campus disciplinary system" and (2) the "very active policies pursued by the university in forging faculty and student unity in support of forward-looking university programs. . . ." [17] Formerly Dean of Columbia's School of International Affairs and an executive assistant to the Secretary-General of the United Nations, Cordier inaugurated a containment policy based on the liberal use of court injunctions and the establishment of a new disciplinary system. The disciplinary system combined a hard-line set of "Interim Rules" with an elaborate system of student and faculty participation in the administration of these rules. Although some political analysts have correctly observed that participation schemes are rarely the crux of radical demands, they serve a crucial function in administrative policy. Since the loss of legitimacy is the most important result of a large-scale student rebellion for a university administration, "restructure plans" serve to re-establish administrative legitimacy by creating new constituencies for the administration within the university community, which are involved in local government on a token basis.

[16] McGeorge Bundy, "The End of Either/Or," *Foreign Affairs*, January 1967, p. 192.
[17] "Testimony of Andrew W. Cordier," *Hearings, Permanent Subcommittee on Investigations, Committee on Government Operations,* U.S. Senate (Washington, 1969), Part 23, p. 5266.

This tactic was also the linchpin to Cordier's reform program to "forge student and faculty unity." After an elaborate series of consultations, committee deliberations, and negotiations, Columbia produced a bold plan for a "University Senate" which provided for 20 percent student representation and which, although technically advisory, might acquire the *de facto* prerogatives of most faculty senates. This senate almost immediately became embroiled in the "arrows" portion of Cordier's policy. Acting President Cordier informed the University Senate that he was supplying the U.S. Senate's Committee on Government operations with the *names* of student radicals. Faculty liberals in the senate obtained a commitment from Cordier that the administration would not furnish the names of members of the "moderate" Students for a Restructured University and Students' Afro-American Society, but only those of the Students for a Democratic Society. The faculty representatives referred to this compromise as a victory, while student representatives were outraged. Many other administrations—Harvard, CUNY, Cornell, University of California among them—also responded to the McClellan Committee's subpoenas without a whimper.

This action is consistent with the standard university policy of selective repression. On the basis of their perception of the hard core and responsible dissent, university administrations selectively enforce disciplinary procedures and other sanctions to serve their political purposes. After the radical demonstrations at Harvard in 1969, the disciplinary committee expelled sixteen students of Progressive Labor's Worker-Student Alliance, which it termed "hard-core Maoists and wreckers," while putting on probation the more "moderate" New Left Caucus members for essentially the same offenses.

The Fabian strategy, then, requires (1) the avoidance of the radicalizing police bust; (2) a waiting game in the choice of the right moment of student demobilization for moving against the hard core; (3) a program of reform. Other necessary components are a law-and-order alliance with a reliable faculty on the left flank, and successful resistance to the pressures for excessive repression from the trustees, politicians, and public opinion, on the right flank. Without university autonomy, repressive forces will let the radical genii of popular effervescence out of the university bottle—by breaking the bottle. Excess repression can lead to a mutual escalation which might, sure enough, lead to the destruction of the university. Without a faculty mandate, on the other side, the administration loses its main legitimation from the university community itself, and will be regarded as the agent of the exurban plutocrats and their suburban auxiliaries.

In university politics, the faculty, especially the tenured gentry, are the high conservatives, the aristocrats who are more royalist then the king. It is an irony of university confrontations that the public and politicians—sometimes even the trustees—should regard faculty as ultra-liberals and dangerous radicals. From the point of view of the administration, this misapprehension is a de-stabilizing factor, making for repressive miscalculations which could suddenly forge an alliance between students and faculty. Imperial impositions of the Reagan administration and the state college trustees on faculty prerogatives had exactly this effect in the case of San Francisco State. In reality, most faculty are—given time— natural allies of the administration. For they are unalterably opposed to direct-action politics in a university setting. In every case of student rebellion the general faculty have condemned direct-action political techniques in un-ambiguous terms:

In 1964, the Academic Senate of the University of California at Berkeley resolved that "force and violence have no place on this campus."

In 1968, the Faculty of Columbia College resolved that it "endorses the right to protest, but strongly condemns both obstructive behavior and physical violence on this campus."

In 1969, the Faculty of Arts and Sciences of Harvard University resolved to condemn "obstructions of the normal processes and activities essential to the functions of a university community."

The faculty consensus is that the university is an a-political sanctuary which, in order to serve its purposes of cultural transmission and scholarly creation, must hold itself aloof from Vanity Fair. An organized group of faculty conservatives at Columbia University entitled its 1969 manifesto: "The University as a Sanctuary of Academic Freedom."

In spite of this commitment, the first response of faculty to a direct-action challenge is not strong opposition, but compromising vacillation. Their indecision follows from the nature of their conservatism. Once the radical probe is a *fait accompli*, the focus of attention shifts to the administrative response. Whereas the faculty cannot affect the radical action which may come without warning, there is a tactical pause before the administration acts, during which the faculty can bring to bear its own principles. Consistent with the idea of the university as an academic sanctuary, the faculty opposes the use of police force as an unnecessary escalation and favors a negotiated settlement with the radical students, whose tactics escape with a verbal condemnation. Although the faculty recommendation against police force is (accidentally) strategically correct, the administration may at this stage regard "negotiation under duress" as a sign of weakness. The trustees, the public, and even the radical students often share the administration's sentiment that the faculty is merely obstructive and vacillating. In truth, the faculty is traumatized by the shock of rebellion. In the first place, faculty members have a paternal regard for their students and cannot quite believe it when the "kids" get serious. The faculty has a similar regard for the university itself. For if the university is a "community of scholars," the faculty is that community. Therefore: the faculty is the university.

Accordingly, the policy of liberal faculty members is to "save the university." In the initial disorientation which follows from a condition of insurrection, the impulse of most faculty members is to fall back, without political reflection, upon their basic ideological commitments. They make, almost instinctively, for the high ground of academic freedom and libertarianism between the "putschist" students and the trigger-happy administration. If the radical students have not offended the faculty's quite elastic notion of academic freedom, they may pick up faculty support on the basis of the general absence of due process in disciplinary procedures in universities. In this early stage of faculty "politicization," liberal faculty members often organize to "save the university" by establishing a caucus with a phone chain, unofficial organizers, and quasi-official spokesmen. In the case of the Free Speech Movement in 1964, it was the informal Committee of 200 (actually consisting of some 350 faculty members out of a total of 1,100 or so) which formulated the "time, place, and manner" solution to the crisis concerning on-campus political advocacy—a proposal which pre-empted the administration's own conservative package. Because there was a free-speech issue at stake, the student movement had massive faculty support; it has not been surpassed since, nor in the new era of radical demands may it ever be equaled. By the time of the Columbia strike, the issues of military research and university racial policies were symbolically (if not substantially) radical, and the liberal caucus, the Ad Hoc Faculty Group, correspondingly handled the student movement in a more gingerly fashion. In the case of Harvard in 1969, the liberal caucus actually tried to maintain a common front with the conservative group. The general principles of the liberal policy are a verbal condemnation of radical tactics, an opposition to police intervention, and an insistence on liberal principles of due process in student discipline. It is also the liberal caucus which often produces—usually in good faith—an olivebranch program of reform in university governance and modifications of policies affecting war and race. The university administration often takes over this program, adapts it to accommodate the demands of faculty conservatives and the trustees, and makes it a keystone in its own policy of co-optation and repression.

The liberal hour quickly passes because a student rebellion creates new factors. Foremost of these is the pressure for repression. In the public universities, these ill winds blow from public opinion, the politicians in the state legislatures and in the Congress, and from the governing boards. In the private universities, they come from alumni, trustees, and federal funding sources. In both cases, the constituency of each stratum is one step further to the right and one step further removed from the scene—from faculty to administration, from administration to trustees, from trustees to alumni or state legislatures, from legislatures to public opinion—and each manages to multiply by another factor the new elements of irrationality and misinformation in the political calculus. In the end, it is the media spectaculars which elicit the reactionary consciousness—as the political arena spirals outward, the source of information becomes more and more the printed and electronic media. Political reality is collapsed into the instantaneous moment of electronic transmission which carries the unconditional message of offense and defense, violence and aggression—in the language of television journalism, "bang-bang." For the authorities, political survival comes to depend not on a position of strength, but on a televised posture of strength. Simultaneously, the terms of the struggle are also reversed in the media: the militant image of student radicals and the moderate image of the administrators in the televised moment of conflict are an inversion of the actual balance of power. The conservative definition of aggression prevails, and the Right rides in on an electronic wave.

The demands for repression are registered in ways which concretely affect faculty interests. Pressures mount for reductions of federal subsidy. State legislatures first threaten and then actually proceed to cut university budgets. Trustees intervene against radical faculty members and reclaim rights in faculty appointments. Politicians introduce bills which require mandatory firing of faculty members who engage in radical forms of political activity. Alumni demand that faculty members be screened for political views and trustees carefully review high-level administration appointments. In some of these areas, faculty members have wielded substantial power; in others they have exercised *de facto* control. But in a crisis, authority reverts to the source. In the 1969 Harvard case, the university administration elected to call in the police immediately without any pretense at consulting the faculty. When an administrator was challenged about this procedure, he answered that there was a "problem of security." When, as a result of political struggles in the universities, faculties see that their careful usurpations, accomplished over decades, are undermined in a single spring, they also begin to perceive a "problem of security." In California, the faculties of the university and state college systems are obsessed by the white peril: the barbarian hordes of Southern California led by their primitive chieftains, Ronald Reagan and Max Rafferty (the "Blue Max"), who cheerfully disembowel university budgets and college chancellors.

Once the faculty accepts the notion that the priority problem is university security, the politics of unity takes over. It becomes necessary for the faculty to unite in a common front behind the administration, to emphasize the general interests which hold the university community together, and to deemphasize secondary factional questions. What holds the community together is money, particularly federal money which underwrites 25 percent of higher education. To maintain the level of federal funding for higher education (and even for one's own research), it may be necessary to accept certain federal definitions of political reality. If investigatory committees demand that administrators and faculty members name names of student radicals, it may be necessary to supply these committees with a few names lest the university's standing in Washington be affected. The same considerations apply to state funding. After the 1967 demonstrations organized by Berkeley students against the Oakland draft induction center, the administration suspended, in a highly selective manner, only those participants who were also radical leaders. A liberal professor admitted that there was a liberal issue of due process somewhere, but commented, "It was simply a matter of whether John X (who was making a pest of himself and was probably guilty anyway) would hang, or whether Reagan would dismantle the place."

In this process, the radical student movement begins to lose some of its charm. While the student movement was briefly an interesting lab session in the fields of political theory and revolutionary history, it must now be referred back to those departments rather than be allowed to continue undermining the College of Arts and Sciences. What emerges is the classic pattern of Cold War liberalism. Practicing a new realpolitik, liberal faculty members begin to pre-empt the conservative position and to sacrifice liberal principles to the exigencies of "unity" and "security." As in the Columbia case, this policy may mean in practice the striking of bargains which compromise what should be non-negotiable issues: liberal faculty members agree to the release to investigating committees of the names of the "militant" SDS members if the "moderate" radicals are protected. Internally, they begin to acquiesce in the gradual purge of foreign, anti-university elements among students and faculty.

In the post-rebellion era of faculty politics, faculty members have time to consider the implications of direct action and the relationship between a radical confrontation and police reaction. Upon reflection, the faculty consensus is that student force necessitates counter-force. It recognizes the inconsistency of its first response to force and resolves not to condone "putschist" tactics in the future. As the political content of the student movement moves left and tactics turn more militant, the faculty consensus hardens. At Berkeley, the well-coordinated caucus and the efficient phone chain of the Committee of 200 began to disintegrate in the fall of

1965, when the student Vietnam Day Committee was maneuvering for a possibly bloody confrontation with the forces of order at the Oakland Army Base. Various faculty were put off by this early example of non-pacific protest, and 400 signed a letter of opposition to it. Incidents related to the Peace Rights Organizing Committee in the spring of 1966 and the student strike of December 1966 accelerated the process of disintegration, so that by 1967 the bloc was reduced to a radical rump. At Columbia in 1969, the faculty also began to organize in explicit opposition to the militant tactics of the Columbia SDS.

The final stage of the decomposition of faculty liberalism is the call to arms issued by the faculty right, which, like the liberals, has also mobilized its forces and takes the initiative on the basis of the issue of "academic freedom." The position of the faculty conservatives is to the right of the sophisticated crisis management of the administrations, and may actually obstruct it. In March 1969, after the Columbia administration thought it better tactically not to press disciplinary actions against the rebel students of the previous spring, a group of 100 senior professors announced at a press conference that "justice is denied the community if disciplinary cases go unresolved and all proceedings are subsequently abandoned." The statement of the group, which included such large names of the university as historian Richard Hofstadter, philosopher Charles Frankel, literary critic Lionel Trilling, and cultural critic Jacques Barzun, went on to assert that the university had the "obligation to defend itself" against student disruptions, and that it had to "demonstrate the will to act." Acting President Cordier, always the experienced diplomat, registered his ideological solidarity with the group but his tactical disagreement with its position on amnesty: "The substance of this statement deserves the support of the entire university community."

Under the leadership of Sidney Hook, emeritus professor of philosophy at New York University and author of *From*

Hegel to Marx, the faculty right has established a national organization: University Centers for Rational Alternatives. This group, too, suspects administrations of the "classic pattern of appeasement—which is both morally intolerable and practically disastrous." According to one of its spokesmen, the purpose of the group is to establish "bodies that will constitute permanent lobbies for rational thought and academic freedom in the university community." In its report, *The New York Times* described this process as the establishment of "faculty cells" in various universities. These cells consist in large part of prestigious senior professors and liberal ideologues at the major universities: political scientist Paul Seabury and physicist Edward Teller at Berkeley, political scientists Zbigniew Brzezinski and Samuel Lubell at Columbia, historian Oscar Handlin and sociologist Nathan Glazer at Harvard, social psychologist Bruno Bettelheim and economist Milton Friedman at the University of Chicago, and so on. In a cover letter co-signed by Hook, a leading anti-communist liberal in the palmy days of the Congress of Cultural Freedom, and S. I. Hayakawa, among others, the rhetorical question is posed: "What will be the ultimate consequences of the 'restructuring' of the universities as bases of totalitarian indoctrination and extremist terrorism?"

By academic freedom, the faculty right—and the faculty generally—does not mean only the right to free conduct of educational activities without political *censorship* from any source, but also the guardianship of faculty autonomy, the preservation of faculty prerogatives, and the extension of faculty privileges. "Academic freedom" is the slogan of professor power. Sidney Hook formulated the doctrine in a response to the Free Speech Movement: "The extent to which these implications can be implemented is affected by the fact that in some American higher institutions of learning *legal* authority is vested in a Board of Regents, and in all other institutions in a corporate board of governing laymen. There is no practicable way of reversing this historical trend. Immense progress, however, has been made in winning over those who have legal authority to the acceptance of *enlightened principles of academic freedom* [emphasis added], which in effect entrust the determination and execution of educational policy to the faculties." [18] In this analysis, academic freedom equals *control* of educational policy, not to mention "ultimate control of the educational facilities of the campus, classrooms and meeting halls, etc., and over the conditions of their exercise." Hook hardly mentions the question of political censorship, although the assumption is that faculty automony is a guarantee of academic freedom in this sense as well.

In an even broader interpretation of academic freedom, Nathan Glazer, author of *The Social Bases of American Communism*, has written: "The Free Speech Movement, which stands at the beginning of the student rebellion in this country, seems now almost to mock its subsequent course. In recent years, the issue has been how to *defend* the speech, and the necessary associated actions, of others. The right of unpopular figures to speak without disruption on campus; the right of professors to give courses and lectures without disruption that makes it impossible to listen or engage in open discussion; the right of professors to engage in research they have freely chosen; the right of government and the corporations to come onto campus to give information and to recruit personnel; the right of students to prepare themselves as officers on campus: all these have been attacked by the young apostles of freedom and their heirs." [19] In this account, freedom of speech on campus and free inquiry in the classroom, which are the basic academic freedoms, are assimilated to a quite different class of "freedoms": "free research," "open recruitment," and the "right" of military preparation. Academic freedom is placed in service not only of faculty activities in general, such as military research, but of the *status quo*

[18] Sidney Hook, "Academic Freedom and the Rights of the Students," in Lipset and Wolin, p. 434.

[19] Nathan Glazer, "Student Politics and the University," *Atlantic* (July 1969), pp. 43–4.

arrangements of the institution such as corporate recruitment and ROTC. The "public service" functions of the university are defended on academic-freedom grounds as if they were a species of free inquiry. Any activity of the faculty is protected by academic freedom even if the undertaking is not *academic* at all. Academic freedom, in short, is not limited to freedom of inquiry and to academic functions; it is the freedom of faculty and administration to carry on their business, regardless of its nature. Academic freedom is the freedom of the marketplace.

The Berkeley faculty decided the military-research issue by these criteria in 1967. Invoking the spirit of Galileo, Harvey, and Newton, the Academic Freedom Committee of the faculty justified unclassified war research on the grounds of academic freedom which protects "scholarly work from having to pass moral or political tests," which have proven to have "little or no validity." The committee observed, "Results of striking importance and vast benefit to mankind have emerged from work that appeared at the outset to be mundane or morally suspect—even from research into the instruments of warfare." [20] Earlier, the Academic Senate at Berkeley, like faculties elsewhere, had formulated a policy against classified research, not on the grounds of the questionable academic nature of the research but on the procedural ground that its results were not "freely publishable."

For the faculty conservatives, academic freedom is a war whoop. In their statement, "The University as a Sanctuary of Academic Freedom," Columbia conservatives announced, "The tradition of the university as a sanctuary of academic freedom and center of informed discussion is an honored one, to be guarded vigilantly." [21] Vigilance is also the byword for Glazer, an FSM faculty refugee at Harvard: "These are strongly held commitments, so strongly that my first reac-

[20] 1967 report of the Academic Freedom Committee, cited in Michael Miles and Martin Roysher, "The Berkeley Thermidor," *The New Republic*, March 16, 1968, p. 20.
[21] *The New York Times*, May 29, 1969.

tion to disruption—and it is not only an emotional one—is to consider how the disrupters can be isolated and weakened, how their influence, which is now enormous among students, can be reduced, how dissension among them can be encouraged, and how they can be finally removed from a community they wish to destroy." [22]

This is the view that eventually prevails among the faculty, which becomes haunted by the specter of the "Latin American university." (The tales of student terrorism generally omit to mention other factors in the political calculus of Latin America, such as repressive military regimes, economic underdevelopment and stagnation, the power of landed oligarchies, subservience to American capital, an unprofessional and part-time faculty, educational corruption, etc.) Because it opposes direct action on principle, the liberal caucus can ally with the student movement only tactically and is hostage to the fundamental arguments of the conservatives (who may, of course, be good liberals as concerns other people's business). The democratic liberals either desert to realpolitik liberalism or are driven into silence, pending some unprecedented outrage. All the political factors favor the faculty right. The mild reforms which do emerge from the restructure committees seem to have no effect on the student left and confirm the hypothesis that the left regards reforms only as tactical instruments. There is no lack of Pop Leninism and gutter rhetoric to support this analysis, and, after a great success, the student left may acquire vanguard delusions which lead to self-isolating misadventures. The faculty right exploits this factor to the full and, often led by German Jewish refugees from Nazism, East European refugees from Communism, and ex-Communists turned anti-Communists, denounces the student Nazi-Communists.

The faculty center—the "Marsh"—is by this time bored with the whole business. Once the taboo is broken, the intervention of police does not offend anyone's sensibilities, while

[22] Glazer, p. 49.

a state of turmoil gets in the way of the business of the university, which is education. The party of peace and quiet prevails. The university administration holds the center between the faculty conservatives and the realpolitik liberals, but all agree that the student left may be "removed from a community they wish to destroy." The official liberals of the faculty consider the prospect regrettable but necessary; the university administration regards it as necessary by any means. It is left to the democratic liberals to oppose repressive policies, but this is a thankless task. The student left does not draw careful distinctions between the democratic liberals and the official liberals, while democratic liberals on the faculty may—with some justification—doubt the students' commitment to libertarian principles. In any case, it is never pleasant for those who consider themselves left of center to be outflanked on the left; it may be tempting to relegate the student left to the criminal-anarchist category and join up with the realpolitik liberals or even the conservatives.

A national opinion survey for the Carnegie Commission on Higher Education by Seymour Martin Lipset, Martin Trow, and Everett C. Ladd supports this conclusion concerning faculty politics. Almost half of the 60,000 faculty members surveyed believed that "most campus demonstrations are created by left groups trying to cause trouble," while over half disapproved of the "emergence of radical student activism in recent years." Over three quarters believed that the radical movement was a threat to academic freedom and that disruptive students should be strictly disciplined. Only 15 percent approved of both the means and the ends of the radicals, and only half of this percentage openly supported the radicals on campus.[23]

Only two factors upset the law-and-order alliance of the faculty with the administration. The first is a clumsy repression from outside the university which affects basic faculty

[23] For a report of the survey results, see *Chronicle of Higher Education*, April 6, 1970.

prerogatives. The second is the small faculty left (5.5 percent of the faculty, according to the survey). There is a traditional division in the faculty between those who consider themselves "intellectuals" and those who think of themselves as "professionals." There is a considerable literature about both groups, the critical portions of which are usually contributed by one group viewing the other. It is the nature of a professional to be of service, and this wing of the faculty naturally favors the *status quo*. Social criticism, on the other hand, is a defining characteristic of intellectuals, who are usually men of the left. These men normally come from disciplines which stress—or at least allow in their methodology the possibility of—critical analysis of the fundamental assumptions of the social order. They are generally in theoretical and literary disciplines.

The significant potential for a faculty left, however, rests elsewhere—with the junior faculty. Those who have been educated in the 1960s have probably been affected by the New Left, and some of them, such as the members of the New University Conference, may identify directly with the New Left. Of more importance is the phenomenon of faculty unionism in the form of the American Federation of Teachers. The university chapters of the AFT, which include graduate teaching assistants and faculty, have played decisive roles in political conflicts at Berkeley and San Francisco State. AFT members, like the left faculty generally, tend to be younger, concentrated in the liberal arts, and to have an intellectual self-image. AFT chapters raise the traditional union questions of wages and hours, but incline toward political syndicalism. At San Francisco State, the AFT chapter, including some 20 percent of the faculty, struck simultaneously with the black and Third World students for better wages and hours but also in support of the students' demands for an autonomous black-studies department. In the words of Glenn S. Dumke, chancellor of the California state college system, these were the "trouble-making few faculty who cause the problem." Hayakawa did not pull his punches either: this "handful" of striking professors "read such magazines as . . . *The Nation* and encourage students in their alienation."

II. THE CULTURAL CIVIL WAR

To move from the response of the university authorities to the reaction of the public powers is to pass through the looking-glass. Although the student movement and the forces of order within the university perceive each other through an ideological lens, the ideologically conditioned perceptions are at least the after-images of some commonly recognized facts and events. In the "real world," it is otherwise. The inhabitants of the public world are, first of all, irrevocably *outside* the university community; most of the older generation have never attended a college or university, and of the mainly upper- and upper-middle-class college graduates (whose potential sympathy for radical movements has its limits), most attended colleges and universities predating the emergence of the federal-grant university after World War II and (still more) after Sputnik I. Second, a bemused citizenry relies heavily on inverted media images for what information it does possess on political struggles within the universities; this information usually consists of televised acts of student aggression. Finally, the transition from the anti-world of the university to the real world of the public involves a rightward shift of the political spectrum which can hit with the impact of a shock wave. In the public world there is no left, but only liberalism, a doctrine of the political center with a left afterglow. The abnormality of the university realm is the vigor of its left politics.

University trustees are both a vector of these public realities and a channel for them. Although they are a part of the university—in fact, are the university itself as a legal entity—the trustees have the attitudes of informed laymen. Very few of them are professional educators and very few have informed themselves about higher education through the standard works and journals. As decision-making men of affairs, they prefer 15-minute briefings from the president. Although their constitutional authority over the university is complete, they are certainly not of the university, and only occasionally in it.

The trustees may also depend on the mass media for their first information of student rebellion, and although they later may learn the administration's version of the facts of the case, they are correspondingly more conscious of the importance of the proper media posture—the show of strength. The trustees are a force for the hard line which successful administrations must resist and educate if they are to control student rebellion. The trustees are also representative of the right-center of the foreshortened political spectrum of the United States, and, at the selective public and private universities, they may be the actual proprietors of corporate capitalism.

In a survey conducted by the Educational Testing Service, more than 40 percent of the trustees at selective private universities reported earnings in excess of $100,000 per year, while 90 percent earned over $30,000. Well over half of these men in both types of institutions were in business or business-related occupations. At the best private universities, nearly half were board members of corporations listed on the stock exchange. Reflecting the tendency for the trustees of state universities to be more entrepreneurial and of principally statewide influence, only 14 percent of the trustees at selective public universities were on the boards of listed corporations, but almost 90 percent were on other corporate boards.[24]

Trustee politics flow from these economic facts. Overwhelmingly white, Protestant, and in their fifties and sixties, less than a sixth at public universities and less than a fourth at private ones reported their politics as "liberal." Two thirds

[24] Rodney Hartnett, *College and University Trustees* (Princeton, N.J., 1969).

of these men at selective public institutions and nearly half at their private counterparts believed that all campus speakers should be officially screened, and over half at the former and a third at the latter favored the requirement of loyalty oaths from faculty members. Approximately three quarters of the trustees at universities of both types believed that faculty members should not have the right of collective bargaining. Incredibly, one third at selective public universities and more than a fifth at selective private universities *disagreed* with the following statement: "Faculty members should have the right to express their opinions about any issue they wish in various channels of college communication, including the classroom, student newspaper, etc., without fear of reprisal."

Clearly there is the potential for a serious conflict between trustees and the faculty if trustees move punitively against the "liberal professors" as presumed instigators and allies of student rebellions. In the case of the university and college systems of the state of California, the conflict is actual. In the fall of 1969, some students at Berkeley used a university channel for student-initiated courses to invite Eldridge Cleaver, minister of information of the Black Panther Party, to deliver a series of lectures in a course for credit. The Board of Regents of the University of California intervened to forbid the course, and 300 students responded with the occupation of a building, an action which attracted relatively little support. The episode, minor in itself, led to a proposal by Ronald Reagan, who as Governor sat on the board, that the Regents reclaim the prerogative to approve directly the appointment and promotion of faculty members. The motion failed, but on a board increasingly composed of Reagan appointees, the possibility of its passage was real.

In the same year, the American Federation of Teachers local at San Francisco State struck for better working conditions and in support of the student strike led by the Black Students Union and the Third World Liberation Front. The trustees of the state college system initially fired the striking teachers at San Francisco State and teachers striking in sympathy at San Jose State, although it later reversed itself as part of the price of a settlement. In 1969, the trustees of the university system intervened to fire Angela Davis, an instructor who was a member of the Communist Party and active with the Black Panthers. In similar fashion, the University of Wisconsin threatened to dismiss teaching assistants who struck in support of black students demanding an autonomous black-studies department. In their private business dealings, trustees have always been loath to concede the right to strike. After teaching assistants at Berkeley struck in conjunction with a student strike in late 1966, the Board of Regents of the University of California threatened dismissal for any university employees "who participate in any strike or otherwise fail to meet their assigned duties in an effort to disrupt the University administration, teaching, or research." [25]

Trustees consider student rebellion worth their personal attention. At Harvard in 1969 and Columbia in 1968, the decision of trustees and administration on how to respond to the student challenge was arrived at with little concession to or consultation with the faculty, much to the indignation of its technocratic theorists. One of these theorists, J. K. Galbraith, protested in a faculty meeting: "If there was this lengthy contingency planning, including discussion with the police, and if there was discussion with the people in Chicago, why was it not possible to discuss this matter with the faculty, or some members of the faculty?" [26] The result was more gratifying to student radicals, who see the corporate proprietors and managers as the ultimate antagonists.

The primacy of the confrontation between the men of corporate power on the boards of trustees and the student radicals has increasingly become a matter of fact as well as theory.

[25] University of California, *University Bulletin*, May 1, 1967, pp. 157–8.
[26] Cited in Urban Research Corporation, *Harvard's Student Strike: The Politics of Mass Mobilization* (Chicago, 1970), p. 38.

This was evident at Stanford University when students occupied the Applied Electronics Laboratory in 1969 to force the issue of military research at the lab and at the university-affiliated Stanford Research Institute. Of the Stanford trustees, William Hewlett was president of Hewlett-Packard, a military aerospace company doing $34 million worth of work for the Department of Defense while the co-founder, David Packard, served as Under-Secretary of Defense. Hewlett was also a director of Chrysler ($146 million in Defense Department work) and FMC ($185 million), the San Diego-based military/aerospace firm. Other trustees were the chairman of the board of General Dynamics, the president of Northrup Aircraft, and a director of Lockheed, which was doing $1.9 billion in defense work.

The trustees are a vector of force for the hard line, particularly at public universities, whose boards are often klatsches for the virulently new rich. But, as the legally responsible authorities and the point of connection between the universities and the public world, the trustees also channel repressive forces from public sources. At private universities, these forces emanate from federal funding sources, public opinion, and the alumni, who, as a result of their own alumni power movement in the nineteenth century, often elect up to a third of the otherwise self-perpetuating boards. The structure of public universities makes the boards wind-swept plains for these forces from governors, state legislatures, and public opinion.

The classic social revolutions generated their opposites—counter-revolutions—and, logically, civil war as a result. On a smaller scale, student revolt has generated counter-revolt and a cultural civil war within American society. This "cultural civil war" has several dimensions. Fundamentally, it is simple political reaction, whose point is to suppress a radical movement which by its nature poses a threat to the *status quo* distribution of power and wealth. Although reaction has its basic appeal to the conservative elements of the upper classes, it also appeals to the middle, working, and even lower classes because of its association with patriotism. Since the radical student movement opposes the Vietnam War, the Selective Service System, and implicitly the entire social order, reactionary politicians can mobilize broad sections of the population against the student left on the basis of patriotic appeals. Nationalism is common sense for a generation which identifies the "national interest" with international justice by virtue of the First World War against "German militarism" (and for "democracy"), the Second World War against Fascism, and a Cold War that was originally directed against Stalinism. Nationalism also has a cultural dimension. In a nation which has received almost 40 million immigrants of non-Anglo-Saxon heritage in the last century and which has an uncertain culture and tradition in any case, patriotism takes on the character of a national religion. Nationalism serves as a device of cultural integration, and it is often the white ethnic minorities that lead the cultural counter-revolt.

Race is the second dimension to the cultural civil war. The effect of liberal policy in the 1960s was to sponsor the advance of the racial minorities at the expense of the white working and lower classes, whose neighborhoods suffered the traumas of new culture contact, whose job security was threatened by equal employment opportunity, and whose school systems faced the real prospect of lower quality which substantial integration presented. The racially liberal elements of the upper classes were willing to finance social programs for the racial minorities out of the tax burden of "Middle America" and the white working class, while ignoring the social needs of the latter. Quite aside from the erosion of their real interests, these lower classes are not models of racial enlightenment. They are suspicious of racial and cultural difference. They have regarded urban violence by blacks as criminal and assumed that it was possible for blacks and other racial minorities to organize social enterprises and rise out of poverty by their own efforts on the model of the white ethnic groups. (No one has been more convinced of this proposition than the old immigrant groups themselves.) White America associates all of these problems with the student movement which lends support to an occasionally violent black movement.

Finally, the counter-revolt is directed against "youth culture" and all that it embodies: drugs, rock music, long hair, and strange costumes. The counter-rebels are especially enraged by the youth culture's rejection of the staples of bourgeois culture: property values, the moral value of work, conformity to the norms of social respectability. This rage against radical youth culture can be discovered among all classes because all classes are fundamentally loyal to the militantly bourgeois culture of the United States and its economic foundation: the "free-enterprise system." Although the American working class and lower classes are aware of their economic interests and have engaged in class war in the course of American history, their class consciousness has never transcended the parameters of American capitalism. Popular radicalism has generally taken a Populist form which has accepted "free enterprise" and the class structure, while it has campaigned against "vested interests" and "big business" in the name of "equal opportunity" and a fair shake. Under these conditions, class consciousness is manifested only as class resentment. These classes resent the youth culture both because it is an upper-class phenomenon and because it offends their petit-bourgeois sensibilities. This right-wing Populist combination of cultural conservatism and class resentment is apparent in the American Independent Party of George Wallace, who even-handedly denounces radical demonstrators and the "Eastern Establishment."

The student movement takes the full force of political and cultural reaction because it overlaps the movements of the New Left, youth culture, and black consciousness. The New Left activates and leads the student movement which "threatens" the system of higher education with its promise of equal opportunity and upward social mobility. The radical student movement has deep roots in the youth culture, which generally depends parasitically on a host university community. Students and hippies also aid and abet the fearful black militants. Since the election of Ronald Reagan as Governor of California in 1966 and the national Presidential campaign of George Wallace in 1968, the rhetoric of counter-revolt has become a stock political formula. President Richard Nixon, a McCarthyite politician in the early 1950s, and Vice-President Spiro Agnew, the successful descendant of Greek immigrants, gave this rhetoric of "Americanism" a national dimension in the first year of the Nixon-Agnew administration. As practiced by these politicians, the technique was to build a popular front against the left (and liberalism) on the basis of a cross-class appeal to nationalism, racism, and cultural traditionalism.

Notoriously, California is the front line of the cultural civil war between the "counter-culture" and the faithful of the "American Dream." The new middle classes and the prosperous working classes of Southern California are descended from the inter-war migrants, who came from the lower strata of the heartland states of America: Okies and Arkies, Great Plains farm boys, Midwestern small-townsmen. Poor and ravaged by the Great Depression, they achieved a certain success in the World War II and Cold War industries of Southern California (37 percent of all manufacturing). Still, these *arrivistes* feel threatened by the uppity blacks and Latins who were provided an opening wedge in the 1960s by the Rumford Open Housing Act. In circumstances of high occupational and geographic mobility, the new white suburbanities of Los Angeles, San Diego, and Orange County are an insecure lot. They have a traditional past and a suggestible future. They have learned property values from the suburban life— earning a living, paying off a mortgage on the house, and meeting payments on the car. The precepts of individualism have been further reinforced by a heritage of fundamentalist

Anglo-Saxon Protestantism, while their social integration is ensured for the immediate future by economic growth and general prosperity. Living in the "nuclear family" unit and commuting to work by automobile, they now have, despite a more rooted past, relatively few institutional connections profound enough to provide them with a historically grounded view of the world. They cannot rely on the Democratic Party, which once helped to fulfill this function for their Eastern and Midwestern city cousins. In a fit of Progressivist reform, California Governor Hiram Johnson several decades ago established a system of open primaries without party endorsement and eliminated partisan elections on the county level, thus crippling precinct organization. Since the average California family moves every four and a half years, political workers find it next to impossible to keep accurate precinct lists in any case. The Democratic Party is a weak vessel in California.

The one medium which successfully and systematically penetrates the suburbs is television, and in California the acknowledged master of the art of imagery is Ronald Reagan. As Lieutenant Governor, Robert Finch (now a Presidential Counsellor in the Nixon administration) noted that Reagan "is visceral; he's role-playing; he has a superb political instinct." Finch spent considerable time "trying to figure out why he comes across the tube the way he does." Antagonists at press conferences and University Regents' meetings have testified to the fact that Reagan can be cornered and cut to pieces as far as people present are concerned, and yet the same people can go home and watch the proceedings on the six-o'clock news to discover Reagan walking away unmarked. In any confrontation before the camera, Reagan plays to the camera, not the man. With a bland self-possession, he walks around, under, and through questions in a manner which tranquilizes the passive viewer.

Although Reagan is a consummate TV actor, he is not a political fraud. He is pre-eminently a suburban politician. Reagan is able to communicate the message his audience—largely in Southern California, largely migrant in origin or parentage —wants to hear: the defense of the "taxpayer." This is, in Reagan's words, the "citizen who has no special pressure group to lobby for him. He works and sweats to make ends meet, to pay his bills, and keep his family in clothes and his kids in school. He is the source from whom all the blessings of tax-supported programs flow." [27] Reagan's image is also his reality. Reagan was born in Tampico, Illinois, the son of a failed itinerant shoe salesman, and in his early manhood he left a job as a sportscaster in Iowa to star in Grade B films in Hollywood. A University of California Regent who had observed Reagan in its meetings called him a "small-town and mass-media guy."

Other small-town and mass-media guys vote for Reagan. He is a new kind of Republican winner. In the 1966 gubernatorial election, according to the results of the private opinion survey the California Poll, Reagan also cut deeply into the Democratic Party coalition. In conditions of prosperity but racial conflict and student revolt at Berkeley, blue-collar and low-income, low-educational groups voted on the cultural issues rather than the economic issues.

In Reagan's California, morality is the new cultural issue. The revolt of the blacks in Watts and Hunter's Point—politics in the streets—is crime-in-the-streets. The use of drugs by the drop-out cultures in Haight-Ashbury, Telegraph Avenue, and Hollywood is juvenile delinquency. Radical student politics—"the mess at Berkeley"—is a breach of the peace and criminal anarchy. "Moral decay" is the popular explanation for these phenomena. Moralism is the common man's theory of social change; and Ronald Reagan is a common-sense thinker. After Spencer-Roberts and Associates, impresarios of political technology, discovered that morality was the "um-

27 Interview with Robert Finch, reported in Michael Miles, "Reagan and the Respectable Right," *The New Republic*, April 20, 1968, pp. 25–6.

brella issue" in the 1966 campaign, Reagan rode it very hard to victory by a million-vote plurality. Since that time, Reagan has led the cultural counter-revolt in California and employed this counter-revolt as the key to a new mass base for the right. The coalition consists of the traditional constituency of the right—the lower middle classes, large segments of the upper and upper middle classes—combined with elements formerly left of center—the prosperous elements of the working class, and the white lower classes who now feel under threat from rising blacks and Latins. At the same time, Reagan is sufficiently respectable to have access to the big money.

The "people of California" dislike the blacks and Latins (25 percent of the population) for their cultural foreignness and for the economic threat in employment and housing which they present as a rising group. As cultural conservatives and lower- and middle-income strata, they resent the wealthy, upper-middle-class, white youth which has the luxury of political rebellion and cultural Bohemianism, apparently without any reprisal. If marijuana and rock music are the emblems of cultural revolt, the people of California have their own cultural staples—beer and pro football. It is not surprising that they should actively sympathize with police Tactical Squads who, besides originating in their own social class, resemble scrub football teams with their helmets, boots, uniforms, formations, and fleshy massiveness.[28]

In the fall of 1967, San Francisco Bay Area radicals, including student radicals from Berkeley, organized disruptive demonstrations against the Oakland draft induction center as part of October's Stop the Draft Week. This effort was during the period of esoterically calibrated tactical shifts "from dissent to resistance," and the steering committee was concerned with mass disruption as a "step in the direction of a revolu-

[28] "Their [the Cleveland Browns'] electric blend of brute force and computerlike precision helped make pro football the No. 1 spectator sport of the decade," *Life* Special Double Issue: "The '6os," December 26, 1969, p. 21.

tionary form of protest." For the Oakland police and the California Highway Patrol, however, Tuesday's demonstrations were just the day of the big game. Well trained and in their best physical shape, the cops took over the three-story parking garage across from the draft induction center on Clay Street in downtown Oakland. The signal was for a trap play. Allowing 4,000 demonstrators to mill around in front of the induction center, several hundred police formed a flying wedge and, wielding billy clubs and a disabling chemical spray, mace, they went in for the score: 24 demonstrators hospitalized to one policeman. In 10 minutes they had the area cleared, and the buses unloaded inductees soon after. The *Oakland Tribune*, published by former Republican U.S. Senator William Knowland, headlined: POLICE ROUT PROTESTERS. The manager of the Oakland Plaza Building, which housed the induction center, congratulated the police on their "fine teamwork." Morning-after quarterback Ron Reagan ("win this one for the Gipper") issued a statement noting that the police "displayed exceptional ability and handled themselves with great professional skill."

Berkeley is Reagan's fate. He was elected in 1966 with the impetus of the FSM, the "Filthy Speech" movement, and the Vietnam Day Committee. After his election, he continued to denounce student outrages as they occurred: the student strike of December 1966, Stop the Draft Week, the street riots arising from an attempt to hold a support demonstration for French students in 1968. Since Berkeley supports an underground culture in the Telegraph Avenue section of the town, student and non-student politics has offered a particularly favorable combination of cultural and political heresy for the Reagan counter-crusade. The "street people" of Telegraph tangled with the police in summer disturbances in 1968. Berkeley has also given moral and material support to black militant politics, notably the Oakland-based Black Panther Party. This relationship led to the incident over Eldridge Cleaver's lectures in the fall of 1968.

Berkeley is the national symbol of cultural and political re-volt. Since it harbors the evil trinity of student revolt, underground culture, and racial militancy under the protective aegis of the wealthy Berkeley Hills liberals, Berkeley is the natural focus for the animus of the California right. In his "State of the State" message for 1969, Governor Reagan denounced the student rebels as "criminal anarchists and latterday Fascists," and proposed a number of legislative measures to contain student rebellion. In addition, he emphasized that "education is not a right, but a privilege," and proposed tuition charges for California's traditionally tuition-free system of higher education. In an airport interview, Reagan commented that right-minded students and faculty members should be assured of educational security "at the point of a bayonet, if necessary."

In February 1969 Reagan proclaimed a "state of extreme emergency" at Berkeley as a result of the "Third World strike" undertaken on the model of the San Francisco State strike. After the end of the strike, the proclamation was not rescinded. Then, in May, local police of Alameda County, the city of Berkeley, and the university cleared a lot about the size of a football field of a motley group of 50 hippies and "street people" of Telegraph Avenue. The 200-man police contingent was equipped with shotguns, tear-gas launchers, telescopic rifles, and flak jackets. At a noon rally on campus, 3,000 people marched to the site to protest the police action. There was some rock- and bottle-throwing, to which the police, now numbering 600, responded with tear-gas barrages. Soon after, the police began firing into the crowd and by the end of the day had killed one person and wounded 30 others. The Regents of the University of California, who owned the park, were meeting the same day in Los Angeles and issued a statement: "It is of paramount importance that law and order be upheld."

The lot was a "People's Park." The university had originally cleared the land with the intention of building dormitories, but since students had avoided the university's existing high-rise dormitories, the university had canceled the plan and considered laying out a soccer field instead (although under-utilized soccer fields already existed). Meanwhile, the lot turned into a muddy field which residents appropriated for a parking lot. A number of the underground citizens of Berkeley, including a few student and ex-student radicals, conceived the idea of converting the lot into a park. The project caught on and hundreds of people joined in without any governing structure, social plan, or, of course, mandate from the university, whose property rights were implicitly challenged. Chancellor Roger Heyns later called this an act of "unjustified aggression." Reagan characterized it as a "deliberate and planned attempt at confrontation."

The university had originally bought the site as a part of its Long Range Development Plan of expansion into the south-campus area, home of radicals, hippies, and assorted freaks. In alliance with the university, the city of Berkeley designated the area as "blighted" in 1966, and attempted to launch an urban-renewal project, but was blocked by a coalition of students, residents, and local merchants (see "Urban Expansion" in Chapter III). According to Frederick Dutton, a liberal Regent, Chancellor Roger Heyns of the Berkeley campus explained the acquisition of the property in the south-campus area to the Board of Regents in terms of insurance against a "rising crime rate" and as an "act against the hippie culture."

The day after the clash with police, under the existing proclamation of a state of extreme emergency, Reagan sent in 2,000 National Guardsmen in full battle dress—with fixed bayonets. The combined forces of law and order, under the command of Sheriff Frank Madigan of Alameda County, proceeded to occupy the city and campus for ten days to purposes which still remain obscure. Crowds would gather to observe the military detachments, and, after a time, skirmishing would break out. At one point, the National Guardsmen trapped a peaceful crowd in Sproul Plaza while helicopters buzzed overhead spraying a noxious form of tear gas on the "hard-core dissidents."

Meantime, Chancellor Heyns, author of *The Psychology of Personal Adjustment* and *An Anatomy for Conformity*, had returned from the conference of the National Science Foundation, which he had been attending in Washington. In a television interview, Heyns assured the viewing public that "we haven't stopped the rational process." Later, the Chancellor explained: "Our strategy was to act with humor and sensitivity. For instance, we offered to roll up the sod in the park and return it to the people. . . . We had no reason to believe there would be trouble." Heyns's own Advisory Committee on Housing and Environment later noted that its recommendations for a community-controlled park had been ignored, and criticized a "heavy-handed and unresponsive planning process." Heyns defined the issue differently: "They [the People's Park people] refused to accept the basic premise that the design and use of the area was finally the responsibility of the University, no matter how flexible the design or liberal the use."

Heyns's superior, Charles Hitch, president of the university system and erstwhile Comptroller of the Department of Defense under McNamara, criticized "certain tactics" of the occupying force, but observed that these were "not the responsibility of university authorities." Governor Reagan also allowed that the helicopter gas attack was a "tactical mistake," but attacked Hitch for "trying to weasel" over to the other side. "The police didn't kill the young man," Reagan said. "He was killed by the first college administrator who said some time ago it was all right to break laws in the name of dissent." When the Mayor of Berkeley suggested that Sheriff Madigan had acted clumsily, Madigan put it to him this way: "If the mayor was capable of running the city so well without problems, we wouldn't be here. I advise the mayor to take his umbrella and go to the Berkeley Munich, wherever that might be."

After several days of occupation, 200 faculty members announced their refusal to teach. A local labor council criticized the police, and the press began to change course. On May 23, the Academic Senate resolved to demand the withdrawal of the "massive police and military presence on campus" and the "cessation of all acts of belligerency and provocation by demonstrators," and to propose a compromise plan by which part of the land would become an "experimental community-generated park." In a student referendum, 85 percent voted support of the original People's Park. By the time of the Regents' meeting on June 20, Hitch and Heyns were telling their superiors that the People's Park was a "popular issue" and suggested setting aside part of the land for a community park. The Regents, many of them Reagan appointees, accepted Reagan's proposal for student housing on the site inasmuch as compromise, the Governor noted, would "appear as nothing but a cop-out on this issue." [29]

By early 1970, California had passed more repressive legislation against student revolt than any other state in the country, including laws providing for denial of state financial aid to student demonstrators and establishing criminal trespass on campus. Pending legislation provided for automatic expulsion of disruptive demonstrators, the regulation of public-address systems, and the dismissal of faculty demonstrators. Under the Reagan administration, the University of California system has been appropriated only enough funds to cover basic operating expenses without provision for any new programs or construction.

By the measure of repressive legislation, Wisconsin is the second most active front of the cultural civil war. Like California, the state is politically volatile and a traditional fastness for both left and right. Influenced by the immigration of northern Europeans which brought leftist European politics into the Great Lakes region, Wisconsin supplied the Socialist

[29] See Robert Scheer, "The Dialectics of Confrontation," *Ramparts,* August 1969, pp. 41–54; and Sheldon Wolin and John Schaar, "Berkeley: The Battle of People's Park," *The New York Review of Books,* July 19, 1969, pp. 24–32.

Party of America with significant support at the turn of the century. As Mayor of Milwaukee, Victor Berger put together a socialist political machine, based on the city's German immigrants, which ran the city for 10 years. Also in the first quarter of the century, the University of Wisconsin—the "Wisconsin Idea"—fashioned the first team of political brain-trusters for Robert La Follette, a Progressivist Governor of the state. (As a U.S. Senator, La Follette later ran for President on a third-party Progressive ticket in 1924.) In the 1960s, Wisconsin elected two left-liberal senators. Political combinations in Wisconsin, however, are capable of producing other animals: in the late 1940s and early '50s, the state elected Senator Joseph McCarthy, who needs no introduction.

The counter-revolt in Wisconsin has been directed against the black movement in the state, including the militant welfare demonstrations led by Father James Groppi in Milwaukee, and against the student left at the University of Wisconsin. After a student demonstration in 1967 against Dow Chemical recruitment on campus, the Republican-controlled state legislature became interested in ferreting out the influence of SDS and the Communist Party youth group, the W. E. B. Du Bois Club (which had no chapter on campus), and set up an investigating committee to subpoena students to get the names of subversives.

In late 1968, racial militancy became a *cause célèbre* in the state after 90 black students disrupted the office of the president of Wisconsin State and were forthwith expelled. The same fall, black students at the University of Wisconsin had carried out a series of disruptive demonstrations for their demands for more "relevant" courses. After a symposium on the "black revolution" in late January 1969, featuring Nathan Hare, a Black People's Alliance appeared to lead class disruptions by black and white students in support of demands for an autonomous black-studies department, an increase in the number of black students and faculty members, student control of a black cultural center, and the admission of the black students expelled from Wisconsin State. After disruptive demonstrations in the following days, Warren Knowles, the Republican Governor, sent in some 2,000 National Guard troops—the first time that National Guardsmen had ever been used against a major university. In later days, Governor Knowles made a point of lunching with National Guard troops in the gymnasium, while radical students held a rock-music festival to raise scholarship funds for black students. State officials maintained that white leftists were "in full control" of the strike—led by the Black People's Alliance—and were manipulating the black dupes. Students meanwhile marched in protest to the state capitol, which, like the university, was located in Madison.

In the spring after the black-studies demonstrations, student and non-student hippies fought police in Madison for several days in an effort to hold a "block party." The next fall, Father Groppi led welfare demonstrators, including Wisconsin students, in an actual occupation of the state legislature in protest of state welfare policies.

The authorities had ready answers to these impositions. Groppi was ordered to serve a formerly suspended sentence for previous demonstrations. Governor Knowles and the state legislature cut the university budget by $38 million. The Governor signed into law a bill providing for the expulsion of students involved in disruptions, and other bills were pending in early 1970 which provided not only for the dismissal of disruptive faculty members but also for the regulation of public-address systems and for charges of criminal trespass. Nonetheless, the momentum of student militancy continued into 1970 with militant demonstrations against General Electric and the Army's Mathematics Research Center and pitched battles with police and National Guardsmen during the national student strike in May.

Although California and Wisconsin lead the league in repressive legislation, they are not untypical. A number of

Southern states—North Carolina, South Carolina, Tennessee, and Texas—have passed harsh legislation directed mainly against the black student movement. Massachusetts and Pennsylvania have measures pending and others on the books, while Illinois has even more efficiently expedited the creation of its system of legal containment. The New York legislature has passed numerous measures for the control of student disruption, most of which have been vetoed by a liberal governor sensitive to the dangers of "counter-productive" effects. The same consideration has inhibited the passage of federal legislation, despite the countless bills which have been offered. After a report by a Congressional task force, the Nixon administration decided not to sponsor legislation to withhold federal aid from student demonstrators on these grounds. By early 1970, such a bill had nonetheless passed the U.S. House of Representatives.[30] By mid-1970, thirty states had passed eighty laws governing student rebellion.

In the cultural civil war, the university administrations are hoisted on their own rhetorical petards. Once they convince the public that the radical students represent a "small minority" of the student population, they are quite helpless to explain why they are unable to discipline the recalcitrants in a thorough and ruthless manner. Administrative caution and selective discipline are interpreted as "appeasement." Rhetorical inconsistency conveys an image of weakness and builds support for repressive legislation. As a result, state legislatures have passed measures which not only violate university autonomy but interfere with the administrative strategy of containment by requiring mandatory penalties for all student offenders. These measures can hardly serve the administratively defined cause of peace.

[30] For a tabulation of legislation pertaining to student demonstrations as of early 1970, see Urban Research Corporation, *Legislative Response to Student Protest* (Chicago, 1970).

2 THE IDEOLOGICAL DIMENSION

DURING THE COLUMBIA REBELLION in the spring of
1968, numerous faculty members offered to lend their services to radical students on a consultant basis. While students
stood on the ledges of Low Library, one very agitated faculty
member ran up to the building and shouted, "I teach *Marxism!* I teach *Marxism!*" He was pulled inside through a win-
dow. His advice was: the time is not ripe. At another point, a
musicologist succeeded in penetrating the lines of counter-
demonstrators, the police cordon, and the interior lines of the
rebels, and made his way into the building. He went to the
piano in the rotunda and began to play various tunes, while
offering cautionary political commentary. And so it went.
The art historians demonstrated that, art-wise, the confrontation was unaesthetic. The sociologists asserted that, sociologi-
cally speaking, the confrontation pointed to insufficient socialization. The political scientists suggested that from the

point of view of comparative political structures, the confrontation was impolitic.

The faculty and students were unable to make common cause against the university administration. This was no surprise, since the two groups had different interests to advance or to protect within the university. But the student left and the liberal faculty members were also destined to part ways because of the fundamental opposition between liberal and left politics. Since liberal theorists are often the political leaders of the faculties of major universities, this opposition is all the more inevitable. University conflicts release transforming passions because all parties understand, if only intuitively, that the rebellions are not exclusively "student" rebellions and that the stakes are not only university "policies" and "structures."

In the case of Columbia, radical students took and occupied five buildings in late April. During the first week of May, even before the ensuing student strike had run its course, the Columbia faculty's newly fashioned "Executive Committee" had fielded a commission of five educational and legal personages (including one Negro) from Harvard, the University of Pennsylvania, Brooklyn College, and a leading New York law firm to investigate the events and consider the "underlying causes of those disturbances." In a brief statement at the open hearings of this Cox Commission, a student representative of the Strike Coordinating Committee offered, as the group's only testimony, excerpts from a standard work on American politics:

The public hearing is usually a haphazard and unsatisfactory device for giving and receiving information. This is one function of such proceedings, but it alone would not account for their continued vitality. A second use is a propaganda channel through which a public may be extended and its segments partially consolidated or reinforced. A third function is to provide a quasi-ritualistic

means of adjusting group conflicts and relieving disturbances through a safety valve. . . .[1]

The passage was taken from *The Governmental Process*, an
exposition of the political theory of democratic pluralism, by
David Truman, Vice-President and Provost of Columbia
University, who, with Grayson Kirk, the President, had been
the chief representative of the university authorities in the
conflict.

Student rebellion is both real and symbolic. Materially,
student rebellion is a struggle between the local interests of
students and administration/faculty within the university
and a struggle *for* the university between the forces of a re-
nascent left and those of the center and right. Symbolically,
campus confrontation represents a potential and to some degree actual struggle between the left and the center/right for
supremacy within the wider social order, as well as a conflict
in theory and social vision between a critical, left-oriented intelligentsia and the "mandarins"—the scholarly and technocratic professionals. The symbolic dimensions of student
rebellion account for the extraordinary passions and resentments that otherwise trivial events may release. These passions have led some analysts to regard student rebellion as
"psychodrama," a politically meaningless catharsis of group
emotions. To the contrary, student revolt is an actual drama
with an authentic political conflict whose meaning and implications outrun the immediate scene.

This point is illustrated by the protagonists who have so
often symbolized antagonistic political forces. During the
Free Speech Movement at the University of California at
Berkeley in 1964, a leading FSM spokesman was Mario Savio,
a philosophy student and an organizer for the Student Non-
violent Coordinating Committee during the Mississippi
Summer Project of 1964. Savio denounced the university as a

[1] Quoted in Jerry L. Avorn *et al.*, *Up Against the Ivy Wall* (New
York, 1968), p. 236.

"knowledge factory" and argued that the "conception that bureaucrats have is that history has in fact come to an end. No events can occur now that the Second World War is over which can change American society substantially." [2] The chief representative of the university authorities was the president of the university system, Clark Kerr, who was co-author of *Industrialism and Industrial Man*, in which he advanced the thesis that Western societies were examples of "pluralistic industrialism" where the essential social distinction was between the "managers" and "the managed." In a series of lectures published as *The Uses of the University*, Kerr popularized the concepts of the "multiversity" and the "knowledge industry" which emphasized the research-and-development role of the university in the processes of economic innovation and growth.

In his struggle with the student movement, President Kerr created a Council of Departmental Chairman as a faculty ally of the administration. The spokesman for this council was Robert A. Scalapino, chairman of the political-science department, a specialist in Asian politics, and a defender of U.S. policy in Vietnam. Scalapino, who was a possible heir to the Berkeley chancellorship, introduced an administration proposal to solve the FSM crisis as "our maximum effort to attain peace and decency." Against Kerr and Scalapino, the FSM often cited Paul Goodman, a social critic with a utopian anarchist perspective, who regarded students as the "major exploited class. The labor of intelligent youth *is* needed, and they are accordingly subjected to tight scheduling, speedup, and other factory exploitative methods." [3] In *Growing Up Absurd*, Goodman had attacked the "organized system" and its social priorities and foreign policies.

The Columbia rebellion of 1968 likewise engaged political theorists as political actors. The ruling-class sociology of

[2] Mario Savio, "An End to History," in Seymour Martin Lipset and Shelden S. Wolin, eds., *The Berkeley Student Revolt* (New York, 1965), p. 217.
[3] Quoted in "We Want a University," Lipset and Wolin, p. 208.

Marxism and the power-elite thesis of C. Wright Mills, a Columbia sociologist before his death in 1962, symbolically confronted the pluralist theory of David Truman, Vice-President of the university. Like Scalapino in the case of the Berkeley chancellorship, Truman was in line for the presidency of the university and had to suffer the disintegration of his prospects in the revolt. Daniel Bell, professor of sociology and later member of the governing Executive Committee of the faculty, was meanwhile instrumental in the formulation of the Ad Hoc Faculty Group's proposals for tactical compromise—the liberal alternative to the hard-line, unyielding policy of the administration. Formerly labor editor of *Fortune*, Bell promulgated the "end-of-ideology" doctrine in the early 1950s and did polemical battle with Mills in the latter part of the decade and with the Marxists before that. The pragmatic radicalism of Paul Goodman survived in the occupied Avery Hall, where architecture students were greatly influenced by Percival Goodman, a Columbia professor of architecture, who was co-author with his brother Paul of *Communitas*, an unconventional investigation of urban planning.

These examples illustrate the peculiar quality of university revolts. Each side has not only immediate interests and political strategies but also large theories of political forms, socioeconomic structures, and social change. These intellectual constructions are all-inclusive, so that the antagonists can produce theories which explain their own (and their opponents') situation as intellectuals, experts, and students in the context of the large movements of history. The explanations and counter-explanations with the implicit value judgments they carry are not generally flattering to the opposition, which is, of course, the point.

This theoretical combat cannot be dismissed as simply polemic and propaganda. A major thesis of this book is that the student movement can only be understood as a challenge to social ideology as well as to social policies and political establishments. The social ideology under challenge is liberalism.

In the 1960s the claim of liberal politics to progressive standing suffered a major setback as a result of the prosecution of the Vietnam War by the Democratic administrations of Kennedy and Johnson. There were from the beginning, however, liberal opponents to an interventionist policy in Southeast Asia and Latin America, so that the interventions in Vietnam, Cuba, and the Dominican Republic were not in themselves sufficient to discredit liberalism. By waging a campaign against the Vietnam War as a necessary consequence of liberal politics, not to mention capitalist society, the student left forced the issue of liberalism as a doctrine. The meaning of the student movement consists in the challenge not only to the balance of power within society, but to the cultural hegemony of liberal social thought. The student movement is also a movement within culture and among the intelligentsia whose roots are in the university system, which becomes a cockpit of political conflict in the several realms of culture, thought, education, science, and social policy.

It is true enough that the student left has never had a systematic alternative to liberal thought and consequently has increasingly fallen back on the Marxist tradition—no sin in itself but subject to vulgarization and false analogy. The enterprise of positive social construction is inevitably the task of left intellectuals; the ideological force of the student movement in the 1960s consisted primarily in its critique rather than in its changeable doctrines. Often enough, this critique took the form of vague denunciations of people called "liberals" and something called "liberalism." This rhetoric does not carry much weight, since liberalism covers contradictory ideas: the radical individualism of Thomas Jefferson and the social engineering of John Dewey, the laissez faire of the nineteenth century and the governmental interventions of the New Deal.

In practice, the passion of the student left is directed primarily against a contemporary mutant in social thought: official liberalism. Official liberalism is the postwar precipitate of several historical experiences of liberal democracy: the state intervention of "New Deal Liberalism," the reconciliation to corporate supremacy during World War II or "corporate liberalism," and the anti-communism of "Cold War liberalism." The result is a liberalism that has disengaged from reform passions and approaches a high conservatism that expresses itself mainly in Victorian prose and frequent quotations from Edmund Burke. Although the integration of the federal government and the dominant corporations, as well as anti-communist policies at home and abroad, may be traced at least as far back as World War I, official liberalism seemed to come of age in the 1960s. The Kennedy administration inaugurated the first concerted effort to employ Keynesian principles of state intervention to regulate economic growth, and carried to new levels of sophistication the judicious mix of schemes for "economic development" with capabilities for "counter-insurgency" to determine the course of history in the Third World. In their approach to government, the Kennedys brought to Washington a new spirit of technocratic planning on the French model; its exemplar was Robert McNamara, Secretary of Defense and later President of the World Bank.

Official liberalism is not a mass ideology but an official doctrine which grows in influence as the higher circles of power are approached. The Vietnam War has precipitated another, oppositional liberalism which is in closer touch with the popular wellsprings of traditional democratic liberalism. This new reform liberalism has been called the "New Politics," which is defined by its opposition to the Vietnam War, interventionist foreign policy, and the military/industrial complex and by its "concern" for popular participation in government and for the new fields of social reform: racial justice, urban reconstruction, and environmental quality. The new reform liberalism, of which the unsuccessful effort to nominate Senator Eugene McCarthy for President on the Democratic ticket in 1968 was an expression, harks back in many ways to the Progressive movement before World War I. New Politics liberalism is, like Progressivism, a mass movement of the middle class, which in the field of foreign policy seems to long for a return to Wilsonian principles.

It is to the credit of reform liberals that they take classical democracy seriously. They defend civil liberties and work for democratic government in the tradition handed down from John Locke and Thomas Jefferson. The weakness of democratic liberalism is that its concern for democratic principles and social reform does not necessarily supply it with the means of implementation or with a theory of social change. The theories of Locke and Jefferson were based explicitly on the social realities of property rights, individualism, and agrarian society. But the history of capitalist growth and state power in the nineteenth and twentieth centuries does not afford much comfort for classical democratic theory. For lack of an alternative, reform liberals combine eighteenth-century theory with twentieth-century social reality; they are, consequently, democratic capitalists. The possibility of a contradiction in terms is inconceivable for democratic liberals. Although democratic liberals generally reject "New Deal liberalism," they ultimately must fall back on its "welfare state" principles as the only means of implementing social reform. Whatever nostalgia they may have for antagonisms between the state and the corporations, they must also face the functional integration of the two systems of power and the social priorities they require. The split between official and democratic liberalism is, accordingly, provisional. The democratic liberals are ultimately dependent upon official liberal thought for theories of social change, concepts of planning, and for social programs, although they may demand greater emphasis on social mechanisms for the redistribution of income and from this direction approach social democracy.

The main enemy of the student left is official liberalism. Although the left may with some justification denounce democratic liberalism as the cohort of official liberalism, the left also recruits from the ranks of democratic liberals. It is official liberalism which takes up the active defense of corporate capitalism against the generally socialist conceptions of the left. If there is an official ideology in Karl Mannheim's sense of the thought of ruling groups which are "so intensively interest-bound to a situation that they are simply no longer able to see certain facts which would undermine their sense of domination," this ideology is official liberalism. As an ideology, official liberalism is a total explanation of society and all its contents and discontents, including students and intellectuals. The social explanations for these dissident strata, the political responses of university administrators to student protest, and the official understanding of the purposes of educational institutions follow from the main premises of official liberalism. For this reason, it will be worthwhile to examine the doctrines of official liberalism in more detail.

I. OFFICIAL LIBERALISM

Official liberalism has two characteristic social hypotheses: the pluralist conception of the political system and the technocratic characterization of the socio-economic realm. Democratic pluralism is a response to the failure of classical theory to explain the political realities of "industrial society." As a revision of democratic theory, pluralism concedes a great deal of ground to critics of the left. It grants that the people are not sovereign; that the citizen as an individual is virtually powerless; that the mass political parties are mainly collections of interests, not voters; that elections are a very limited expression of popular power; that the means of social control and public manipulation are extensive. According to pluralist theory, all of this is inevitable—a consequence of population growth, industrialization, and urbanization. But democracy is not a farce. Besides exercise of his voting franchise, the individual citizen has the important option of joining a "voluntary association," such as a professional society, a civil-rights group, a veterans' organization, where he can concert his resources with others of like mind to effect a political end. It is the operation of such voluntary associations and the organized "interest groups" on the political parties and governments which makes up politics in America.

According to pluralist theory, there is no single dominant interest group, such as "big business," but rather shifting coalitions of various groups among which politicians mediate as "power brokers." Although strict pluralists often maintain that the "public interest" is a vacuous concept, they generally assign an important role to "public opinion" in the democratic stabilization of interest-group competition. The consensus among interest groups and the public on the "rules of the game" protects modern democracy from the potential depredations of the coercive techniques of a "totalitarian democracy." Although many interests such as racial minorities, consumers, and the poor are admittedly unorganized, this presents no problem in principle. If unrepresented groups organize as coherent interest groups, there is always room for them, always another "piece of the action." In pluralist theory, the center of power is not an organized "power structure" but a phantom marketplace, dominated by the "free competition" of interest groups which money is powerless to command.

In a sense, pluralism is self-validating. A close-focus view of any social system uncovers a multiplicity of interest groups that are invisible to the naked eye. Where the casual observer in Russia might see only the power of the party, the military, and the bureaucracy, a Soviet pluralist might point to the countervailing power of consumer-oriented manufacture against heavy industry, of agricultural interests against both, of technical managers against party operatives. The issues are the class base of interest-group politics and the relative power of the interests. No social system is "monolithic." Historical investigations of "totalitarian" systems such as the Nazi re-

gime have discovered not a single, omnicompetent bureaucracy but a cacophony of conflicting authorities which the dic-
tator manipulates as the ultimate power broker. Without a
specification of the distribution of power and wealth among
social classes, a political analysis of institutional structures
and interest groups is meaningless. The issue, then, for the
pluralist explanation of American politics is the social base of
the interest groups.

It turns out that the large majority of powerful interests are
based in the upper and upper middle classes. There are ex-
ceptions—urban political machines (in decline), farm organizations (dominated by the rich farmer), the AFL-CIO (rep-
resenting a privileged minority of the labor force)—but most
of the "voluntary associations" are middle- and upper-class organizations. Although these interest groups may exercise considerable influence over official policy relevant to their specific
interests, some questions of greater import are essentially beyond the reach of their influence, such as foreign policy, military programs, and economic management. Unfortunately for
pluralist theory, these are the realms which determine the
course of national and even world history. They are directed
by the Presidential nucleus, the federal bureaucracy, and the
national and international corporations, with only occasional
interloping by tribunes of the people.

In *Democracy in America*, Alexis de Tocqueville, who is
often cited as a proto-pluralist, was careful to specify certain
social conditions which made pluralism viable in America: a
Western frontier, to which the masses could escape from the
ossification of the class structure; the widely dispersed ownership of the press, which helped to ensure the free circulation
of information; and an isolationist foreign policy, which prevented the central government from growing strong through
the prosecution of war. Since the 1830s, when Tocqueville
wrote, the frontier has disappeared, the press and electronic
media have been organized by media corporations, and the
state prospers in a condition of permanent war.

Tocqueville also took careful note of the "manufacturing aristocracy which is growing up under our eyes"; it was "one of the harshest which ever existed in the world" but was also in 1831 "one of the most confined and least dangerous." Tocqueville advised the friends of democracy to "keep their eyes anxiously fixed in this direction" since "if ever a permanent inequality of conditions and aristocracy again penetrate into the world, it may be predicted that this is the gate by which they will enter." [4] Instead, political pluralists have deprecated the influence of corporate interests within the government and ignored the public powers wielded directly by private corporations. They have also failed to consider the import of powers left unassumed and planning left undone because of governmental consideration of private interests. Instead of keeping "their eyes anxiously fixed" in the direction of the corporate rich, the pluralists have kept their eyes anxiously fixed on Tocqueville.

It is to explain the pre-eminent realities of state and corporate power that official liberalism falls back on the technocratic line of argument. The lines of force of this reasoning often conflict with pluralist theory. Whereas pluralism attempts to salvage a democratic polity from the complex of industrial society, technocratic logic assumes that democratic control is impossible in the wider reaches of the social realm, including the governmental. This contradiction does not prevent official liberals from maintaining both theories simultaneously. In *Industrialism and Industrial Man*, Clark Kerr and his co-authors predict the worldwide triumph of "pluralistic industrialism":

> Industrialism is a system of social organization where industries, including many large-scale industries, are the dominant method of production. Such a system cannot be an atomistic one with infinite fractionalization of power and distribution of decision-making. Authority

[4] Alexis de Tocqueville, *Democracy in America*, Vol. II, (New York: Knopf, 1956), p. 161.

must be concentrated, although individuals may still have areas in which they can make free choices. Authority may be concentrated in a monistic or pluralistic arrangement. It is our view that the dominant arrangement will be pluralistic. Where there is one locus of power, there will be several; where there are many, there will come to be fewer.[5]

The logic of pluralistic industrialism is contained in the sentence: "Authority may be *concentrated* in a monistic or pluralistic arrangement" (emphasis added). In the United States, "pluralism" consists in the *incorporation* of private interest groups into the governing apparatus of society and in the dissolution of the distinction between public and private authority.

Technocratic logic is reductionist in spirit. Its subject is industrial society; capitalist and socialist models of development are generally discussed only in reference to the Third World, since the more or less socialist and the more or less capitalist countries in the West are "converging." It is implied that the capitalist organization of an industrial society has no consequences of great import. Its authoritarian premise is derived from an interpretation of the basic developments of the last century: massive industrialization, accelerating population growth, the traumatic impact of science and technology. Under these conditions, bureaucracy is a necessity, and where there is bureaucracy, there are structures of authority and hierarchy: "elites." This is the "iron law of oligarchy," in the classic formulation of Robert Michels. A related factor working against democratic social organization, technocrats argue, is the ever greater role of specialized knowledge, especially scientific knowledge, in the management of the great bureaucracies and of society at large. There is inherent hierarchy, whether institutionalized or not, in the

[5] Clark Kerr, John I. Dunlop, Frederick H. Harbison, and Charles A. Meyers, *Industrialism and Industrial Man* (Cambridge, Mass., 1960), pp. 288–9.

relations of the knowledgeable and the ignorant, those possessing relevant information and those not. The increasing role of research and development in an expanding economy necessarily results in the union of expertise and bureaucracy in such roles as the technical advisor and the research manager.

Technocratic theory does not entirely abandon the defense of democratic values. Although the industrial state is authoritarian in structure, it is democratic in recruitment. Positions of authority are open to men of any class or income level, if only they have the requisite intellect and training. The state and corporate bureaucracies create the social conditions of a rationalized capitalism: equal opportunity, high social mobility, and the dissolution of class lines. But there are problems with this theory. Equal access to positions of authority in the bureaucracies presupposes an educational system which provides approximately equal opportunities to all income groups. Investigations which have set out to prove this point have discovered the opposite. Likewise, studies of social mobility and the distribution of income have discovered no significant changes since World War II. "Meritocracy" also presupposes the "separation of ownership and control" within the corporations, sometimes known as the "managerial revolution." This thesis has never been proved empirically by a systematic investigation of stock ownership and control within American corporations.[6]

Official liberalism also has a theory of social change for the contemporary epoch, a theory which is crucial to its explanation of opposition movements. This notion is of a contempo-

[6] For a discussion of educational opportunity, see Christopher Jencks and David Riesman, "Social Stratification and Mass Higher Education" in *The Academic Revolution* (New York, 1968). On social mobility, see Peter M. Blau and Otis Dudley Duncan, *The American Occupational Structure* (New York, 1967); for trends in the distribution of income, consult Herman P. Miller, *Income Distribution in the United States* (Washington, D.C., 1966). The thesis of the separation of ownership and control was promulgated by Adolph A. Berle and Gardiner C. Means in 1932 in *The Modern Corporation and Private Property* (New York, 1932), but has never been proved in an empirical investigation of the major corporations in the United States.

rary transition from prosaic industrial capitalism to "post-capitalism," the "technetronic age," or whatever. As evidence for his variant, the "post-industrial society," Daniel Bell cites three economic trends. The first is the decline of the manu-facturing sector of the economy—the focus of industrial capi-talism—and the growth of the "service" sector (government, trade, finance, utilities, etc.), which now accounts for approx-imately half of employment and gross national product. The second trend is the change in the composition of the labor force so that white-collar employees have come to outnum-ber blue-collar workers, and the category of professional and technical occupations has come to grow faster than the other occupational categories—from 6.6 percent of the total in 1940 to an estimated 14.9 percent in 1975. (Like the other occupational categories, however, the professional/technical category is loose and non-exclusive.) Finally and crucially, *knowledge* has become the major source of innovation and economic growth, and now constitutes approximately 30 per-cent of total production. (Again, "knowledge" is defined loosely.)

If knowledge in a general sense is the motor of economic growth, then the university, the producer of original and the-oretical knowledge, is on its way to becoming the dominant institution in the society. The university, Bell concludes, will be the "primary institution of the new society," and the "husbanding of talent and the spread of educational and in-tellectual institutions will become a prime concern for soci-ety; not only the best talents but eventually the entire com-plex of social prestige and social status will be rooted in the intellectual and scientific communities." [7] In this account, power creeps noticeably closer to the professoriate, especially to those engaged in work of potential economic and political use—in the sciences, engineering, the professions, and the so-cial sciences.

Although the university is hardly the origin of the 30 per-

[7] Daniel Bell, "Notes on the Post-Industrial Society: I" in *The Public Interest*, Winter 1967, p. 30.

cent of the GNP categorized as knowledge (all of higher education accounts for 2 percent), there is no doubt that its operations have practical effects. This evolution is the result of two historic events of the century—World War II and the Cold War—which created the federal government's interest in the resources of the university. The applied-physics laboratories, the policy-studies institutes, the nuclear-explosives laboratories, and the other varieties of research institutes (especially medical) of the universities, as well as grants direct to individual faculty members, are a nuclear core which stimulates economic growth by spinning off other research institutes, experimental laboratories, and information corporations in the region. Military technology is central to the process, since almost half of the research subsidy to universities is military-related. The apotheosis of the university—traditionally associated with left-of-center politics—through the agency of military technology, Bell calls "ironic."

We have by now surely passed into the realm of technocratic ideology. The university, crucial to the technocratic vision of a bureaucratic (but meritocratic) social order based on equal educational opportunity, is invested with a second crucial function—the research and development necessary for economic growth and national security. Before it is even established that managers have taken power from propertied wealth, the technocrats take over from the managers. All that is left is the ceremonial gesture of handing power over to the university men. "To speak rashly," Bell writes, "if the dominant figures of the past hundred years have been the entrepreneur, the businessman, and the industrial executive, the 'new men' are the scientists, the mathematicians, the economists, and the engineers of the new computer technology. And the dominant institutions of the new society—in the sense that they will provide the most creative challenges and enlist the richest talents—will be the intellectual institutions. The leadership of the new society will rest, not with businessmen or corporations as we know them (for a good deal of production will have been routinized), but with the research corporation, the industrial laboratories, the experimental stations, and the universities." [8] But just as the National Academy of Sciences is about to seize power and to inaugurate the Hundred-Year Mandarinate, Bell draws back. Most of the research is, after all, done under contract to the federal government: "It is not the technocrat who ultimately holds power, but the politician."

There are, of course, political differences within the technocratic consensus. If Bell holds the center, John Kenneth Galbraith leads the loyal opposition. In *The New Industrial State*, he envisions a split in the technocracy between the conservative "techno-structure" of the corporations and the "educational and scientific estate" in the universities, government, and foundations, which will occasionally take up liberal causes. The right, unquestionably, belongs to Zbigniew Brzezinski, a "communist affairs" expert at Columbia University and former member of the Policy Planning Council of the U.S. Department of State. In his *Encounter* article "America in the Technetronic Age," Brzezinski caricatures the standard notions of technocratic thought:

> On the social level, American innovation is most strikingly seen in the manner in which the new meritocratic elite is taking over American life, utilising the universities, exploiting the latest techniques of communications, harnessing as rapidly as possible the most recent technological devices. [9]

In the same article, Brzezinski explores, with some alacrity, the possibilities for the dictatorship of the professoriate:

> Moreover, the rapid pace of change will put a premium on anticipating events and planning for them. Power will gravitate into the hands of those who control the infor-

[8] Bell, p. 27.

[9] Zbigniew Brzezinski, "America in the Technetronic Age," *Encounter*, January 1968, p. 23.

mation, and can correlate it most rapidly. Our existing *post*-crisis management institutions will probably be increasingly supplanted by *pre*-crisis management institutions, the task of which will be to identify in advance likely social crises and to develop programs to cope with them. This could encourage tendencies during the next several decades towards a technocratic dictatorship, leaving less and less room for political procedures, as we now know them.[10]

Official liberals have ready in the vision of a post-industrial society a theory of social and economic change by which they can dismiss in advance any opposition to the corporate state. A left ideology, for instance, might be classified as a "disease of the transition" from industrial to post-industrial society analogous to W. W. Rostow's characterization of communist ideology in countries moving from pre-industrial to industrial societies. The dislocations which must result from such a transition will provide the makings of an explanation of opposition in terms of social pathology—especially, historical "obsolescence." In like fashion, the new social order will be described as historically inevitable, and those who make it as the "real revolutionaries of our time," in another Rostow formulation. The leading concept—the transition from one social order to another based on a change in the dominant mode of production—is taken from Marx, but the concept of the transition is *reduced* to purely technological and economic terms. Although the technocrats are the true revolutionaries, they do not create culture or new values. The ideology is a vulgarized and inverted Marxism of the ruling class—a true case of convergence.

This technocratic realism is a crackpot realism. This does not prevent it from becoming official doctrine. The political eminence of Rostow, foreign-policy advisor to Presidents Kennedy and Johnson, and Brzezinski, who was Hubert

10 Brzezinski, p. 21.

Humphrey's foreign-policy advisor in the 1968 Presidential campaign, attests to its influence in foreign policy, while Galbraith, a former ambassador to India, and Bell, a member of a Presidential commission on technology, now survey the whole range of social policy as members of the Democratic Council, the policy-making body of the Democratic Party.

The technocratic solution to the social problem of the leftist intellectuals follows from the logic of post-industrial obsolescence: the age requires specialists and technicians; the intellectuals are not specialists and technicians; therefore, the intellectuals are obsolete. In Brzezinski's formulation:

> A profound change in the intellectual community itself is inherent in this development. The largely humanist-oriented, occasionally ideologically-minded intellectual-dissenter, who saw his role largely in terms of proffering social critiques, is rapidly being displaced either by experts and specialists, who become involved in special government undertakings, or by the generalist-integrators, who become in effect house ideologues for those in power, providing overall intellectual integration for disparate actions. A community of organization-oriented, application-minded intellectuals, relating itself more effectively to the political system than their predecessors, serves to introduce into the political system concerns broader than those likely to be generated by the system itself and perhaps more relevant than those articulated by outside critics.[11]

Although social critique is outmoded, Brzezinski finds a place in his hyphenated prose for the "generalist-integrator" and the "house ideologue," who are also more "effective" because they work from the inside. The intellectuals, on the other hand, tend to be humanists and thus committed to the traditional (therefore obsolescent) values of freedom and social justice which are irrelevant to the New Era. In this spirit,

[11] Brzezinski, p. 22.

Raymond Aron, a French exponent of the end-of-ideology doctrine, said of the French students after the May Rebellion that their revolt was a "refusal of modernity."

As it constitutes the left opposition and operates within the dominant institution of the "technetronic" society, the student movement could no more expect to escape the critical attention of official liberals than the left intellectuals. From the previous exposition, it is not difficult to anticipate the forms of explanation and criticism. In an article in *The New Republic*, "Revolution and Counterrevolution (But Not Necessarily About Columbia!)," Brzezinski compares student rebellion to the inchoate rebellion of English workers —the Chartists or the machine-smashing Luddites—under the impact of early industrialization. These rebellions were "essentially counterrevolutionary" because they could formulate no alternative vision of the future, but relied on traditional values and the preservation of past social organization. Similarly, peasant uprisings and anarchist revolutions have failed to formulate a social vision adequate to the social facts. On the same grounds, Brzezinski consigns the student movement to the proverbial dustbin of history:

> On the contrary, it is revealing here to note that some of the recent upheavals have been led by people who increasingly will have no role to play in the new technetronic society. Their reaction reflects both a conscious and, even more important, an unconscious realization that they themselves are becoming historically obsolete. The movements they lead are more reminiscent of the Red Guards or the Nazis, than of the Bolsheviks or the French revolutionaries. Thus, rather than representing a true revolution, some recent outbursts are in fact a counterrevolution. Its violence and revolutionary slogans are merely—and sadly—the death rattle of the historical irrelevants.[12]

12 Zbigniew Brzezinski, "Revolution and Counterrevolution (But Not Necessarily About Columbia!)" *The New Republic*, June 1, 1968, p. 25.

The claim that radical students will "have no role to play" in an advanced society apparently derives from the fact that these students are in the liberal arts. The unstated assumptions are that in the "technetronic age," technicians are the men of power; that in the university the talented men of the future are in technical and professional fields; and therefore that liberal-arts majors are concentrating in declining fields. Brzezinski's arguments are specious, because generalists, not specialists, manage a "technological society"; managers, not technicians, dispose of technical resources; while politicians, not their advisors, make political decisions. On the undergraduate level, the generalists, managers, and politicians more often come out of the liberal arts than the technical fields. Liberal education is a characteristically elite education. Student radicals, majoring in liberal-arts subjects, could hardly rebel out of the "unconscious realization" of their obsolescence, since they have the option of becoming men of power —lawyers, politicians, corporate managers, financial executives. The explanation for the origin of most student radicals in liberal-arts fields is that political questions are raised in the course of study in these areas and the basic legitimations of a society may be challenged in the literature of the field. Accordingly, the highest percentage of student radicals comes from explicitly political fields—political science, sociology, and history. Other radicals are likely to come out of disciplines where social critique has a prominent place: philosophy, modern literature, and the like. There is evidence that contemplative students select these fields for exactly this reason, while careerist students opt for technical and professional fields for reasons of job security.

The sociological evidence concerning student radicals provides little comfort for the theorists of social obsolescence, much less for the egregious notion of the "death rattle of the historical irrelevants." These surveys indicate that student leftists have their social origins in the more educated sectors of the society: the urban, affluent, upper middle class—

especially politically liberal professionals with Jewish or liberal Protestant religious affiliations.[13] The technocratic argument is also a distortion in its own terms. There is radical activity in the professions and in the pure sciences. For example, the students who occupied Avery Hall at Columbia were students of architecture and urban planning.

The technocrats also have a theory of cultural nihilism, which explains student revolt as a species of alienation (really, boredom) based on affluence. Herman Kahn, director of the Hudson Institute and former military analyst for the RAND Corporation, suggests this scenario in *The Year 2000*:

> Thus there may be a great increase in selfishness, a great decline of interest in government and society as a whole, and a rise in the more childish forms of individualism and in the more anti-social forms of concern for self and immediate family. Thus, paradoxically, the technological, highly productive society, by demanding less of the individual, may decrease his economic frustrations but increase his aggressions against the society. Certainly here would be fertile soil for what has come to be known as alienation.[14]

Clearly, this is not a pleasant "alternative future" for a future-planner to contemplate, even for one who managed to keep cool through a treatise *On Thermonuclear War*. The "post-industrial" society will provide the population with high income, vast stretches of leisure time, and a longer, healthier life. At the same time, the social system will of necessity be

---

[13] Cf. The studies of Somers, Selvin and Hagstrom, and Lyonns in Lipset and Wolin; Richard Flacks in the *Journal of Social Issues* (July 1967); Watts and Whittaker in *Journal of Applied Behaviorial Science* (1966, 2); Block, Haan, and Smith in James F. Adams, ed., *Contributions to an Understanding of Adolescence* (Boston, 1968); Paul Heist in O. A. Knorr and W. V. Mintner, eds., *Order and Freedom on the Campus* (Boulder, Colo., 1965).

[14] Herman Kahn and Anthony J. Wiener, *The Year 2000: A Framework of Speculation for the Next Thirty-Three Years* (New York, 1967), p. 199.

increasingly bureaucratic, remote, and incomprehensible, so that mass loyalty to it could decline drastically as it fulfilled its promise of affluence. The population would include a high percentage of youth which, as a result of mass education, would make large, possibly unreasonable demands on the social system. The prolongation of adolescence in educational institutions would encourage social irresponsibility in combination with psychological frustration caused by the unnatural postponement of adulthood. In the universities, the young would be learning the anti-bourgeois tradition of modern culture, itself based on the failure of a secular society to provide transcendental values. All of these conditions pose the possibility of a crisis of values and aimless rebellion on the model of Raymond Aron's "psychodrama" in France in May 1968.

The defect of this theory is that alienated youth and radical youth are distinct, not identical groups, so that alienation based on affluence does not necessarily explain the activities of the young radicals.[15] The radical preoccupation with "alienation" is founded on the young Marx's notion of alienation in the *work process*, not on the idea of alienation growing out of affluence. Although Kahn predicts more meaningful work based on the higher levels of skill and education in an advanced society, he also envisions a decreasing necessity for work and the pensioning off of a large percentage of the work force. In this way, the same social dislocations which Kahn would explain as affluent idleness, radicals would attribute to the unavailability of interesting work for most people and the lack of autonomy when good work was available. Two theories of alienation are competing: consumer's alienation against producer's alienation.

"Generational conflict" draws on some of the same social hypotheses as the affluence/alienation theory. If mass higher education prolongs adolescence and even creates a new stage of life ("post-adolescence" or "youth"), the postponement of

[15] Cf. Kenneth Keniston, *Young Radicals* (New York, 1968); Watts and Whittaker study cited above.

adulthood might also create psychological frustrations and increase the urge to take on the authorities as a father surrogate. A "quickening rate of social change" might open up a widening cultural gap between the generations and enhance the potential for conflict. In his *Conflict of Generations*, Lewis Feuer, social psychologist and editor of a standard anthology of Marx's writings, grounds the explanation historically by arguing that unconscious forces of generational conflict are released only if the "generational equilibrium" is upset by a large historical event or circumstance which "deauthorizes" the older generation. This factor raises the possibility that student revolt is objectively justified, although Feuer, who was an active opponent of the FSM at Berkeley in 1964, emphasizes the "irrationality" and "unconscious sources" of student movements.

The notion of Oedipal rebellion depends on Freudian concepts and thus, as a scientific explanation, rests on rather shaky foundations. What is decisive, however, is that the empirical evidence contradicts the theory. Once again, the sociological surveys indicate that radical students, unlike alienated students, *share* in high degree the political opinions of their parents and, compared to non-activist students, share fundamental family values as well.[16] Although radical students are naturally to the left of their parents, they are also acting within a cultural and family tradition.

Some elements of these explanations are undeniable facts of the student movement. The student movement did emerge from the elite universities, and student radicals are often enough the children of affluence. From this fact, the Movement's critics readily conclude that the young leftists suffer the alienation of the sated and the radical instincts of the lib-

[16] Cf. studies of Keniston and Flacks cited above; also Richard Braungart's study, the results of which are reported by Seymour Martin Lipset and Philip G. Altbach in a volume edited by Lipset, *Student Politics* (New York, 1967). On the other side, Block, Haan, and Smith in the *Journal of Social Issues* (Fall 1969) find evidence of rebellion against parents among "dissenters," although not among "activists," who are less protest-oriented than dissenters.

ertine, while its sympathizers argue that the affluent young have transcended materialism through conspicuous consumption and now long for spiritual things. As we have seen, however, the correlation between affluence and radicalism is indirect; the young left is descended from educated professionals rather than from wealth per se. Similarly, it is true that students may acquire a critical bent from the anti-bourgeois currents in modern culture and may also suffer a crisis of values in a secular society which banishes transcendent values. But cultural modernism and religious crisis (and affluence as well) are familiar features of Western society; they are as characteristic of the 1950s—or, for that matter, the 1920s, when there was no student movement—as they are of the present era.

Explanation of the student movement based upon affluence, crisis of values, and cultural modernism lacks a historical foundation. The same is true of generational conflict—a characteristic feature of industrial societies, which needs to be related to the emergence of youth culture in order to apply to the American student movement of the 1960s. "Permissive" family socialization is another frequently cited cause of the student movement which, if it were crucial, might just as well have had powerful effects before the late 1960s. Family socialization is more a function of social and cultural background—in this case, the educated upper middle class—than an independent factor. Some sociological studies indicate a pattern of inconsistency in the family socialization of radicals in which parental expectations are permissive in some areas and demanding in others. An emphasis on competitive mettle, together with a certain liberality, which these surveys reveal in the child-rearing of the parents of radicals, seems a more realistic reflection of life among the liberal professions than the Roman image of indulgence and permissiveness which the Movement's critics depict.[17] Taken together, all of these fac-

[17] See the studies of Block, Haan, and Smith cited above. In their 1969 study, these writers find that the upbringing of the "dissenters" exhibits an inconsistency between permissiveness and competitive de-

tors—affluence, crisis of values, cultural modernism, generational conflict, and permissive upbringing—tend to lack a historical dimension and have only a marginal explanatory force. What is remarkable is that each of them has been pushed forward by academic analysts as the sole cause of the student movement.

II. ORIGINS OF THE STUDENT MOVEMENT

To arrive at a historical explanation of the student movement, it is necessary to examine the Movement's history, which begins as an on-campus phenomenon with the Free Speech Movement of 1964. In the academic year of 1963–64, the civil-rights movement arrived in the San Francisco Bay Area when the city of Berkeley's CORE launched a campaign for equal employment opportunities. In the fall of 1963, students participated in the direct-action movement, consisting primarily of picketing, sit-ins, and "shop-ins," to force local merchants to increase their hiring of racial minorities. This campaign culminated in the Sheraton Palace Hotel demonstration, when 2,000 students violated a court order restricting the number of pickets and 800 were arrested. In the early 1960s, many Bay Area students, including Berkeley students, had gone south to participate in the civil-rights movement; it was this movement which activated the formerly desultory student protest at the university, raising the level of participation from handfuls to hundreds and occasionally thousands, and leading toward direct-action tactics.

In the early fall of 1964, campus civil-rights groups were planning to continue the direct-action campaign against local

---

mands, while the upbringing of the "activists" is in significant respect not permissive at all. The "permissive" family socialization of young radicals may also be regarded as education in freedom and responsibility, which conflicts with the repressiveness of authoritarian bureaucracies (see studies of Flacks and Heist cited above).

merchants and businesses, including the *Oakland Tribune,* when the university forbade the further use of a campus area that had been used to publicize and organize political activity. The university authorities argued that there was a distinction between "free speech" and "political advocacy." Since the university was an "educational institution," President Clark Kerr asserted, it was "not right to use the University as a basis from which people organize and undertake direct action in the surrounding community." Student activists considered this policy merely a capitulation to the demands of outside powers—particularly local businessmen affected by the civil-rights campaign, such as the rightist publisher of the *Oakland Tribune,* former U.S. Senator William Knowland— that the student-based civil-rights movement be repressed. On the grounds that political advocacy was also a free-speech issue, student organizations—including Young Democrats and Young Republicans, but also socialist youth groups, and pre-eminently Campus CORE and University Friends of SNCC—founded the Free Speech Movement and eventually, under the leadership of the civil-rights activists, organized mass sit-ins against the university.

The civil-rights movement, then, activated not only the Free Speech Movement at Berkeley but the white student movement generally by bringing white students into political motion with the sit-ins, freedom rides, and voter-registration campaigns of the early 1960s. Black students meanwhile were the cutting edge of the civil-rights movement; black college students originated the sit-in tactic in North Carolina in 1960 and generated a spontaneous student sit-in movement throughout the South that led to the formation of the Student Nonviolent Coordinating Committee (SNCC) the same year. Since the early 1960s, a black student movement has continued to evolve within the context of a larger black social movement, while the white student movement has developed within a mainly white anti-war movement, but has continued to be strongly influenced by the black movement even after the black-power declarations of 1966. The postwar social forces—urbanization of the black population, the expansion of the Negro middle class, the rise of Third World nationalism—which have influenced the black movement have influenced the white student movement by extension. Although black students did not play a direct role in the FSM, the black movement and the white student movement symbolically intersected from the beginning.

The civil-rights activists were a nucleus of the nascent New Left movement and many already subscribed to socialist politics, as indicated by a sociological survey of a militant demonstration during the FSM. The following year the New Left took off at Berkeley and throughout the country when President Lyndon Johnson escalated the counter-insurgency operations in Vietnam into a full-scale "limited war." The Students for a Democratic Society brought 25,000 people to Washington in 1965 in the first mass protest against the war, and although SDS later effectively dropped out of the anti-war movement, the New Left gained strength from the momentum of the anti-war movement among students and the upper middle class. At Berkeley in 1965, the Vietnam Day Committee organized a mass march on the Oakland Army Base and an attempt to stop troop trains.

The escalation of the war in the years 1964–68 was a constant impetus to campus-based radical action throughout the country. The Selective Service System compounded the radicalizing effects of the war by drafting individuals from elements that were most likely to oppose the war. Conscription bore increasingly heavily on students after 1967, when graduate and professional school deferments were eliminated. Before 1967, opinion surveys did not reveal greater opposition to the war among students than among the general population. Ironically, students launched the campaign of the middle '60s for greater equity in the draft, to which the 1967 alterations in conscription policy were largely a response.

Protest actions against the war took the form of draft resistance, opposition to the military presence on campus, and mass anti-war demonstrations. "Stop the Draft Week," an assault on the Oakland induction center in 1967, was an example of the increasing militancy of the latter. On-campus action was directed against university contributions to the war effort, such as military-related research-and-development and manpower services, such as ROTC and military and defense-industry recruitment. By 1969, arson and bombings of ROTC buildings and other military installations were common occurrences. Although the Nixon administration began to withdraw troops from Vietnam in 1969, its extension of the war into Laos and Cambodia precipitated a national student strike in May 1970. The war in Indo-China is a second major political cause of the student movement.

One of the main themes of the FSM was the denunciation of the "knowledge factory" and of the "multiversity." Mass lectures, the low priority of teaching, the dominance of the values of research, and the university as a "service station" to the industrial economy were all elements of the student left's critique of the multi-function university. The widely proclaimed objective of the FSM was to bring the "machine" to a "grinding halt." In the year after the FSM, there was an abortive effort to organize a student syndicalist movement that would advance student interests within the institution through the tactics of a labor movement. After the FSM, a "free university" movement arose in Berkeley and throughout the country. Although these free universities generally failed for lack of financing, serious subject matter, or educational direction, their existence alone was a challenge to the bureaucratic system of education, characterized by a system of standard units of input and output enforced by several levels of authority. Although opinion surveys of Berkeley students after the FSM indicated that they were not especially dissatisfied with the quality of their education, the drop-out rate for the University of California at Berkeley—the great experiment in large-scale elite education sponsored by state government—was 50 percent for its undergraduates, who comprised some 15,000 of its 27,500 students. This rate compares with a figure of less than 10 percent for the smaller, private universities of comparable stature. Although the undergraduate colleges of the large public universities are usually less selective than the private universities, their much higher drop-out rates are prima-facie evidence for student dissatisfaction with the undergraduate education and mass society of these multiversities.

The big three of these public multiversities—California, Wisconsin, and Michigan—have been leading centers of radical initiative. Among the private universities, only Columbia and Howard (also notably large and impersonal institutions) have played a comparable role, while the big three among the private institutions—Harvard, Yale, and Princeton—have tended to follow initiatives developed elsewhere. The central role of the public multiversities in the development of the radical movement, along with the free-university movement and the wide popularity of educational reform, strongly suggests that the advent of mass higher education since World War II has contributed as a fundamental social precondition, and not only as a political catalyst, to the rise of a student movement. Statistically, mass higher education means that 50 percent of the college-age population now receives some higher schooling, compared to 16 percent after the war. Current enrollment is over 7.3 million, compared to 2.2 million in 1947, while expenditures have increased from slightly over $1 billion to more than $20 billion. This rapid expansion has transformed the higher educational system as it affects students. Increasing enrollments have resulted in standardized testing and regular examination at all levels and in rising competition for admissions, grades, honors, and emoluments. The mass conditions of student life have contributed to the rise of large, impersonal bureaucracies to administer the student masses, and have opened the way to various forms of commercial exploitation by inflating local prices and tightening the housing market. Some of the recent responses to these mass conditions have been the 1969–70 rent strike at Berkeley and the popular uprisings in the Isla Vista, the student compound of mass high-rise dormitories at the University of California at Santa Barbara.

The national surveys of student protest have generally found a close correlation between the size of educational institutions and the probability of student protests.[18] The same surveys have indicated, however, that educational issues have been secondary protest issues, while other opinion surveys have not uncovered great student dissatisfaction with the quality of education. For these reasons, many analysts have discounted education and the conditions of student life as fundamental causes of student rebellion. It is often maintained that the correlation of institutional size and student protest is a function of the necessity for a "critical mass" of radical students, who form an activist subculture which is self-reinforcing and catalyzes protest. While it is evident that there must be a minimum number of radical students for protest to occur, it is doubtful that this thesis can account for the correlation between size and protest. In its survey of 1969 protests, the Urban Research Corporation found that the incidence of protest greatly increased with the size of the institution: 1 percent for schools of less than 500 students, 3 percent for schools of less than 1,000 students, 8 percent for schools of less than 5,000, 27 percent for those of less than 10,000, and 54 percent for those of more than 10,000 enrollment. If it were a question of a "critical mass," one would expect the incidence of protest to level off after a certain institutional size, rather than to increase steadily. Similarly, Richard Peterson found in a survey of 1967–68 protests that there was a generally positive correlation between size

[18] E.g., Richard Peterson, *The Scope of Organized Protest in 1964–65* (Princeton, N.J., 1966) and *The Scope of Organized Student Protest in 1967–68* (Princeton, N.J., 1968); Alexander Astin and Alan E. Bayer, *Campus Disruption During 1968–69* (Washington, D.C., 1969); Urban Research Corporation, *Student Protests 1969* (Chicago, 1970).

and protest, and a large increase in the probability of protests at the large public universities (a principal growth sector of mass higher education) compared to the national sample. In a study of protest in 1968–69, Alexander Astin and Alan Bayer also discovered the highest incidence of protest at the medium and large universities and at the large community colleges—the institutions most affected by the postwar expansion of higher education. Since there have been no efforts to correlate the incidence of protest with the rate of expansion of enrollments, the evidence of national surveys does not conclusively prove the relevance of mass education to student protest.

Another fact that seems to argue against the mass-education thesis is the strength of the student movement in the elite institutions. Although the elite institutions among the state universities have been centers of radical activity, the mediocre state universities lagged until 1969–70. As a rule, the private universities, most of which are elite, have experienced more protest than the public universities as a group. Institutional size and expansion of enrollments do not explain all the variations in the incidence of protest. Although the large community colleges had many protests in 1969, the smaller public two-year colleges had almost none.

Nonetheless, the higher probability of student rebellion in elite institutions, both public and private, has roots in the postwar transformation of higher education, which has been qualitative as well as quantitative. Under the pressure of the economic demand for higher degrees, the undergraduate colleges of the elite institutions have increasingly become *preparatory* institutions for graduate and professional schools. This transformation has intensified the competition for grades, admission, and preferment, which was already exacerbated by the expansion in enrollments; it has also undermined the traditional role of the college as a moratorium on secular pressures and a time for reflection, cultural exploration, and the search for self.

The elite institutions have been affected by a postwar *industrialization* of education, which consists not only in the expansion of enrollments but in the transformation of the internal character of educational institutions. Higher education has been industrialized in three respects. (1) Funds for the entire system, increasingly coming from the federal government, have been allocated to serve economic purposes, mainly manpower development and basic and applied research. (2) Among the elite institutions, research has taken priority over teaching and graduate education over undergraduate education, while the "service" functions of the universities overshadow both scholarship and education. (3) The higher educational system, whether large universities under corporate forms of organization or state systems managed by superboards, has been subjected to industrial methods of operation. The national results of educational industrialization are the rise of publicly subsidized, research-oriented universities, the decline of the liberal-arts colleges (which are starved of funds), and the appearance of factory-like community colleges to undertake routine manpower functions. Traditional student-oriented functions, such as undergraduate teaching and liberal education, have declined as a result of the financial weakness of liberal-arts colleges and the priority of research and service functions in the universities. The national student/faculty ratio, which stood around 12.5 in 1960, rose to 13.5 in 1970 and is estimated to increase to 14.5 by 1980. Within the major universities, the priority placed upon original research and scholarship has reinforced this decline on the elite levels. As less faculty time has been available for teaching and the quality of the effort has declined, these institutions have employed industrial solutions: high inputs of educational technology and the sweat labor of graduate teaching assistants. The reality of industrial methods of mass instruction is reflected in the rise of teachers' unionism among graduate teaching assistants and regular faculty members as well, particularly at community colleges. Teaching assistants at Berkeley and the University of Wisconsin have in recent years launched protracted strikes for better working conditions, educational reforms, and political objectives. Faculty members have increasingly unionized in the community colleges, where they have the standing of white-collar employees. These community colleges, which now educate 20 percent of all students, are projected to educate 33 percent by 1980.

Since the industrialization of higher education has affected the elite institutions as much as the rest of the system, there is no reason why student protest should not have originated in the elite sectors. Although the rate of expansion of enrollments is not as high as on the lower levels, the elite institutions feature the most intense competitive pressures and perhaps the greatest relative decline in undergraduate teaching and liberal education. Even if the erosion of student interests in these schools were less than elsewhere, it would still affect the most intelligent, most politically conscious students and thus have the most explosive potential. The interaction of educational industrialization and the young intelligentsia is the key to the leading role of the elite public universities in the origins of the student movement. All of the institutional surveys of student protest report correlations between the quality of the institution—and thus the quality of the student bodies—and the likelihood of protest. The quality and political consciousness of the student bodies is also a particularly important factor in determining the frequency of protest at the elite liberal-arts colleges.

Another factor making for student unrest in these elite institutions and in large universities generally is their heterogeneous combination of students of varying cultural backgrounds—urban and rural, WASP and non-WASP—and life styles—academic, Joe College, vocational, and Bohemian. This heterogeneity contributes to the disintegration of a single university community and to the rise of an educational "city" with more subcultures, ferment, and personal options but also with more impersonality and less loyalty to the central administration. The combination of less institutional legitimacy and more social ferment is likely to facilitate student rebellions. In his study of student protest from 1958–59 to 1968–69 for the Carnegie Commission on Higher Education, Harold Hodgkinson found that, compared to the national sample, high-protest institutions had a greater proportion of out-of-state students and a more heterogeneous student body in terms of age, ethnic composition, and socio-economic background.[19] Taking into account factors such as the ratio of out-of-state students to in-state students and the ratio of foreign-born students to native-born students, Joseph Scott and Mohamed El-Assal discovered that 87 percent of the "complex" institutions in their sample reported protests in 1964 and 1965, compared to 43 percent of the "simple" institutions. Protests were also more likely to occur in institutions located in large cities rather than in small towns.[20]

In classifying institutions as complex or simple, Scott and El-Assal also attempted to judge the effect of the bureaucratization and functional diversity of multiversities on student protest by calculating in their measure of complexity such factors as the number of departments and degrees, the student/faculty ratio, the ratio of undergraduate to graduate students, and the ratio of dormitory to non-dormitory students. Thus the typically bureaucratic and specialized multiversities were twice as likely to have protests as simpler institutions. These authors found that 100 percent of the complex, large, high-quality institutions in their sample had protests, compared to 34 percent of the simple, small, low-quality schools. The results of Hodgkinson's study also tend to support the industrialization-of-education thesis. Com-

[19] Harold Hodgkinson, "Student Protest—An Institutional and National Profile," *Teachers College Record* (Columbia University), May 1970, pp. 537–55.
[20] Joseph W. Scott and Mohamed El-Assal, "Multiversity, University Size, University Quality, and Student Protest: An Empirical Study," *American Sociological Review*, October 1969, pp. 702–10.

pared to the national sample, the high-protest institutions
were more likely to have faculty members who spent increasing time on research and decreasing time on teaching, who
were increasingly subsidized by federal agencies, and who
were committed increasingly to research and decreasingly to
the institution.

Both the Hodgkinson and the Scott-and-El-Assal studies
found institutional size to be the best single predictor of student protest. While the high-protest four-year colleges were
approximately the same size as the norm, Hodgkinson found
that the high-protest community colleges and universities—
those institutions most affected by industrialization—were
usually twice as large as the norm. Hodgkinson also discovered a continuous rise in the probability of protest with the
size of the institution: 14 percent for small institutions
(under 1,000 students), 32 percent for medium (1,000–
5,000), 58 percent for large (5,000–15,000), 75 percent for
the giants (15,000–25,000), and 88 percent for the supers
(25,000 plus). "With regard to student protest," Hodgkinson
concluded, "the data does not seem to reveal any kind of
'critical mass' beyond which size the institution is more likely
to have increased protest than any other. . . . There seems
to be no single point at which the curve jumps sharply towards increased protest; rather it is a steady increase in protest
as the enrollment of the institution increases." [21]

Historically, there is a correlation between expanding educational systems and student movements. After its defeat in
the Crimean War in 1854, the Czarist regime in Russia established several new universities in its policy of modernization
and was soon faced in the 1860s with a radical movement
among the students and intelligentsia. In China, the May
Fourth Movement appeared in 1919 after a 15-year period in
which Westernized schools had increased their enrollment
from 100,000 to 4.5 million. The nature of the social disloca-
tion engendered by these educational transformations was

[21] Hodgkinson, pp. 543–4.

naturally different from the effects of educational change in modern America. In the former, the expansion of the higher educational system was associated with a general process of industrialization, cultural trauma from contact with the West, and, often, nationalist revolt against imperial domination.

Although the student movements in Russia and China were given an impetus by educational expansion, they did not direct themselves to educational conditions. As movements of the young intelligentsia, they made a universal, revolutionary claim and opposed the social order as such. Similarly, it is not necessary for the student movement in the United States to orient itself to educational issues for it to be conditioned by the educational environment. As a movement of intellectuals and ideologues, the American student movement, like other student movements before it, directs itself to questions of national and world import, such as the Indo-China War, racism, imperialism, and the like. Nonetheless, the relevance of many of its issues to the educational context is clear. Although the demand for "student power" was originally raised by SDS as a pale echo of black power, its staying power as a political question is related to the dominance within the educational establishment of bureaucratic administration and the disregard of student interests in the areas of undergraduate teaching and general education. In its survey of 1969 student protests, the Urban Research Corporation found that student-power issues were raised in 44 percent of the cases of protest, second only to issues of black recognition. The principal student-power issues raised were student participation on decision-making committees and a student role in the hiring and firing of faculty members. The third major category of protest was "quality of student life," which ranked ahead of war-related protest in frequency. The major demand raised under this heading was for revision of the system of grades and courses. In their study for the American Council on Education, Bayer and Astin also found that student participation and "instructional procedures," relating to class size, quality of instruction, grading system, and student evaluations, constituted a major category of protest, on a par with war-related issues and clearly ranking behind only black demands.

Finally, the industrialization of education not only affects the conditions of student life and education; it also creates many of the local examples of national issues. For instance, the role of the major universities in research and development is the basis for their relationships with the military/industrial complex; the expanding enrollments and functions of these institutions account for their aggressive expansion into surrounding communities which are often inhabited by the non-white poor. The reality of the political issues raised by the student movement cannot be discounted as a factor in the occurrence of protest at large, research-oriented universities.

The direct influence of educational industrialization cannot by itself explain the student movement. The expansion of the educational system has combined with the general advance of the industrial economy to produce another factor favoring the rise of a student movement: youth culture.

In pre-industrial societies, there is a more or less direct transition from childhood to adulthood, with only short stages of "adolescence" and "youth." In these societies, the family is a basic unit of economic production and the various generations are integrated in an organic family-based system of personal life, religious tradition, economic production, and social ritual. The effect of industrialization is to separate the family from the division of labor and the allocation of social roles. This separation weakens the solidarity among the generations. The generations, without the integration of a family-oriented social system, face each other as organized antagonists in stratified bureaucratic systems, and confront one another with the self-evident truths of different collective histories. Since the premium is on specialized skills and organized knowledge which requires extensive preparation, educational systems are corollaries of industrialized systems. The result is the prolongation of adolescence, particularly for the middle and upper classes. Instead of moving immediately into adulthood—that is, into full-time employment and marriage—the educated classes must defer these responsibilities pending the completion of their social and educational preparation. This is sometimes called a "role moratorium."

By the 1950s, the United States was known for its youth culture. This was a natural result of its advanced degree of industrialization and a mass system of secondary and higher education unique in the industrialized world. In those days, the adolescent youth culture was preoccupied with expressive values, such as "personality" and "sincerity," to enliven the bureaucratic systems they inhabited, sexual rituals in the face of continued sexual prohibitions, and assumed identities in the absence of real social roles. The cultural tokens of the teen-agers were clothes, automobiles, rock music, and a special slang. An autonomous primary group, such as the clique or the gang, usually set the normative standards and attempted to fill the void left by the increasing irrelevance of the family past childhood. Culturally, all of this was thin stuff. Youth culture is not a culture at all, but a subculture which is economically and socially parasitic on the main culture. But it does create a subsociety that copes, after a fashion, with the difficulties of the youth situation which other social institutions, such as the family, the educational system, and the military, either ignore or exacerbate. These difficulties consist in enforced immaturity well after sexual, physical, and intellectual maturity, identity crisis in the absence of specified social roles, and regimentation by authoritarian bureaucracies without the minimal rights associated with political democracy.

Even in the 1950s the adolescent youth culture was latently a culture of opposition. The effect of its rituals was to exclude adult society and to forge bonds of group solidarity in the common plight. In the 1960s, the New Left and the anti-war and black-liberation movements activated this latent opposition and made it explicit. In this period, youth culture began to spin off various youth movements, such as the hippies and rural communes. The "cult of immediacy" remarked upon in the 1950s was superseded by a cultivation of sensuality and mysticism. The clique was superseded by the hippie commune. The cult of conventional clothes was transformed into a cult of costumes. Hard rock music developed into a variety of forms, many of which carried an explicitly anti-bourgeois message. Generational conflict, an aspect of the basic youth situation, was supplied with a specific radical political content. New Left politics, generational conflict, and revolt against bureaucracy tended to reinforce and invigorate each other and add momentum to student rebellion in the high schools and colleges.

The continued expansion of the educational system into the 1960s (projected into the 1980s) also reinforced the interlocking adolescent youth culture and student movements. The pre-war necessity for a high-school diploma limited the youth culture to the late teens, but the postwar necessity for a college degree effectively extended the youth culture into the early twenties and created a new pre-adult stage of life beyond adolescence: "youth." By the late 1960s, one fifth of college graduates—and thus approximately 5 percent of all college-age youth—were going on to some form of graduate or professional education, drawing out the stage of youth into the middle twenties and beyond. The influx of students into graduate and professional schools resulted in duplication of the same mass character and bureaucratic forms in education at the higher levels. Although college-age youth experiences less of the transitional turmoil of adolescence, the college-age youth culture has much of the same generational solidarity and the frustration of less than adult status.

During the 1960s, as a result of the maturation of the "war baby" generation, college-age youth also began to grow rapidly as a percentage of the population. The proportion of youth in the population, which had actually declined from

12.5 to 9 percent between 1940 and 1960, rose in the following decade to 11.5 percent and was projected to rise to 12.5 percent by 1980. (This trend does *not* represent, however, some modern development toward the demographic domination of youth, but a recovery from the low birth rates of the Depression years. By 1970, the percentage of college-age youth in the population had only equaled that of 1930 and remained well below the 14 percent of 1900. If anything, the effect of modern society is to extend the average life span and thus the influence of the aged.) Still, rapid expansion of the youth population in the 1960s, together with mass education, was a powerful stimulus to the development of youth culture. This was also a $30-billion consumer "youth market." In the process of exploiting this market, the mass media, record companies, and other corporate producers had the ironic effect of marketing an oppositional youth culture and New Left ideology.

Together, these interrelated developments of educational industrialization, youth culture, and population trends constitute a strong basis in the social structure for a student movement in the 1960s. These changes did not, however, have equal impact on all sectors of the population. They had most influence on urban sectors, because rural society is less affected by industrial change and mass higher education. Since youth culture ultimately depends on the prolongation of adolescence resulting from mass higher education, youth culture is class-based to the same degree as the secondary and higher education system. The student movement most affects the middle and upper classes, which dominate the higher educational system. Any revolutionary youth movement based on youth culture only reaches other members of these same classes, and does not carry radical politics into different social classes. The working class is particularly resistant to youth culture because its offspring enter adulthood much earlier through marriage and full-time employment. Black youth, however, develop a youth culture of their own because unemployment rates of 20 percent or more prevent them from entering into the standard relationships with society. As they are often the children of black migrants from the rural South, young blacks in the urban ghetto also develop the group solidarity typical of second-generation immigrants who must reject the values and culture of their parents, which are irrelevant to their new situation.

The social character of the higher educational system and the youth culture suggests the nature of the constituency for the student movement: urban, middle class or above, and usually Jewish or Protestant. This is a limited, hardly proletarian sector of the population, but highly significant in the economic development of postwar American society. The economic growth of the United States in this period has depended in large degree on technological innovation and the exploitation of new markets in the "knowledge industry"— that 30 percent of the economy which, broadly défined, has to do with the production and distribution of information and knowledge. Crucial sectors of this knowledge industry are such fields as education, electronic data-processing, and research and development. Research and development now constitute 3 percent of the total gross national product. The "education industry," of which higher education composes one third, constitutes 6 percent of the GNP. Higher education, science-based industry, information machines and services, research and development, and mass communications are closely related to one another, and depend on a professional class to administer them. As it happens, professional and technical workers are the fastest-growing occupational sector in the economy. In 1965 this category constituted over 13 percent of the labor force. According to estimates, it will constitute 15 percent of the labor force by 1975—a 50-percent increase in absolute terms.

The student movement exists in symbiotic relationship with this new stratum. Although neither student radicals nor their families are generally rooted in the technical sectors of this stratum, both they and their parents are often either employed by, or headed for, the verbally oriented sectors of the knowledge industry. It is the liberal wing of this stratum which gives strong support to the anti-Vietnam War movement, while their offspring often support radical politics.

The student movement is ultimately a product of the changes in the political economy of the United States from World War II on. This argument is not a "technological society" thesis, with the implicit judgment that these consequences follow from neutral and inevitable processes of technological innovation. In this case, the technology is based on the military-aerospace industry, a product of World War II and the Cold War, while the higher educational system is supported by massive federal subsidy for government purposes, often military. It is also not a "post-industrial society" thesis. Although advanced industrial capitalism in the United States may depend increasingly on growth in the "tertiary" or service sector of the economy, especially in knowledge-based fields, it has not necessarily gone beyond industrial society and implicitly industrial capitalism. Rather, the student movement is a product of the industrialization, under capitalist forms of organization, of new areas of human enterprise: education, knowledge, and culture among them. The methods that were originally applied to manufacturing and agriculture are now applied to those fields. These methods involve corporate forms of control, as in institutes, think tanks, and multiversities; mass organization, as in research labs, planning departments, and commission reports; technological inputs, as in "intellectual technology," educational technology, and information technology. There is now an education industry and a knowledge industry, as well as an entertainment industry, a publishing industry, and so on. This is not post-industrial society; it is super-industrial society.

Dependent upon educational systems and applied knowledge, this hyper-industrialized society has produced the new opposition in the student movement and the left-of-center elements among salaried professionals. Historically, the students and intellectuals are notoriously the dangerous classes. They have been dangerous because they were temporarily or permanently declassed. As "marginal men" without fixed loyalties who trafficked in ideas as a pastime, they were the groups most susceptible to purely ideological and political currents. Fortunately for the old orders, however, they were also few in numbers; they were potential vanguards for other social forces or mainly symptoms of social malfunctions, rather than threats in themselves. The unique feature of modern society is that it requires an entire class of educated people which is capable of producing bona-fide mass movements. The modern social order lessens their alienation by defining their class position and integrating them into bureaucratic systems. But it also exploits their labor in the knowledge industry. If this exploitation of educated labor is less onerous than that of manual labor in the course of the first industrial revolution, it affects a more volatile stratum with a higher political consciousness.

In any case, students remain temporarily declassed and, by the evidence of the student movement, are susceptible to radical ideology. The evolution of a youth culture reinforces this political volatility. However, the structural effects of the industrialization of education, the rise of youth culture (and youth markets), and demographic change do not in themselves produce a radical student movement. Political causes are required to trigger a political movement. We have seen that the black social movement and the Vietnam War are two of these political triggers.

A third political factor in the activation of the student movement in the 1960s was the decomposition of the Cold War structure of international politics. The emergence of national communisms in such countries as Yugoslavia, North Vietnam, and Cuba and the development of the Sino-Soviet split not only disintegrated the "Communist bloc" under Soviet hegemony but undermined the bloc's opposite number:

the "Free World" in both its international and domestic manifestations. As the United States and the Soviet Union moved toward détente after the traumatic Cuban missile crisis of 1962 and the gap between the standards of living in the West and the rest of the world continued to widen, there was a tendency toward the formation of new international antagonisms along the lines of the rich and the poor nations, the Northern and the Southern hemispheres.

The domestic effect of these developments was to erode the nationalist political climate of the United States which was the reflection of the international Cold War. The anticommunist containment policy against the only nuclear power that posed a serious military threat was diluted, while the newly fashioned containment policy against China was not nearly as plausible as a defensive policy. Although the rationale for militant anti-communism was weakened, the United States nonetheless freely undertook counterrevolutionary interventions in Cuba, the Dominican Republic, and Vietnam. One result of this foreign-policy contradiction was an impetus to the formation of a New Left.

The re-emergence of a vigorous left in the 1960s was natural; the anomaly was its absence in the 1950s. Cold War foreign policy created the domestic political climate for the suppression of the Communist Party and the silencing of the left in the 1950s. The decline of the anti-communist crusade eroded this nationalist climate and generated an opening to the left in the middle 1960s. The old left began to resurface; the New Left took form; and leftist attitudes became not quite treasonable. This opening to the left was favored by the de-legitimation of liberalism as the Vietnam War developed. The sponsorship of counter-revolution in Cuba and Vietnam by the Kennedy and Johnson administrations forced most left-of-center students abruptly left and out of the regular orbits of the Democratic Party. The minimum politics became at least a new form of democratic liberalism (or "New Politics"), while the far left turned toward active advocacy of "people's war." The re-emergence of the old left under the impact of these political events helped to move students to the left. One form of this influence was direct: the politics of the parents of student activists. A survey by Samuel Lubell discovered that one sixth of the sample had left-wing parentage. In a survey of University of Chicago students who demonstrated against the ranking of students for purposes of Selective Service in 1966, Richard Flacks, a co-founder of SDS, found that 16 percent of the students were from radical families.[22] The black social movement after 1954, the *détente* with the Soviet Union taking form after 1962, and the Vietnam War after 1965 were sufficient politically to activate a student opposition latent in the social structure of the United States. Some social conditions favorable to the rise of a student movement, such as inconsistent family socialization, a crisis in transcendent values, and the subversive thrust of cultural modernism, were constant factors in postwar America. Other typically postwar structural forces gathered increasing momentum in the 1960s. The educational system expanded rapidly in the 1955–65 decade and created the conditions for youth culture, while youth increased rapidly as a percentage of the population after 1960. The lines of force of these political detonators and general social conditions affecting students and youth crossed at Berkeley in 1964, again at Columbia in 1968, and then increasingly rapidly throughout the country in 1969–70. Protest issues often unified the political and social causes of rebellion in a single symbol—as in the issues of urban expansion and the militarization of research and development. These political issues were not "pretexts" but causes of revolt.

[22] See the Flacks study cited above, and Lipset and Altbach for a report of Lubell's results.

3 THE MARKETPLACE OF IDEAS

WHEN HE DESCRIBED the "corporation of learning" in *The Higher Learning in America* in 1918, Thorstein Veblen allowed that the "perfected type . . . has doubtless not been achieved hitherto, unless it be in one or another of the newer establishments with large ambitions and endowments, and with few traditions to hamper the working out of the system." [1] Student radicals argue that the system of "academic control under business principles" has by 1971 been perfected in some of these "newer establishments" (such as the state-wide university systems on the California model), and in not a few of the older establishments as well. The radical theory of the university postulates a corporate enterprise which turns out trained manpower and research-and-development. Each of the local contenders in student rebellion—student radicals,

[1] Thorstein Veblen, *The Higher Learning in America* (New York: Hill and Wang, 1965), p. 69.

faculty, and administration—has its own theory of the university. Such a theory is a necessary combat issue, along with contingency plans, walkie-talkies, press conferences, protective helmets, helicopters, and study commissions. The conflict of theory has parity with the political struggle, since the veil of legitimate authority in a community of wordsmiths wears only as well as its verbal defense.

During student rebellions, radical research groups have issued detailed briefs describing the corporate operations of the university. But Veblen's account is still the classic statement of the radical position, although the developments of the last 50 years have dated his analysis in various respects. It was Veblen's conviction that the businessmen-trustees—those dusty, stuffed men whose boardrooms have been turned by informed modern opinion into museums of nineteenth-century capitalism—did indeed control the university, because the higher learning naturally took its character from the business society in which it operated. One of the determinants of this society, Veblen continued, was the "state of the industrial arts, the technological situation," but the other was the "pursuit of business." When businessmen began to gain place on university boards in the nineteenth century, replacing clergymen and reproducing their own kind through the self-perpetuating mechanism of board recruitment, they imposed the usages of corporate organization and control which had been employed for the pursuit of private gain by businessmen in joint-stock companies with limited liability. Accustomed to an economic calculus of value and possessed of complete authority, businessmen-trustees were likely to respond only to the "popular sentiments" and the "practical interests" of the general community. These "popular" sentiments in favor of practical education actually originated in the university's real constituency—the "well-to-do laity" and "that more select body of substantial citizens who have the disposal of accumulated wealth." As community leaders and national notables, these businessmen-trustees valued, as qualifications for board membership, "a 'businesslike' facility in the management of affairs, an engaging address and fluent command of language before a popular audience, and what is called 'optimism'—a serene and voluble loyalty to the current conventionalities and a conspicuously profound conviction that things are working out for good, except for such untoward details as do not visibly conduce to the vested advantage of the well-to-do businessmen under the established law and order." [2]

University boards invested full operational authority in a single executive officer—the president of the university. An intelligent board, Veblen explained, would give its general manager full discretion, and not obstruct him with too close an accounting of the details of his administration, as long as he showed gratifying results. The "captain of erudition" would be chosen for business qualifications such as commercial sense and executive ability. "As to the requirements of scholarly or scientific competency," Veblen added, "a plausible speaker with a large gift of assurance, a businesslike 'educator' or clergyman, some urbane pillar of society, some astute veteran of the scientific *demi-monde* will meet all reasonable requirements." [3]

Although the captain of erudition was invested with autocratic powers, he was subject to the "moral wear and tear that comes of arbitrary powers exercised in a tangle of ambiguities." Although the board of trustees met only occasionally, it did have its committees to keep more abreast of things and there was always the reservation that the president was limited by the specifications of the budget. On the other side, the star executive had to deal with the pretensions of the faculty. To facilitate the latter task, the academic executive gathered about him a junta of senior faculty to serve as advisors, expeditors, and especially parliamentarians whose assignment would be to "save the formalities, but secure the sub-

[2] Veblen, p. 180.
[3] Veblen, p. 61.

stance" of acquiescence in executive policy from occasionally reluctant faculty senates. These "coadjustors and vehicles of executive policy," necessarily men of "zealous serviceability" and "high (putative) rank as scholars and scientists," were selected on the "same general grounds of fitness as their chief —administrative facility, plausibility, proficiency as public speakers and parliamentarians, ready versatility of convictions, and a staunch loyalty to their bread." [4]

The final result of these arrangements, Veblen concluded, was a "business concern dealing in standardized erudition." The ineradicable view of the businessmen-trustees and their captains of erudition was that "learning and university instruction are a species of skilled labor, to be hired at competitive wages and to turn out the largest merchantable output that can be obtained by shrewd bargaining with their employees. . . ." The mental bent of the board of directors required, as a first principle of sound business practice, that the academic executive "show by itemized accounts that the volume of output is such as to warrant the investment. So the equipment and personnel must be organized into a facile and orderly working force, held under the directive control of the captain of erudition at every point, and so articulated and standardized that its rate of speed and the volume of its current output can be exhibited to full statistical effect as it runs." [5] Thus, there was the necessity for "standardized units of erudition"—courses, credits, grades, and degrees—and "bureaux of erudition": departments, schools, and colleges. Veblen argued that this apparatus followed less from the level of the enrollment and educational operation in themselves than from the requirements for central control of the educational system. Central administration of the university was an end in itself, serving chiefly to make central administration possible and to impose administrative purposes on the autonomous activity of scholars. In this enterprise, the ad-

[4] Veblen, p. 69.
[5] Veblen, p. 64.

ministration cleverly enlisted the faculty as petty bureaucrats and cheap labor in the name of faculty autonomy: In matters of "administrative routine and punctilio," the faculty exercised a degree of initiative and discretion. The entire process of "bureaucracy and scholarly accountancy," Veblen noted, was undertaken under the banners of "efficiency engineering" and "scientific management," popularized by Frederick Taylor and Charles Babbage.

The university establishment, Veblen believed, most resembled the retail trade. There was the same concern with the firm's "immaterial capital"—the "good will" and public reputation which were indispensable in attracting customers and capital. The universities were also highly competitive, bidding against each other with fellowships and salaries for the best graduate students and the most notable faculty members. In plying this trade, the business-oriented directorate of the university was nevertheless concerned, by dint of its experience, with investing in durable goods and extensions of the plant—matters of monumental importance. The criterion of educational success was a business criterion: "an uninterrupted growth in size and other tangible features." Diversification and expansion were the keynotes, Veblen observed, as the university moved into "new fields of scholastic enterprise"—extension courses, law schools, business schools, adult education, medical schools, vocational training. Such a policy only reflected the fundamental reality of the university: "The seat of discretion is in the directorate; though many details of administration may be left to the deliberations of the staff, so long as these details do not impinge on the directorate's scheme of policy." [6]

This was Veblen's critique of the corporation of learning circa 1918. The analysis accords closely with that of student radicals a half century later; Veblen's reform program, however, was informed by a cultural conservatism which remains the common faith of liberal-arts faculties. Business control of

[6] Veblen, p. 173.

the university was objectionable because the leading principle of sound business practice—return on investment—could not apply to the educational enterprise. Investment management required fairly precise measurement of inputs and outputs so that investment could be counted on to maximize output. But Veblen argued that there was no way to measure educational "production"; consequently, university management tended to substitute educational hardware which could be measured—plant and equipment, enrollment, numerical output of scholarly works—for education itself. There was no "return" on educational investment because education did not—or should not—have any commercial value. A university did not produce goods and services; it produced something other—and more important—than goods and services: *culture*. Culture was pre-eminently the preservation and advancement of knowledge and the transmission and creation of values. The university could very well expand and diversify without serving culture. The only judges of the cultural success of the university were *autonomous scholars*, whose requirements—freedom, community, intimacy—were precisely the opposite of the purposes of the university managers. "The staff is the university," Veblen thought, or so the guiding principle would have to be if the university was to serve civilized purposes.

The *community of scholars* is also the modern faculty's theory of the university. The difference is that the modern liberal-arts faculty regards the existing institution as the approximate realization of the community of scholars, while Veblen regarded the *status quo* arrangements as a "skillfully devised death of the spirit." Veblen's program for achieving a community of scholars was to eliminate the governing boards and central administration: "All that is here intended to be said is nothing more than the obiter dictum that, as seen from the point of view of the higher learning, the academic executive and all his works are anathema, and should be discontinued by the simple expedient of wiping him off the slate;

and that the governing board, in so far as it presumes to exercise any other than vacantly perfunctory duties, has the same value and should with advantage be lost in the same shuffle." [7] The modern liberal-arts faculty, on the contrary, believes that the community of scholars has been approximately realized.

The faculty theory of the university was first formulated in 1852 by Cardinal Newman in *The Idea of the University*. The university, Newman said, is a "place of *teaching* universal *knowledge*," and this knowledge is "its own end." While advocating the "culture of the intellect," Newman placed unequivocal emphasis on the primacy of teaching; the "diffusion and extension of knowledge rather than its advancement." [8] In 1930, in another classic exposition, *Universities: American, English, German*, Abraham Flexner revised this idea: "It is, however, creative activity, productive and critical inquiry—all in a sense without practical responsibility—that must bulk ever larger and larger in the modern university." [9] The "idea of a modern university" required that the advancement of knowledge take precedence over the conservation of knowledge, although each complemented and invigorated the other. Research and teaching—in that order—are regarded by faculty members today as the essential functions of the university—that is, of the community of scholars. Flexner, however, advanced a purist conception of research, especially social research:

> I have been urging that universities maintain contacts with the actual world and at the same time continue to be irresponsible. Are the two attitudes incompatible? Can they really take an objective position in reference to social, political, and economic phenomena? Can they

[7] Veblen, p. 209.

[8] John Henry Cardinal Newman, *The Idea of a University* (New York: Image Books, 1959), p. 7.

[9] Abraham Flexner, *Universities: American, English, German* (New York: Oxford, 1968), p. 8.

study phenomena without wanting to tell legislatures, communities, municipal authorities, and chambers of commerce what they ought to do at any particular moment about some particular thing? I think they must and can. It is a question of ideals and organization. For experimental purposes they may, without sacrifice of intellectual integrity, make suggestions and watch results; but this is different from running a city government or a political party, involving, as such responsibilities do, compromises of principle that are fatal to fearless thinking.[10]

Like Veblen, Flexner had a reform program to implement this attitude. He wished to eliminate non-intellectual schooling from the university premises—namely, schools of business, journalism, education, religion, and the like. "Practical importance," Flexner said, in exact agreement with Veblen, "is not a sufficient title to academic recognition: if that is the best that can be said, it is an excellent reason for exclusion.[11] Among the modern faculty, however, there is no consensus on this deduction from the idea of a modern university.

The contribution of the modern faculty to the ideal of the community of scholars is not theoretical; it is organizational. The modern faculty has *professionalized* the community of scholars. This development has been, among other things, a political response to a political threat to the community of scholars in an earlier period of radical ferment. In the several decades preceding the First World War, university trustees intervened actively to suppress the threat to religious orthodoxy, industrial capitalism, and the militant state posed by iconoclastic professors such as Richard T. Ely, John R. Commons, and Scott Nearing. On his resignation from Columbia University after a political dispute with the university authorities, Charles Beard, originator of the economic interpretation of the Constitution, was moved to comment: "I have

10 Flexner, p. 15.
11 Flexner, p. 27.

been driven to the conclusion that the university is really under the control of a small and active group of Trustees who have no standing in the world of education, who are reactionary and visionless in politics, narrow and medieval in religion. Their conduct betrays a profound misconception of the true function of a university in the advancement of learning." [12]

In 1915, academicians organized the American Association of University Professors (AAUP), an organization dedicated to the propagation of the professional doctrines of tenure and academic freedom. Since that time, faculties have generally won their campaign for tenure systems and recognition of academic freedom, although the onset of a new radical era has, as always, reactivated the repressive instincts of university trustees. Faculties have also established the leading principles of faculty professionalism—if not as the reality of university practice, then as a program for action: (1) vigilant surveillance and control of the *standards* of teaching and research, and (2) the clear primacy of research; (3) a claim to the control of their own personnel policy and of (4) the entire range of educational policy. This four-point program of scholarly professionalism goes under the slogan of "academic freedom."

Academic freedom is a militant ideology. Faculty members commonly believe that the professionalization of academicians has resulted in an "academic revolution" which has left them in effective control of the essential educational functions of the university. The academic revolution is a revolution of technocracy. It presupposes a "managerial revolution" in which the governing boards have been pensioned off by the university presidents and their executive apparatus. In such a situation, faculty specialists come to exercise real authority by virtue of their specialized knowledge and collective *élan* and the university administrations become mere caretakers specializing in building and grounds. The faculty is

---

[12] Quoted in *Who Rules Columbia?* (New York: North American Congress on Latin America, 1968).

reputed to control educational policy—the essential function of the university, after all—from the academic strongholds of its departments. Educational policy under faculty sway covers such critical matters as course content, curriculum, methods of instruction, research policy, and degree requirements.

The faculty also claims autonomy. Although university presidents and governing boards, the academicians argue, may technically control personnel decisions regarding teacher-scholars, the faculty makes the decisions in practice through committees and departmental meetings, and the higher-ups merely review and concur. Senior faculty members also have tenure, while the talented and scholarly junior members have a very strong market position. The doubling and redoubling of student enrollments in higher education have meant a high demand for Ph.D. faculty members; moreover, the national community of each professional *discipline* determines the reputation of scholars, not the institutional bureaucracy, which has no choice but to accept the criterion of professional reputation if it is to remain a "first-rate university." Finally, the faculty points to its conquest of administrative ground. Departmental chairmen are either elected or appointed according to the wishes of their colleagues, and the academic deans and officers are increasingly the faculty's choices, though the administration's formal appointees. The president himself, the professors continue, is usually an academic professional whom the trustees have found to be acceptable to the faculty. If it can maintain a united front and an effective committee system, the faculty senate can survey general educational policy and even challenge the administration on its own ground. The possibilities for usurpation are unlimited.

University management ordinarily suffers in silence the pretensions of its professional staff. In fact, to encourage delusions of power, which can facilitate the smooth and unchallenged management of the enterprise, is in the interests of management. But sometimes it becomes too much. In a response to an essay by a former AAUP president which propagated the notions of the "Age of the Professor" and the "Age of the Department," John Oswald, President of the University of Kentucky, asked, "What department of chemistry has voted to have a department of biochemistry that is coordinate and autonomous? Which department decides whether or not a new medical school is to be developed? Does a vote by the English Department to increase salaries produce the money by which increases can be realized? Is an expansion of a department of infectious diseases to precede or follow the expansion of Middle English Studies? Many decisions for the whole institution are beyond the purview of a particular department; indeed, they involve not only the faculty and the president, but the trustees and also the student body." [13]

Writing in 1918, *before* the professionalization of the faculty, Veblen had already encountered the academic-revolution thesis and taken note of it: "So it will be held by the spokesmen of content that virtually full discretion in all matters of academic policy is delegated to the academic head of the university, fortified by the advice and consent of the senior members of the faculty; so that the scholarly interests of the university are, by the free choice of the governing boards, in practice drawn out from under the control of these businessmen in question and placed in the hands of the scholars." [14] Although one of the founders of technocratic theory, Veblen was not disposed to accept the faculty's distended version of the doctrine: "This complaisant view overlooks the fact that much effective surveillance of the academic work is exercised through the board's control of the budget. The academic staff can do little else than what the specifications of the budget provide for; without the means with which the corporate income should supply them they are as helpless as might be expected." [15]

[13] John W. Oswald, "The Inherent Authority of the President," in Charles G. Dobbins and Calvin B. T. Lee, eds., *Whose Goals for American Higher Education?* (Washington, D.C., 1968), p. 125.
[14] Veblen, p. 58.
[15] Veblen, p. 58.

University administrators reject the idea of the university as a community of scholars. In his introduction to a recent edition of Flexner's *Universities*, Clark Kerr criticizes the faculty's theory in the following terms: "Flexner did not realize how many functions can be combined within a single university—even apparently inconsistent functions. Particularly, he did not see how service functions might draw support and money to a university, so that it could perform better also in advanced teaching and research. American universities did not 'break beneath the incongruous load placed upon them.' He saw too much in unity and cohesion, and too little in pluralism and diversity." [16] Administrators have sponsored, particularly since World War II, this third function of the university: public service. They have added or improved programs in engineering, public administration, applied scientific research, public and international affairs, and agricultural research and education. Since the public-service function is not in harmony with the traditional functions of teaching and research, university administrators may even reject the "idea" of the university as such. "Flexner thought of the university as an 'organism,' " Clark Kerr noted in *The Uses of the University*. "In an organism, the parts and whole are inextricably bound together. Not so the multiversity—many parts can be added and subtracted with little effect on the whole or even little notice taken or any blood spilled. It is more a mechanism—a series of processes producing a series of results—a mechanism held together by administrative rules and powered by money." [17]

University administrators, however, do not reject the community of scholars as such, only the "idea" of the university *as* a community of scholars. The community of scholars is one of a number of communities within the multiversity. This conception betrays the fact that administrators actually have their own "idea" of the *multi*versity as the "pluralist university." "Pluralism in higher education matches the plu-

16 Flexner, p. xviii.
17 Clark Kerr, *The Uses of the University* (New York, 1963), p. 20.

ralistic American society," Kerr writes. "The multiversity in particular is the child of middle-class pluralism; it relates to so much of the variety of the surrounding society and is thus so varied internally." [18] The genius of this principle is that it cannot, in principle, be violated. As long as one is adding new functions to the university and not subtracting, the honor of the university is still plural. For instance, social psychologist Kenneth Keniston has argued that a fourth function—social criticism—has taken its place among the traditional functions of teaching, research, and public service. This argument was verified by the official support of the Vietnam Moratorium on October 15, 1969, by a number of colleges and universities. Not only the advocacy but also the opposition to this political stand was led by faculty members, not administrators, because the doctrine of academic freedom, as formulated by the AAUP in 1915, posited institutional neutrality as a condition for the realization of free inquiry. MIT faculty almost defeated a resolution to support the Moratorium, but Howard Johnson, President of the institute, cast a tie-breaking vote on a procedural point, which led to the anti-war resolution.

The faculty theory of the university, the community of scholars, gives the faculty pride of place; the administration theory of the pluralist university naturally favors the administrators. University management arrogates to itself responsibility for matters of *institutional* import. "But someone must be concerned with the institution as a whole," former Cornell President James Perkins writes, "the activities it supports, the public face it presents, and the private concerns with which it is occupied. This job cannot be divided among disparate elements of the university. So it is the administrator—the president and others with managerial responsibility, cooperating with faculty and student leaders—who must be concerned both with the apparatus of the university and with the idea it represents." [19] While conceding faculty pre-eminence in their

[18] Kerr, p. 118.
[19] James A. Perkins, *The University in Transition* (Princeton, N.J., 1966), p. 57.

educational specialties, Perkins notes the converse of specialized competence: "Partial views which are based upon increasingly specialized interests make it difficult for the faculty
as faculty to have a point of view on broad institutional matters." [20] Institutional management, moreover, is also a specialized competence, and the administrators are the specialists. It
is their responsibility not only to maintain the institutional
integrity of the university, but also to provide *educational*
leadership. This is known in the trade as "innovation." Innovation on the university level is most significant in the establishment of new programs, schools, and colleges. But it may
also involve direct intervention in faculty territory—namely,
the departments. The department, according to Perkins, is a
"conservative unit"; to enhance quality, it may be necessary
to intervene in the feudal baronies occasionally. Intervention
is a "delicate art." The academic deans can exercise control of
quality through the appointment of departmental chairmen;
the "task of innovation will be easier if he has arranged for
the rotation of chairmen." The innovator-in-chief is the president—"his access to funds gives him an even more powerful
lever in effecting change." This interpretation of the role of
the administration has official standing. In a joint policy
statement on university governance in 1966, the AAUP, the
American Council on Education, and the Association of
Governing Boards of Universities and Colleges assigned to
the administration a responsibility to "infuse new life into a
department" and to handle "problems of obsolescence." [21]
These retooling operations in other departments do not
arouse the general faculty, since they are always undertaken
in the name of "standards." Thus do the dogmas of specialization consume the specialists.

[20] Perkins, pp. 54–5.
[21] "Statement on Government of Colleges and Universities," *AAUP
Bulletin* (Winter 1966), p. 378.

I. THE CONGLOMERATE UNIVERSITY

Contemplating the music schools, art schools, vocational training programs, summer schools, education schools, and extension programs which universities were operating in 1918, Veblen was moved to observe: "On its face, this enterprise in assorted education simulates the precedents given by the larger modern business coalitions, which frequently bring under one general business management a considerable number and variety of industrial plants." [22] Veblen's program for the "dissolution of the trust" naturally never made headway, although universities dropped many of the less glamorous and more huckstering enterprises they had undertaken. Modern university management operates on a grander scale, avoiding the narrow prestige margin of petty commerce, but it is clear that its organizing principle is similar. In Veblen's time, the educational trend was toward vertical integration; colleges added graduate programs, professional schools, and sometimes even projects in secondary education, christening themselves "universities." In the post-World War II era, the universities expanded horizontally by taking on research laboratories, schools of public and international affairs, urban-affairs institutes, areas studies, policy research programs, federally funded research-and-development centers, computer centers, black-studies programs, public-opinion institutes, and all manner of applied scientific-research units, while simultaneously expanding more traditional programs in engineering, medicine, law, agriculture, and education. "Acceptance of these responsibilities," John J. Corson has observed with approval in *Governance of Colleges and Universities*, "may make of the university an intellectual holding company. Even as it has subsidiaries, known as colleges, concerned with teaching and research, it may also have subsidiaries, known as institutes, laboratories, or centers, engaged in research and in

[22] Veblen, pp. 140–1.

the application of new knowledge to current problems. Within this holding company structure may exist many non-profit institutions. Now many of these valuable institutions float in unproductive space, lacking the umbilical cord to an institutional setting." [23]

Noting the vertical integration of the university in his day, Veblen compared it to a trust; observing the horizontal diversification of more recent date, James Ridgeway suggests in *The Closed Corporation*: "Whereas it was once common among radicals to view these institutions as captive technical schools, preparing workers to take up jobs in companies whose ideals were represented by the businessmen-trustees, today it is apparent that the modern university more nearly resembles a conglomerate corporation on its own." [24] There are barriers to this theory, but they are not insuperable. A conglomerate corporation is a profit-making enterprise, while a university is not. But modern management techniques, such as input-output analysis, make it possible to run a multiversity on precisely the same principle as a business corporation: return on investment. A university is centered in the education field, while a conglomerate purports to operate in a wide range of non-related activities. But most of the largest conglomerates are heavily into one market—military-aerospace—while the universities also run non-educational enterprises, including university presses and investment trusts, weapons research and riot-control projects, poverty programs and counter-insurgency studies, real-estate offices and cigarette-filter promotions. Both are dependent on the "public market"—state and federal contracts and subsidy, especially for military-aerospace operations. Both are "going international." The conglomerate corporation establishes its subsidiaries in Athens, Madrid, and Caracas, while the

[23] John J. Corson, "Public Service and Higher Education: Compatibility or Conflict?" in Dobbins and Lee, p. 90.
[24] James Ridgeway, *The Closed Corporation* (New York, 1968), p. 13.

conglomerate university organizes its international-affairs programs and sets up its campuses abroad: Columbia-in-Capetown, Stanford-in-Seoul, Berkeley-in-Bangkok, Harvard-on-the-Himalayan-Border.

This is not to say that the university is an industrial corporation, much less a "factory." The independent power of the faculty within the university, though far short of dominance, has no parallel in the manufacturing world. The position of students is not the role of a proletariat but, on the closest analogy, the role of consumers. Without question, higher education—at least in its elite sectors—has special cultural functions which no commercial enterprise assumes, and special significance for the democratic claims of the social order. The university is *sui generis* among social institutions. The thesis of the conglomerate university does not imply that the modern university is somehow other than a university. The point of the argument is to suggest the ultimate primacy of the economic functions of the conglomerate university, whose concentration on basic and applied research resembles that of conglomerate corporations specializing in research-and-development markets. Similarly, the outputs of the higher educational system are educational credentials, which determine their holders' place in the labor market on the presumption that they represent mental skills and intellectual training. In this enterprise, the major universities certify the elite cadres, while the lesser institutions turn out trained manpower. Although these degrees and credentials are the main products of educational institutions, students are in a sense not only consumers of the products but the products themselves.

These economic functions militate for corporate organization. The organizing center of the conglomerate university is university management. Although various subsidiaries of the university have their own administrative apparatus and a measure of autonomy, university management is the central core which determines the flight pattern of its orbiting centers, institutes, and laboratories. Central management controls the budget and finances, provides information services, acts as a broker for contracting with outside agencies, directs long-range planning, and represents the institution in its public relations and political operations. In "meeting its responsibilities," a university administration utilizes the latest innovations in management theory, organizational techniques, and managerial technology. The technological nucleus of the operation is now the computer center. Although university management employs the computer to expedite routine clerical processes and information gathering, the critical role of electronic data-processing is in the preparation of the budget. In order to put the computer to work on the problems of policy priorities and resource allocation which budgeting entails, it is necessary to employ various forms of quantitative analysis. A rigorous cost analysis must determine standards of efficient performance for instruction, central services, admissions, registration, payroll, and research program. Various budget formulas—student/faculty ratio, courses per faculty member, square footage of space per student per type of program, dollars per student for faculty compensation—may be used to determine rational allocations for various programs. The formulas are subject to extensive deliberation and may be changed from time to time, since their rationality is critical to the rationality of the whole budgeting process.

Although quantification and computerization are of the essence, they do not exhaust the modern managerial style. Efforts to define purposes complement the quantification of technique. "Program budgeting," which organizes the budget by program and adjusts the budget formulas to differing programs, replaces the line-item budget, which allocated funds to general categories of salary, maintenance, and the like. The "systems approach" involves an effort to adjust quantitative analysis to the cut of problems and purposes, rather than to allocate funds on the procrustean bed of bureaucratic convenience. The method encourages the definition of the purposes of the general organization—the better to establish general policy, to make quantitative measurements of performance, and, most important of all, to facilitate long-range planning. The planning-and-budgeting process—known as Program Planning and Budgeting Systems (PPBS)—obviously cannot function unless the system processes accurate information. As part of their data-gathering apparatus, universities have established offices of "institutional research" which study university operations and do statistical research on its programs and personnel. There are also offices of "space management" which attempt to develop objective criteria for the allocation of building space to various programs within the present and projected university plant.

The "new science of management" corroborates Veblen's theory of the "corporation of learning." The allocation of resources in the budget is determined by input-output analysis which involves provision for cost-efficient expenditures, *measurement* of educational output (usually in dollars), a resulting determination of return on investment, and finally an adjustment of input to increase output and to ensure an optimum return on investment in the future. In short, input-output analysis makes it possible, even in the absence of profit margins, to run a university on economic principles.

The criterion of success is efficiency. Although the determination of the goals which are to be efficiently achieved does not have to be an economic determination, the goals must be quantifiable for the systems analysis to work. This fact encourages the choice of measurable economic effects as goals. "Except in matters of degree (e.g., the operations researchers tend to use rather high-powered mathematics)," the management theorist Herbert Simon comments, "it is not clear that operations research embodies any philosophy different from that of scientific management. Charles Babbage and Frederick Taylor will have to be made, retroactively, charter members of the operations research societies." [25] The logic of the "new science"—like the old "scientific management" of Bab-

[25] Herbert A. Simon, *The New Science of Management Decision* (New York, 1960), p. 14.

bage and Taylor—also moves in the direction of a "single organizational system" under central control. "What seems to have happened in many universities," say Rourke and Brooks, "is a simultaneous centralization of the *preparation* of the budget and a decentralization of the *administration* of the budget once the funds are appropriated or allocated." [26]

Some of the more future-oriented universities—the University of California and Purdue University among them—have attempted to apply computerized management techniques not only to budgeting but also to general problems of policy planning in the university. To substantiate the claim to "scientific" status, management scientists must make *predictions* about the development of the university. To this end, university management designs a statistical model of the university which includes as many quantified variables as seem to affect the outcome. The computer is programed with this model and thereupon makes projections of the future state of the university. Presumably, university management is left in a position to control future developments by altering variables in suitable ways; what ways are suitable can be determined through "simulations" on the computer. The model itself is also perfected in this process, which may feature numerous "administrative games" played on the computer and with live actors.

Social "scientists" are usually deeply involved in these computer simulations. The major obstacle to the application of the scientific method to society has always been the unavailability of experimental conditions under which social scientists could control relevant variables in order to make predictions, verify their hypotheses, construct their theories, and develop their "laws of human behavior." Since history tends to happen quickly, chaotically, and irretrievably, conditions have not militated to the advantage of social "science."

[26] Francis E. Rourke and Glenn E. Brooks, *The Managerial Revolution in Higher Education* (Baltimore, 1966), p. 84. This book explores the applications of management methods to universities.

Game theory, mathematical models, and computer simulations have opened a way, so social scientists think, out of the impasse. The quest for a social science has made for a natural alliance between the social scientists who make predictions and the managers who can make use of the predictions while financing the technology of prediction. "And with the growing sophistication of computer-based simulation procedures," Daniel Bell writes, "—simulations of economic systems, of social behavior, of decision problems—we have the possibility, for the first time, of large-scale 'controlled experiments' in the social sciences. These, in turn, will allow us to plot 'alternative futures,' thus greatly increasing the extent to which we can choose and control matters that affect our lives." [27] "We" are the "new men"—the "scientists, the mathematicians, the economists, and the engineers of the new computer technology"—in alliance with the managers (and owners) of the institutional bureaucracies.

These social scientists often call for a "new political theory." But the theory already exists in the form of "modern management." The new practice of management should not be confused with the bureaucratic technique described by Max Weber. The model institution of the year 2000 is not a rigid hierarchy on the line-and-staff model. Ideally, it will not be heavily freighted with regulation manuals and unvarying procedures and it will have neither a single chain of command nor a system of departments and bureaus to handle all its duties. Instead, it will be organizationally fluid, with different groups—teams, task forces, and working parties— forming *ad hoc* as a problem arises and dissolving upon the solution of the problem. According to expectation, these teams will bring to bear precisely the right mix of specialized talents to meet the unique requirements of a particular problem. They will have a high degree of autonomy because unique problems would require original solutions and be-

[27] Daniel Bell, "Notes on the Post-Industrial Society: I," *The Public Interest* (Winter 1967), p. 30.

cause team players—mainly professional staff—will be highly educated, cultured, and liberally oriented; they will demand autonomy as a condition of employment. A diversified enterprise of the new type could accommodate within it many autonomous institutions and divisions which might be working in quite different fields. The unifying theme would be a common concern with new technologies, social innovation, and economic growth.

The prototypes of the new-model corporation already exist, in the organizational forms of the high-technology companies, the conglomerates, the research organizations, the universities, and the more progressive sectors of foundations and governments. The embryonic future, it is often claimed, is represented by the university which houses a large professional and technical staff and operates a diversity of enterprises on the principle of delegation of responsibility. This is a convergence thesis of the business firm and the university.

The organizing principle of the new-model institution will be centralized control through decentralized structures. Authority will repose at the center. However, administrative responsibility will be radically decentralized and even some significant policy-making (though never authority) will be farmed out. The central authority will, however, establish certain controls, probably budgetary, on the "autonomous" subsidiaries in its domain. It is the central authority that will set the parameters of decision-making for its subordinates and require them to produce results to certain general specifications. It will not be necessary to supervise the operation directly or to control budget expenditures, once appropriations are made. The management core will also arrogate to itself control of resource allocation and establish a process of centralized planning, utilizing elaborate systems of organized research-and-information technology. As insurance against misinformation, management might develop a complex "communications system" of consultative committees, advisory bodies, and study commissions which would link it to all levels of the enterprise. The political advantages of this "social theory"—suborned to organizational theory—would be legion. While the corporate communications system provides information to central management, it also constitutes an elaborate co-optation structure to assimilate potential opposition with the lure of "participation." The institutional apparatus commits itself to social progress, or rather "social innovation"—that is, social change sponsored by the dominant institutions within the limits necessary for systems maintenance. The hang-loose organizational style should reconcile conflicts between management and the professional staff. In the event of system malfunction, one could fall back on a co-management scheme to assimilate opposition with substantive, though minority, shares of power and wealth.

This variety of "social theory" is pseudo-scientific. Systems analysis requires that all "relevant variables" be reducible to numerical values. It vacuums human volition out of the social process—the "data"—and deposits it at the other end of the social microscope. It generally lacks the dimension of historical explanation and may even ignore the political economy that its institutional models and social-psychological case studies inhabit. It is social theory reduced to organizational theory and is, accordingly, a species of administrative reductionism. Scientism can safely be added to pluralism and technocracy, discussed in Chapter II, as characteristic of official liberalism. Scientism is the common methodological style of both technocratic analysis and pluralist theory. The technocratic claim to power rests upon its scientific pretensions, while pluralist analysis often attempts to incorporate a pointless apparatus of graphs and quantification to polish its surface. Pluralism also tends to the positivistic by avoiding significant generalization and taking un-analyzed data as final.

The political engine which drives these rather eviscerated abstractions is nationalism—the fourth characteristic of official liberalism. If the "national interest" does not require some particular policy advocated by official liberals, then it is the "national purpose" or "national needs." The national-interest criterion defines the priorities of state-and-corporate capitalism; these are pre-eminently economic growth, military security, and social control. Individual freedom, economic equality, and social justice do not rank high on this list, if indeed they are on the list. "The state," Galbraith writes, "is strongly concerned with the stability of the economy. And with its expansion or growth. And with education. And with technical and scientific advance. These are *the* national goals; they are sufficiently trite so that one has a reassuring sense of the obvious in restating them." [28] The political passions of official liberalism are nationalist passions: the Cuban missile crisis of 1962, technology and the growth rate, the space program and the successful moon landing of 1969.

The university managers obtain powerful leverage from their pivotal position in conglomerate organization; the president and his officers have the responsibility—in the formulation of the governance statement of the AAUP, the governing-boards association, and the American Council on Education—of "operating the communication system which links the components of the academic community." The implementation of operations research and the new technology of management have shifted additional power to the center. In their study, Rourke and Brooks attribute this shift in the institutional balance of power *not* to "technological imperatives" (in the sense of specialized knowledge) but to the political and economic realities which govern the use of technology. University administrations have generally maintained an "administrative monopoly of information" that the computer facility has processed on the institution. Institutional research has been a "means of implementing courses of action already decided upon" and thus an "instrument in the hands of the decision-maker rather than a source of decision." Centralized management of building space has eroded

[28] John Kenneth Galbraith, *The New Industrial State* (New York, 1968), p. 316.

departmental control of their own scheduling and of office, research, and classroom space. Large powers in the university are now exercised by a new officialdom—the financial vice-president, the budget officer, the space manager, the director of the computer center, the head of institutional research. This is not to mention an array of vice-presidents—for finance, for public relations, for academic affairs, for research, etc. These corporate bureaucrats—along with men responsible for other centralized functions, such as admissions, registration, athletics, buildings and grounds, security, counseling, placement, alumni affairs—constitute the executive branch of the university.

The most powerful members of the bureaucracy are probably the budget officer and the financial vice-president. But the whole apparatus is the operational arm of the chief executive officer, the president of the university—although there is a trend to team management. It is the president and his administration which establish the new computer facility and the research organization, and they are not likely to neglect their political interests in setting the terms for the operation. The prohibitive cost of computers also favors a single facility under central direction. Finally, the dense vocabulary and magic technology of modern management can serve to mystify other elements inside and outside the university. The assumption of a professional mystique can be put to good political use: "a large state university is often forced to put on a dramatic show of scientific objectivity in its budgetary process in order to justify its requests for continued support, even though the dramatic props—elaborate formulas, statistical ratios, and so on—may have very little to do with the way in which decisions are actually made within the academic establishment. In such a context the new science of management serves not so much to manage the university as to manage the impression that outsiders have about it." [29]

The faculty "component" must suffer a decline in power in

[29] Rourke and Brooks, p. 98.

a conglomerate arrangement. There is, of course, a system of "dual power" in the university, and the faculty has very significant discretion in determining the form and content of education. But it exercises this discretion within parameters established from above. The power to decide departmental policy cannot, in addition, compare with the power to establish new departments. The faculty wields minimal leverage in institutional decisions. In a period of extremely rapid growth in the educational establishment, the control of the *processes of growth* is the decisive power. The university managers literally control social change in the field of education; they can afford to wait out their opposition, secure in the knowledge that the tides will go out, leaving the traditionalists and the *enragés* stranded in their enclaves. The faculty senates—the institutional organizations of the scholars—can hardly compete with the executive branch. Their efficacy has not improved since Veblen described them as "deliberative bodies charged with power to talk. Their serious attention has been taken up with schemes for weighing imponderables and correlating incommensurables, with such a degree of verisimilitude as would keep the statistics and accountancy of the collective administration in countenance, and still leave some play in the joints of the system for the personal relation of teacher and disciple. It is a nice problem in self-deception, chiefly notable for an endless proliferation." [30]

Because of this lack of authority, senate meetings are not well attended. Many educational writers have, like Corson, remarked on the "enigmatic attitudes of the faculties—a catholic concern and a comprehensive claim of competence on the one hand, and an indifference and unwillingness to take part on the other. . . ." [31] The solution to the enigma lies in the professional loyalties of the faculty members. Their meal tickets depend on their scholarly output, the quality of

[30] Veblen, p. 206.

[31] John J. Corson, *Governance of Colleges and Universities* (New York, 1960), p. 99.

which is judged by a national community of professionals. There is little incentive for faculty members to formulate institutional policy beyond the protection of their realm of "research" and the progressive abrogation of their teaching (and other) responsibilities. Theirs is a craft-unionist mentality. They seek privilege, not power.

Contemplating this professional bias, Ruml and Morrison suggest, in an essay notorious among faculty members, that the trustees should disestablish faculty control of curriculum: "The departmentalized structure gives a prevailing and powerful vocational bias. It stimulates recruiting and the offering of highly specialized content courses attractive to a highly specialized student constituency. As a consequence, there is a pervasive deterioration of instruction that should be of a general and liberal character." [32] The narrow perspectives of professionalization and the inherent conservatism of the departmental baronies, Corson suggests (in a view representative of administrations), "substantially disqualify most faculties for a large role in governance."

This is not to say that administrations freeze out the faculty entirely. "But if faculty as a corporate body cannot be expected to manage the university," Perkins writes, "individual faculty members are indispensable to the management process. Indeed, I would put high on any university priority list the identification and support of the faculty whose viewpoint is broad, who have that rare quality of seeing problems in operational terms, and whose faculty standing is solidly based on specialized competence." [33] In short, it is necessary to develop a camarilla of like-minded "faculty leaders" who may share in the formulation, popularization, and execution of presidential policy by virtue of their "rare quality" of understanding problems in "operational terms." The faculty masses are likely to regard this arrangement, with appropriate

[32] Beardsley Ruml and Donald H. Morrison, *Memo to a College Trustee* (New York, 1959), pp. 8–9.
[33] Perkins, p. 56.

accents of tough talk, as "real power." The logic of faculty politics in the university, as elsewhere, is built on the schema of co-management. In the tripartite statement on governance cited above, the accent is on "interdependence," "adequate communication," "joint planning and effort," and "participation." The faculty should participate, everyone agrees, in the university operation at all levels. "Distinction should be observed," the statement nonetheless warns, "between the institutional system of communication and the system or responsibility for the making of decisions." [34] In a statement on faculty strikes, the AAUP cautioned against militant tactics that would imply that faculty members are "mere employees" rather than "officers of their colleges and universities."

Educational expansion and university growth, which the educational managers have both directed and profited from, have also had the ironic effect of concealing the shift in institutional power. As long as they are able to finance growth in a generous manner, the managers do not have to play a "zero sum game"—that is, they do not have to take from the traditional sectors of university life in order to feed their new priorities. In the 1960s, university administrations avoided serious conflict with sectors of the faculty because state and federal subsidy financed a period of affluence. But the 1970s will continue to require large increases in financial allocations merely to finance growing student enrollment. If funding sources dry up for the universities, as they already have for the liberal-arts colleges, the new apparatus of control will surface into plain sight even for the shuffleboard-playing passengers. Hostility to the higher educational system resulting from student rebellion and an inflationary economy have encouraged this possibility on the governmental levels. In 1969 and again in 1970 President Nixon vetoed a huge education-appropriation bill as inflationary.

Although the adverse effect on the influence of faculty is unmistakable, Rourke and Brooks do not speculate on the

[34] *AAUP Bulletin* (Winter 1966), p. 378.

effect of the "managerial revolution" on the power of regents and trustees. Most likely, it is not very great. The signal power of the governing boards is their authority to appoint the president, who has the responsibility to "see to it that the standards and procedures in operational use conform to the policy established by the governing board and to the standards of sound academic practice." [35] Although the president prepares the budget, the governing board normally has a committee to review its particulars. On the other hand: "Relatively few faculties, as a body, play any substantial, formal role in budgetary formulation. . . . More often, the deans are given an opportunity to present estimates of their needs; and while department heads and faculties have an opportunity to make their demands, entreaties, or urgings, they have no decisive part to play. The trustees, or more often a committee of them, take a more active, and in some instances a commanding, position in determining what shall be included in the budget." [36]

Normally, the trustees also elect an executive committee to oversee the university between full meetings of the board. Besides the budget and executive committees, most boards also have committees on curriculum, finance, development, and building and grounds. While retaining control of budget priorities, the governing boards simultaneously determine, together with their administrative bureaus, long-range planning for the institution and the related matter of the expansion of the plant. They also oversee the financial management of the university endowment and investment portfolio. This responsibility can have specifically educational consequences, since financial management involves a choice of future returns against present gains. "Academic revolution" theorists have often argued that the educational ignorance of trustees has effectively disestablished them and transferred power to the administration and faculty. But the controlling decisions per-

[35] *AAUP Bulletin*, p. 378.
[36] Corson, *Governance of Colleges and Universities*, pp. 65–6.

tain to the *economics* of education, not to the theory of education. The governing boards know finance, business, and economics; they also know the effects of such decisions on the character of an institution and the techniques of managerial control. These matters are their *specialty*.

The expansion of education has not undermined the power of governing boards from below; it has eroded their power from above. Educational policy-making moves ever upward. Among public institutions, this process has led to the development of statewide systems of higher education in over 40 states. One reason for this event has been the *economics* of technology. The costs of computerized budgeting favor the centralization of expensive computer facilities; the development of objective data on universities provides political authorities with handles for control. The dominant cause, however, has been the enormous growth of the educational establishment in terms of student enrollment, educational program, and costs per student. In the decade between the late '50s and '60s, student enrollment in higher education nationally doubled and the expenditures tripled. The states financed one fourth of higher education in this period. Not unnaturally, the state governments have been unwilling to make a free gift of one of the largest segments of their budgets. The spirits of the time have demanded accountability, the efficient use of public funds, the elimination of waste and duplication, the rational allocation of monies, and, more recently, the surveillance of the liberal professors and their radical charges. Central direction has been exercised from the office of the governor, which recommends appropriations and appoints educational officials, and from the legislature, which appropriates money. The trend has moved from the appropriation of funds to the supervision of specific allocations and expenditures of funds. This supervision has in many cases been exercised from the state bureaucracy consisting of central building agencies, purchasing departments, auditors, comptrollers, and especially the budget offices. Educators consider these practices rather crude from the point of view of liberal principle and managerial strategy.

The major device for central control has been statewide coordinating boards, which have allowed a measure of "autonomy" for the institutions, while undertaking statewide planning functions. These super-boards and other statewide boards for specific types of institutions have taken over much of the authority associated with the traditional governing board for a single institution: budget and program review; determination of admissions standards, tuition rates, and room and board fees; establishment of new programs, departments, and schools; building and construction. They have also assumed entirely new authority: the creation of new campuses and "master planning." Often modeled on the first California Master Plan of 1960, the master plans have tended to emphasize community-college systems offering technical and vocational programs, and to set high-level tracks for higher education which channel the secondary-school population into universities, colleges, or junior colleges through the manipulation of admissions standards and tuition rates. Commenting on the statewide systems in *The Dimensions of Academic Freedom*, Walter Metzger (a member of the Ad Hoc Faculty Group during the Columbia strike) notes, "These vertical and horizontal combinations of plants in similar and diverse lines, these unequal allocations of power between the central office and the local branch, this division of territorial markets state by state, make the integrated academic organization and the modern business corporation seem very much alike, if not of kin." [37]

This process of educational integration—what James Perkins, a director of the RAND Corporation, calls the movement from "autonomy to systems"—grinds inexorably toward a national policy for higher education. The key agency in the development of such a policy is the federal government,

[37] Walter Metzger, *The Dimensions of Academic Freedom* (Urbana, Ill., 1969), p. 16.

which has moved rapidly in the last decade toward dominance of higher education. Through its subsidization and
control of national research and development, the federal
government financed some 13 percent of higher education by
the end of the 1950s. The education acts of the Kennedy and
Johnson administrations raised this percentage to 21 percent
by the 1960s, while the Carnegie Commission for Higher Education, chaired by Clark Kerr, estimates that the federal
government must finance 33 percent by the end of the 1970s
to support the continuing expansion of the system. These figures suggest powerful influence short of dominance, but they
understate the case. They exclude funds for veterans' education, management contracts for federally funded research-and-
development centers, and loans for construction and student
aid. Furthermore, this percentage represents the federal share
of the whole of higher education, which includes 2,300 institutions. But more than two thirds of federal money goes to
just 100 of these institutions, and a third goes to 25 out of
this 100.

In its study of "Twenty-Six Campuses and the Federal Government" [38] for the academic year 1959–60, the Carnegie
Foundation for the Advancement of Teaching discovered
that, among the 12 elite universities in its sample, federal-
project research within academic departments accounted for
between 18 and 76 percent of the campus-proper expenditures of these institutions, with 30 percent as the median. If
federal support for special-research institutes was included,
the Carnegie Foundation discovered that federal research
subsidies alone accounted for between 14 and 83 percent of
the total institutional expenditures, with 40 percent as the
median. Among these "federal-grant universities" (Clark
Kerr's phrase), the most federalized were Princeton (75 percent), Stanford (41 percent), MIT (82 percent), Cal Tech
(84 percent), and the University of Chicago (64 percent), all

[38] "Twenty-Six Campuses and the Federal Government," *Educational Record* (April 1963), pp. 95–137.

nominally private institutions. If the research institutes, which are not always university-owned, are excluded, federal research subsidies still supported 40 percent of the budgets of these leading federal-grant universities. This was in an early period of federal influence when the government's share of total higher educational expenditures stood at only 13 percent. Federal aid is more evenly distributed now, but the federal share has doubled, so that federal influence on the major league is no less. The government commands the heights of higher education, and it can depend on the nature of the educational market and the instincts of imitation to disseminate "national policy" throughout the higher educational system. In the "private sector" of the major league, many of these universities have, in effect, only management contracts on their own institutions.

It would be an overstatement—though not a gross one—to say that the federal government has nationalized higher education. For one thing, the nationalization thesis ignores the "partnership" between the federal bureaucracy and the state governments called the "New Federalism." The states finance 27 percent of higher education and run the statewide systems, which are in many ways the pace-setters of the educational establishment. The states have a limited tax base, however, and their role has been declining (formerly their share was 33 percent) and will continue to decline, perhaps to below 20 percent, in the 1970s. The nature of the New Federalism points to state assumption of routine operations, such as day-to-day administration, and sufficient expansion to cover increases in enrollment and costs, while the initiative for *new* programs and *qualitative* expansion originates elsewhere. The agents of change are the federal agencies and the foundations with their "seed money" techniques. In sum, the federal government, together with the states and foundations, has assumed control of higher education through the weight of its funding, its command of the heights, and, most important, its direction of the processes of growth. It has taken over a large share of this function from the governing boards and university managements, but not from the educational communities—students and faculty—who have from the very beginning been unable to pay the ante.

It is sometimes argued, nevertheless, that contract research with the federal government has increased the power of the faculty, mainly the scientific faculty, to the detriment of university management. Certainly the members of the scientific faculty cultivate their connections with federal funding agencies and so increase their leverage in the university communities. One of the new men in this arrangement is the "research entrepreneur," who with federal funds, builds up a personal enclave—an institute, special program or whatever—which has a quasi-independent budget, professional staff, and payroll. Academic scientists point to the "peer-and-project system" as a guarantee of autonomy. Under the terms of the project system, scientific researchers may make proposals of their own design for federal support, while an elaborate system of advisory panels of leading scientists—the peers—advises federal agencies on the scientific merit of the proposals. On the basis of the peer-and-project system, scientists have considered themselves to be both free agents and men of influence in Washington. This self-image received a rude shock in October, 1969 when it turned out that the Department of Health, Education and Welfare, presumably the least security-conscious of the major agencies, was blacklisting hundreds of leading scientists from these panels. The criteria of "security" and "suitability" were mainly applied to opponents of the Vietnam War, members of leftist political organizations, and men who had antagonized Congressional investigating committees.

Ultimately, the research entrepreneurs are not independent figures, but agents of a foreign power. This result is ensured by the structure of the basic research market, which is "monopsonistic" (characterised by a single buyer). Far from operating like true entrepreneurs, the research empire-builders are captives of their funding source, the federal government. The Department of Defense, for instance, receives five times as many proposals as it funds, and thus by rewarding its friends and punishing its enemies, may determine research priorities in the scientific world. The research entrepreneurs may attempt to maneuver among federal agencies, but this ploy has limited possibilities, since the various agencies specialize in certain fields of research.

The argument that the scientific faculty as a body gains power from federal influence also ignores the circulating elite among the education and research managers. The universities, foundations, and federal agencies tend to exchange their top personnel and thus develop a common point of view and a community of interest. Any influence university management loses on the scene it is likely to recoup through its influence in Washington and New York. The rise of men such as John Gardner (Carnegie Corporation, U.S. Department of Health, Education and Welfare, Urban Coalition), Clark Kerr (University of California, Carnegie Corporation), James Perkins (Carnegie Corporation, Cornell University), and McGeorge Bundy (Harvard University, White House, Ford Foundation) is a structural result of the interlocking governments of the corporate state.

The educational managers in the universities, in the state systems, in the foundations, and in the federal agencies have been groping toward a "new idea of the university." It is generally agreed among them that the phenomenon is very "diverse": there are many universities; there are many state governments; there are many private foundations; there are many federal agencies that fund; there are even more corporate donors; and there are more wealthy individual donors still. The sheer diversity of it all has inspired some observers to hail the "new pluralism," but this nomenclature is too vague. Its lack of positive content is inherently unsatisfactory to the systems managers, who are the vanguard of technocracy. "We are only beginning to understand the enormous, even revolutionary power that has been created by this combination of interests," Perkins explains. "It has contributed to the evolution of the service state; to the idea of the private corporation with public concerns; and to the development of the modern university itself, which is responsible for much of the vitality of both." [39] The combination of interests is defined by the "joining of hands of state, corporation, and university"—in short, the corporate state.

If the corporate state is the stomping ground of the university, there is still lacking an idea of the university. Perkins suggests that the university is the "great pumping heart that keeps this system fresh, invigorated, and in motion." He explains: "The university and the other institutions of society—including the corporation, the farm, the cultural center, and the government agency—have now been joined together by a new kind of blood stream, made up of the ideas, the trained intelligence, and the manpower which provide the driving agency of our society." [40] The pluralist idea of the university is that it is the "great pumping heart" of economic development and social management. The new idea of the university is that of a motor of economic growth. Higher education has been nationalized, not by the federal government alone, but by the forces which manage economic growth. These are preeminently the state apparatus, national and local, and the corporations, national and international, including their philanthropic wing, the private foundations. This is the genius of the American system—a numberless "diversity" of institutions, yet coordinated through regional and national associations and compacts, and operated under the principle of a "mixture of private pursuit and public purpose."

The economic importance of the university consists, first of all, in its dynamism as a market. In the last decade, higher

[39] James A. Perkins, "The New Conditions of Autonomy," in Logan Wilson, ed., *Emerging Patterns in American Higher Education* (Washington, D.C., 1965), p. 9.
[40] Perkins, *The University in Transition*, pp. 18–19.

education has proved its mettle as a growth industry. In the late 1950s, expenditures for higher education stood at $5.2 billion, which amounted to 1 percent of the gross national product. In the 1960s, while student enrollment doubled, total expenditures more than tripled to reach the sum of $17.2 billion—2 percent of the GNP. It is further estimated that expenditures for higher education will more than double again in the 1970s, and eventually come to constitute 3 percent of the GNP. Barring a political malfunction in the appropriations systems, higher education should continue to be a growth industry into the 1980s. The rise of higher education is a part of the general rise of the knowledge industry. Interpreting this industry in the broadest sense, Fritz Machlup estimated in the early 1960s that the knowledge industry accounted for 29 percent of the gross national product and was growing at twice the rate of the non-knowledge economy.[41]

Higher education bulks large in the economy and in the federal budget—the largest item after defense, space, agriculture, and science and technology. Its special economic significance consists not in its bulk, however, but in the stimulating effect it is alleged to have on the rest of the economy. Higher education is, the argument runs, the key factor in economic growth in an advanced economy. In studies for the Committee for Economic Development and the Brookings Institution, Edward Denison has attributed almost half of the growth rate of the United States in the 1950s and early '60s to factors related to higher education. One fifth of the growth rate, Denison has maintained, is a result of improvements in the quality of the labor force, namely education, and almost a third more has resulted from "advances in knowledge" applied to the production process.[42]

[41] Cf. Fritz Machlup, *The Production and Distribution of Knowledge in the United States* (Princeton, N.J., 1962).
[42] Cf. Edward F. Denison, *The Sources of Economic Growth in the United States* (New York, 1962) and *Why Growth Rates Differ* (Washington, D.C., 1967).

As queen of the schools, the university takes the leading role in economic growth. In terms of output, the larger university systems promise to enter the realm of the billion-dollar corporation in the 1970s. In the area of trained man-power, the university produces the leading technical and professional cadres—the Ph.D.'s, the M.D's, the LL.B.'s, the B.A.'s, and the B.S.'s. In the area of advances in knowledge that are beneficial to the economy, the university leads the field in basic research, which is believed crucial to research and development and technological innovation. The social function of the university is no longer ornamental. The ideologues of official liberalism have increasingly honored education—and allied sectors of the knowledge industry such as information systems, communications media, and research and development—with the Siege Perilous in their social vision. The educators and scientists, Galbraith argues, "stand in relation to the industrial system much as did the banking and financial community to the earlier stages of industrial development. Then capital was decisive, and a vast network of banks, savings banks, insurance companies, brokerage houses, and investment bankers came into existence to mobilize savings and thus to meet the need. In the mature corporation, the decisive factor of production, as we have seen, is the supply of qualified talent. A similar complex of educational institutions has similarly come into being to supply this need." [43] In like fashion, Daniel Bell writes: "In all of this, the university, which is the place where theoretical knowledge is sought, tested, and codified in a disinterested way, becomes the primary institution of the new society. Perhaps it is not too much to say that if the business firm was the key institution of the past hundred years, because of its role in organizing production for the mass creation of products, the university will become the central institution of the next hundred years because of its role as the new source of innovation and knowledge." [44]

[43] Galbraith, p. 291.
[44] Bell, p. 30.

II. THE MILITARIZATION OF
RESEARCH AND DEVELOPMENT

The new idea of the university has social consequences. Mc-George Bundy, president of the Ford Foundation, has noted that "federal investment in the higher learning has been extraordinarily productive, both for the national security and for the quality of our civilization," and that these investments have "been such as to enhance the freedom and independent strength of American colleges and universities." These propositions, Bundy observes, are "self-evident to responsible scientists, responsible university administrators, responsible Government officials, and responsible members of the leading committees of Congress." [45] Let us investigate.

The role of the university as a research-and-development center for the corporate state was a result of World War II and the ensuing Cold War, and the political character of the research still reflects this fundamental reality. Before the war, universities and scientists were only cultural varnish and a manpower pool for a business "civilization." During the war, university laboratories established their claim to a responsible position by developing radar and the atomic bomb under the direction of the Office of Scientific Research and Development (OSRD). Since the relationship between the universities and the government proved so fruitful, the educational nationalists who led wartime science—Vannevar Bush, President of the Carnegie Institute of Washington, Frank B. Jewett, President of Bell Telephone Laboratories and the National Academy of Sciences, James B. Conant and Karl T. Compton, Presidents of Harvard and MIT—favored the continuation of the relationship after the war. In his report to this effect, *Science, the Endless Frontier*, Bush, who was director of OSRD, expounded the military, economic, and cul-

---

[45] McGeorge Bundy, "Of Winds and Windmills: Free Universities and Public Policy," in Charles G. Dobbins, ed., *Higher Education and the Federal Government* (Washington, D.C., 1963), pp. 89–90.

tural benefits of the sponsorship of science. Like his compa-
triots at Los Alamos or MIT Instrumentation Laboratory,
however, Bush desired federal subsidy without federal control. Natural scientists, like their confreres in the humanities,
subscribe to the Veblen-Flexner thesis of cultural creativity:
research and scholarship can flourish only under conditions of
autonomy for the producers. On the other hand, scientists
want the money. For these reasons, Bush proposed a National Science Foundation which would fund basic science
with minimal bureaucratic constraints.

The National Science Foundation proposal initially
aborted. But federal subsidy for research and development
(R&D) proceeded under the direction of the "mission-
oriented" agencies—namely, the Department of Defense and
the Atomic Energy Commission (and later, the National Institutes of Health). The primary—but by no means exclusive
—role of the universities was to undertake basic research
within the larger scheme of government sponsorship of research and development (which encompasses basic research,
applied research, and development). The relationship of the
universities to the federal government was only a special case
—until the 1960s—of federal policy toward research and development. And, just as R&D policy had initially been determined by the war against the Fascist powers, the postwar
policy was determined by the Cold War with the Communist powers, pre-eminently the Soviet Union. An original result of the first collaboration of government and science was a
new military technology; the circumstances of the postwar
confrontation—an unlimited arms race with the Soviet
Union—underscored the military priority of technology.
After Sputnik I in 1957, research and development received
an enormous impetus from the Cold War's new dimension
of competitive space exploration. The imaginary "missile
gap" of John F. Kennedy in 1960 and an aggressively counter-
revolutionary foreign policy in the Third World in the ensuing years created new political demands for militarized re-

search and development. Although the arcane techniques of counter-insurgency created new markets (electronic barriers, computerized pacification, defoliation and anti-crop chemistry), nuclear technology and delivery systems have remained the staples.

The initial rationale for federal support of research and development, then, was military, not economic. Under the imperative of "national security," the federal government not only subsidized R&D, but nationalized it. In the 1960s, the state sponsored 70 percent of all research and development. In the process of nationalizing R&D, it *ipso facto* militarized it: 85 percent of federally supported research and development in the 1960s was in the fields of defense, space, and atomic energy. In the last 15 years, moreover, the subsidy for research and development has increasingly been justified by a second rationale: economic growth. The credibility of the economic-growth criterion has been supported by arguments that economic growth in an advanced industrial society depends upon progress in technical knowledge which raises productivity. In addition to raising productivity in traditional industries, technological innovation creates entirely new markets, which contribute to the stabilization of an erratic capitalist economy. New technologies are among the "new frontiers" of investment for corporate capitalism. The social priority of science and technology reflects this reality. Since military security and economic growth are the passwords of American politics, science and technology fare well in federal budgetary allocations. The field now constitutes 12 percent of the federal budget and amounts to 2 percent of the GNP. This is the big money.

Although the nationalization and militarization of research and development were accomplished under the auspices of the corporate state, science and technology also helped to create that apparatus. Early on, the favored instrument of federally supported R&D was contractual relationships with the profit-making industrial corporation or the non-profit institution. The accomplishment of public purposes through contractual connections with private enterprise is the defining characteristic of the corporate state. During the Eisenhower administration, the federal government moved beyond research and development to contract out many of its productive functions, and lost its in-house capabilities in the process. Government procurement has increased enormously; in the late 1960s it amounted in the Defense Department alone to $45 billion annually (out of a federal total of $60 billion). In the area of research and development, scientists and engineers have looked favorably on the system as a means of maintaining the "autonomy" they would lose working on in-house projects.

Contemplating the trackless regions of government procurement, social scientists predictably regard the corporate state as a triumph of pluralism which has prevented excessive government centralization. The American right fears new conquests of the federal government, a loss of business virility, and the decline of "free enterprise." Marxists of orthodox persuasion regard the state as the captive of the corporations. Statists regard the corporations as the instrument of the federal government. These are issues for political theologians. It is difficult to determine where government ends and corporations begin, much less decide who controls whom. The state lets research-and-development contracts, thus converting product development, a high cost for business in the "private sector," into a profitable business for corporations in the "public sector." The state provides the market for the product once it is developed, thus eliminating market risk (though not political risk) from the public marketplace and establishing effective monopolies for companies which may achieve a unique technological capability as a result of the original R&D contract. The public provides the tax money; the Congress appropriates the funds; and the federal bureaucracy supervises the operation. But the prime contractor may make essential managerial decisions and wield the political and economic influence that comes from awarding sub-contracts. The purpose is public, but the operation is for profit.

Although the corporations sometimes appear to be the dominant partners, the federal government owns large portions of their plant and equipment and enforces various controls on corporate policy. The government, the profit-making corporations, and the non-profit institutions of the knowledge industry are so interlocked at the directorial level, so interwoven at the middle levels, so meshed in function, that they are hardly distinguishable. Separately regarded, it is difficult to determine which is dominant; together, they are becoming a new governing apparatus which rules what remains.

The prototype of the emerging social order has been the "military/industrial complex." The Department of Defense was first to sponsor research and development (as a means to develop the military technologies necessary for military supremacy). The Air Force led the way in contracting out essential functions and thus in creating the mechanism of the "complex." Defense management first employed systems and quantitative analysis as a technique of managerial control within government. This originality has had certain interesting social consequences. If research and development and technological innovation are the keys to economic growth, then it is the defense-space complex, which funds over 50 percent of all R&D in the United States, that is sponsoring economic growth. If the "public market" is a highly profitable sector of the economy, it is the Defense Department which bulks largest in this public market. If systems analysis and management theory are the instruments of a new social rationality and the keys to an enlightened social order, then the DoD is a model of rationality and enlightenment. Research and development are largely military-aerospace; the growth industries of the economy which utilize research and development are often military-aerospace; the public market, in which these growth companies (often conglomerates) operate, is largely military-aerospace. The technocratic vanguard has also learned its trade in the "systems engineering" of the military-aerospace industry and the systems analysis of the Department of Defense.

Possibly these connections are merely contingent—fading creations of World War II and the Cold War. Some observers perceive the social initiative passing from DoD (and the related agencies, AEC and NASA) to other sectors of the federal bureaucracy. They anticipate new growth industries, implementing new technologies, in new public markets and predict the relative decline of the military/industrial complex and the dawn of a "reordering of our national priorities."

If such an event should come to pass, it will not occur on terms unfavorable to the military-aerospace interests. From the middle '60s to the late '60s the defense-space dominance of federal research and development declined only slightly, from 90 to 85 percent of the total. This proportion did not represent an absolute decline; on the contrary, it partially represented a proselytizing movement. Disciples of the "systems approach" migrated from military-related operations to other federal agencies—Health, Education and Welfare, Housing and Urban Development (HUD) and the Office of Economic Opportunity (OEO). With them, they carried the good news of R&D, systems, computers, and contract pluralism. Where they did not penetrate, their doctrines did by virtue of their cogency to government administrators. The military-aerospace corporations have waited to cash in on new contracts for educational technologies (teaching machines, audio-visual aids, etc.), urban-development R&D (prefabrication, low-cost housing rehabilitation), ocean sciences (food and raw materials), manpower-development programs, medical electronics, and so on. Any social policy which relies on technological inputs will tend to benefit the military-aerospace corporations because the 300 corporations which perform 97 percent of federal R&D also perform 91 percent of private R&D. All of these 300 are military contractors, and many of them predominantly military-aerospace. If the social priorities shift, the military-aerospace companies will be ready with their organized knowledge, their R&D capability, their technological solutions, their appreciation of the "complex," and their game optimism.

In the field of urban development, for instance, the Defense Department awarded three R&D contracts in 1968 for the development of new low-cost building technologies to General Electric, Aero-Jet General, and Kaiser Industries, all major military contractors. DoD sponsored the program because, with its matchless command and control, builders could experiment in military housing without restrictions by building codes; but military-aerospace firms also bid on R&D contracts awarded by HUD. Lockheed and North American–Rockwell have been awarded contracts by the U.S. Office of Education in the fields of educational technology and information. In sum, a reallocation of federal money will probably consolidate the corporate state under the direction of former military managers if the Vietnam War ends and inflation is halted. On the other hand, a failure to reallocate funds will also benefit military contractors and represent less uncertainty and political risk to the dominant firms. The early decisions of the Nixon administration—the funding of the antiballistic missile and the supersonic transport, the evaporation of the "peace dividend," the vetoes of education and housing bills—suggest the latter course of action. In this event, it will also be necessary, in the long run, for China to replace the Soviet Union in the Cold War scenario.

In their relationships to the federal government, the universities have been carried along by these tidal movements. Most federal aid has been for research and development and, consequently, for the natural sciences and engineering. In the process, academic science and, to a significant extent, the whole university operation have been militarized. It is possible, however, to argue that this process has been reversed in the last decade with the advent of generalized federal support for higher education, and that the Department of Health, Education and Welfare (HEW) has rightly taken control of the federal program. Research and development, one could argue, now constitute only 40 per cent of all federal aid to higher education, and the National Institutes of Health, which support medical science, contribute more R&D funds to universities than any other agency. HEW, so the argument runs, now distributes two thirds of all federal aid to higher education, and the National Science Foundation, which is dedicated to science for the sake of science, is growing in influence. Far from dominating the schools, it is said, the Defense Department contributes only 8 percent of all federal aid to higher education.[46]

This interpretation will not bear examination. Although the share of federal support devoted to research and development has declined, 70 percent of all federal aid still goes to science and engineering because a new priority is support of *science education,* which is obviously necessary to maintain a high-level R&D effort for the long term. Although the Department of Defense contributes only 8 percent of direct aid to higher education, the defense-space complex, including the DoD and the allied agencies of the AEC and the National Aeronautics and Space Administration (NASA), contributes 17 percent. This figure is still not impressive, but all of these percentages exclude the Federally Funded Research and Development Centers (FFRDC), which are key installations of military science. These world-famous Research and Development Centers—Brookhaven, Los Alamos, the Jet Propulsion Laboratory, and the rest—are managed, though not owned, by universities. Although they are "relatively autonomous," the National Science Foundation (NSF) report describes

[46] For figures and percentages on federal support of higher education, see National Science Foundation, *Federal Support to Universities and Colleges Fiscal Year 1967* (Washington, D.C., 1969). For figures on research and development cited in this chapter, see National Science Foundation, *Federal Funds for Research, Development, and Other Scientific Activities 1967, 1968, and 1969* (Washington, D.C., 1968).

them as making "important contributions to the educational and research activities of the parent institution." University management is essential, not peripheral, to their purpose, because these centers must "draw upon the available scientific and technical manpower"—that is, the best talent, which is reluctant to leave the "relative autonomy" of the universities for the government bureaucracies. The NSF report describes the work of these centers in the following terms: Lawrence Radiation Laboratory (University of California for the Atomic Energy Commission): "studies of controlled thermonuclear reactions to generate energy through fusion of light nuclei and important contributions toward improving the efficiency of nuclear weapons"; Lincoln Laboratory (MIT for the Air Force): "defense and other military problems involving ballistic missile defense and offense, radar discrimination, satellite communication, and identification of underground nuclear tests"; Applied Physics Laboratory (Johns Hopkins University for the Navy): "includes research in such areas as naval surface-launched missiles and missile systems and Navy satellite navigation technology"; Los Alamos Scientific Laboratory (University of California for the AEC): "largely concerned with weapons development, also research in rocket propulsion, reactor technology, and physical research in the medium-energy region." [47] These Research and Development Centers received $900 million in federal funds, a sum approximating 25 percent of all federal aid ($3.3 billion in 1967, excluding FFRDC's). Some 95 percent of the money for these centers came from the defense-space complex—DoD, AEC, and NASA.

If the Research and Development Centers are added to the direct aid, then the military-aerospace agencies contribute one third of federal aid to higher education. In the area of research and development, their contribution is still more significant; 30 percent of direct aid, and 50 percent if the R&D Centers are added. In addition, much of the support for sci-

[47] *Federal Support for Colleges and Universities* 1967, pp. 36–7.

ence education which is channeled through HEW is designed to ensure the future of military science.

Another line of defense of the integrity of the university and of academic science is that most of the federal research and development undertaken by universities is basic research and so, by its very nature, immune to corruption. In the area of basic research, the scientific researcher defines the problem, submits the proposal, and undertakes the work according to his own requirements. If the funds originate in a mission-oriented agency, the reasoning goes, it is only a political device to generate the funds to support basic science, not an expectation of results: one must be a political realist. It is true, as this argument suggests, that the universities are the leading performers of basic research for the government. They and the allied research and development centers do almost half of all federally sponsored basic research, including 40 percent of that funded by the military-aerospace group and two thirds of HEW's. The universities do more than a billion dollars' worth out of the more than $2 billion in federally funded basic research (total federal R&D: $17 billion). Including the Research and Development Centers, half of this sum by volume is for the defense-space agencies, one quarter for HEW, and another fifth for the National Science Foundation. The problem, however, with the theory of expiation of sins by basic research is that the universities do over *two* billion dollars' worth of total research and development for the federal government. Less than half of their R&D obligations are for basic research. Only slightly more than a third of the work of the Research and Development Centers is basic research, while an equal amount goes to actual development as well as a large sum to applied research. Of direct-contract research in the universities, only slightly more than half is basic.

The purity-of-basic-research argument is also false in its own terms. The mission-oriented departments of the government are not charitable institutions. They retain the option to fund or not to fund the proposals that are presented to them on the basis of the goals of their operation. Since they receive four to five times as many proposals as they fund, the structure of the market favors their control. Some fields of the life sciences are more likely to produce practical medical results than others; some other scientific fields are more likely to produce chemical-biological weapons and death rays than others. Although the military agencies have funded many projects without an obvious military orientation, the mission-oriented departments still fund that basic research which holds the promise of uncovering knowledge that will contribute to a new line of wares. Government officials make this point annually in the appropriations hearings of the Congress. In 1969, Congress formally prohibited the Pentagon from funding research unless it had a "direct and apparent relation to a specific military function or operation." The next year this provision was amended to require only a "potential relation" to such purposes.

All in all, the defense-space complex contributed in fiscal 1967 more than $1.3 billion to universities and colleges. The result is that military-related funding amounted to 30 percent of the federal subsidy and to 8 percent of the nation's expenditures for higher education ($17.2 billion in 1967–68). Since the military-aerospace contribution was research-and-development money, it was concentrated in the elite universities which lead in science and engineering and was representative of a much higher percentage of the budgets of these federal-grant universities. The leading institutions in the university-military-aerospace complex are those universities which operate the critically important Research and Development Centers. The Lawrence Radiation Laboratory and the Los Alamos Scientific Laboratory are budgeted at $175 million and $102 million, equal to half of the operating budget of the entire University of California system which operates them. The two laboratories employed 7,000 scientific, technical, and administrative personnel. The university is also represented on the board of the Institute for Defense Analyses (IDA), formerly a university consortium which is now technically independent. The Naval Biological Laboratory of the Berkeley campus, the department of agronomy at the Davis campus, and the medical school of the Los Angeles campus have been engaged in anti-crop and chemical-biological warfare (CBW) research. Elsewhere, the California Institute of Technology runs the Jet Propulsion Laboratory on a budget of $222 million from the National Aeronautics and Space Administration, and the University of Chicago manages the Argonne National Laboratory on a $97-million appropriation from the AEC. Both universities are represented on the board of IDA.

When the defense-space agencies fund the universities directly, they still prefer semi-autonomous research subsidiaries. The research subsidiaries can organize scientific talent for large-scale projects and maintain security procedures, but still retain the atmosphere and pay scales which scientific personnel demand. For example, the University of Michigan—the second-largest recipient of federal funds throughout the 1960s with more than $60 million per year ($10 million from DoD in fiscal year 1968)—runs an Institute of Science and Technology which is an umbrella organization for several military-oriented operations. Chief of these is the Willow Run Laboratory, where half of the staff is drawn from students and faculty of the university and which maintains a close relationship with the Advanced Research Projects Agency (ARPA) of the Defense Department. The Institute of Science and Technology's operation also includes the Cooley Electronics Laboratory and three Pentagon-funded "Information Analysis Centers"—the Ballistic Missile Radiation Analysis Center, the VELA Seismic Information and Analysis Center, and the Infrared Information and Analysis Center.

The electronics capability of the University of Michigan has earned it the reputation of the "free world leader in combat surveillance"—a capacity which it has put to work in developing counter-guerrilla reconnaissance in Thailand. In the past, the Pentagon has relied upon its network of Information Analysis Centers, such as the Michigan installations or the University of Wisconsin's Mathematics Research Center (this installation was destroyed in 1970 by a terrorist bombing that also killed a research assistant) to do not only electronics or quantitative research but also social-science research into the human factor. One of these centers at American University undertook a study of "Witchcraft in the Congo" in the middle 1960s. It observed that "insurgent witch doctors" had convinced anti-government troops by means of charms and incantations that they were invulnerable to rifle fire. Gullible government troops had come to share this belief, so that the analysis center had been called into action to investigate the possibility of "counter-magic tactics." The center enumerated the available options, including the development of "counter-insurgent witch doctors" and "counter-charms," but concluded that such a policy might result in an escalation of magic tactics. This eventuality would erode the system of secular belief so necessary for modernization. The center advised that judicious use of automatic weapons would eventually disabuse insurgent troops of the belief in their invulnerability.

In all, the Department of Defense contracts with some 100 universities and non-profit affiliates of universities among its top 500 contractors for research and development. Since these are the major centers of academic science in the country, the list of contractors for the Atomic Energy Commission and the National Aeronautics and Space Administration is similar. The leaders in the field are the University of California, Cal Tech, MIT, Johns Hopkins, and Stanford. The University of California and Cal Tech qualify, as already mentioned, through their respective management of Research and Development Centers in weapons research for the AEC and rocketry research for NASA. MIT and Johns Hopkins—

through their management of the Lincoln Laboratory and the Applied Physics Laboratory for the Department of Defense—are regularly among the leading 100 military contractors for the defense establishment—the militant fraternity of major military/industrial corporations in the United States.

The Stanford Research Institute (SRI), a wholly owned subsidiary of Stanford University, also consistently made this assembly in the 1960s. Stanford is a linchpin of the military-aerospace industry of the West Coast. In addition to ownership of SRI, which does $30 million in R&D work (including CBW research) for the Department of Defense, the university operates the Stanford Linear Accelerator Center, a Research and Development Center which the AEC funds at $30 million, and the Stanford Electronics Laboratory, which did more than $2 million in classified research in fiscal '68. Excluding SRI and the AEC-funded accelerator, the university received $16 million in contracts from the Defense Department in 1969.

In 1969, the Stanford board of trustees was a nexus of the military/industrial complex. Kenneth Pitzer, President of the university, was a director of the RAND Corporation. The Stanford Research Institute, deeply involved in Southeast Asia, ran a counter-insurgency program in Thailand and had an office in Bangkok. Of the SRI board of directors, which is appointed by the university board of trustees, Malcolm MacNaughton was President of Castle and Cooke, which has controlling interests in Thai-America Steel; Edgar Kaiser was part owner of the Thai Metal Works; and Fred L. Hartley's Union Oil had drilling rights off the Thai coast—which, it is to be hoped, will fare better from Union Oil than the coast of Southern California.

The cases above are only illustrative. The Reserve Officer Training Corps, which bulks small on any one campus, is the major source of officer cadres—40 percent of new officers—for the military through its 364-campus system. Academic scientists and social scientists do a large volume of consulting (at fees of several hundred dollars a day) for military-aerospace corporations and the defense-space agencies. University research organizations may meanwhile hold subcontracts from both industrial corporations and non-profit research institutions, which do not appear in the standard inventories of military-related research. Innumerable faculty members do individual project research for the defense-space agencies. All of these relationships are in addition to the favored instrument of the research affiliate.

Because the research organizations are independent and inconspicuous, liberal-arts faculty members will often argue that these institutes have little relation to the university and thus cannot corrupt its function. In many cases, this claim is false, since the research affiliates employ faculty members on their staffs and help to train graduate students and undergraduates. And in all cases the research organizations' appeal for the defense establishment rests in their ability to recruit the right talent by virtue of their university connections. Finally, the line of argument confuses the university with the college of arts and sciences. The research institutes may have little relation to the college of arts and sciences, but they form an integral part of the *university*, insofar as a conglomerate organization can have integral parts.

Yet there have been a number of cases of university disaffiliation from research institutes as a result of political pressure from the left in the colleges of arts and sciences. Without question, the latter exercise great influence because they usually command the largest budget, the greatest number of students and faculty members, and the tradition of being *the* university. Universally, the college still regards itself as the heart of the university, although the reality is that the center of gravity is the managerial core (governing board and administration). As early as 1967, after a two-year struggle, the left at the University of Pennsylvania was able to force disaffiliation from the Institute of Cooperative Research, which did research in chemical-biological warfare for the military.[48] As a result of an SDS campaign in 1968, member universities severed their legal ties with the Institute for Defense Analyses, which incorporated as a non-profit research institution. Columbia University and Cornell University have, respectively, divested themselves of the Electronics Research Laboratory and the Cornell Aeronautical Laboratory (a CBW as well as an aeronautical contractor), which have also become independent non-profits.

The question is whether these disaffiliations are of any substantial significance. It is business-as-usual for universities to spin off knowledge corporations and research-and-development enterprises. There are literally hundreds of these spin-offs in Stanford Industrial Park in Palo Alto and on Boston's Route 128. They are nominally independent, but their directors are often university men; their staff may consist in large degree of university faculty members and research associates; and, at the least, the prestige and connections resulting from university paternity help to produce contracts. Here again we are dealing with a complex. The universities disaffiliated from IDA, but the board of directors still consists of executive officers of universities. Columbia University divested itself of the Electronics Research Laboratory, but university officials still sit on the board of the laboratory in its new incarnation, the Riverside Research Institute, which rents office space from the university. The procedure was much the same in the case of the Cornell Aeronautical Laboratory (whose divestiture was later prohibited by a court ruling). The nature of the case is that university officials could very well withdraw from the boards without affecting the productive relationships between the non-profits and the universities.

The April Third Movement at Stanford addressed itself to this fundamental issue in 1969 by demanding that the university convert the Stanford Research Institute to socially bene-

[48] For a discussion of the role of universities in the military's chemical-biological warfare program, see Seymour Hersh, *Chemical and Biological Warfare* (New York, 1969).

ficial research instead of divesting itself of the institute. While the staff of SRI wished to retain the connection with a prestigious university, the trustees of the university responded to the movement with a plan to divest. Testifying before the Appropriations Committee of the U.S. Senate, Dr. John S. Foster, Director of Defense Research and Engineering at the Pentagon, commented: "At Stanford, for example, a firm decision has been made to separate the Stanford Research Institute from the university itself. Separation alone will have no serious impact on Defense research at either activity. Indeed, we have specific assurances from both organizations that it will not." [49]

On the East Coast, MIT advertised a seven-month "trial" in fall 1969 of the feasibility of converting Lincoln Laboratory and the Instrumentation Laboratory, which collectively do $120 million in research for the Defense Department, to domestic and socially oriented research. Foster observed: "Thus, while we expect to make gradual changes, in cooperation with MIT, in the composition of their effort, there does not appear to be any immediate substantial impact on the critical R&D that MIT carries out for us." This was in accord with the policy of "selective diversification" of the Research and Development Centers. Since the military-aerospace operations anticipate that new markets will open up in education technology, urban R&D, ocean sciences, communications, and so on, they can very well turn their long-range plans to good public-relations effect. Only the percentage of military-aerospace work is likely to decline, while the absolute value of these contracts increases. The statistical trends indicate a steady growth of defense-space research and development in the universities from $885 million in 1963 to $1.3 billion budgeted in 1969. While R&D not related to the military has

[49] Testimony of Dr. John S. Foster, "Department of Defense Appropriations for Fiscal Year 1970," *Hearings before Subcommittee of U.S. Senate Committee on Appropriations* (Washington, D.C., 1969), p. 305.

grown faster, from under $500 million to over $1 billion in the same period, these trends do not suggest that the government and the universities will willingly cut the defense-space research and development at universities, much less eliminate it. Foster explained to the Senate Appropriations Committee that selective diversification did not mean that there was an intention to "dilute our DoD funding to FCRC's [Federal Contract Research Centers, the former name for the R&D centers] for national security work, nor do we expect the FCRC's to reduce or delimit their contributions to defense needs."

Restrictions on classified research at universities have also been illusory. Foster noted that the review committees, established by some universities to oversee classified research, had not actually rejected classified-research contracts to any extent. Amounting to only 4 percent of total defense-oriented research, the impact of these sums, Foster said, "can be reduced through a more discriminating administration of security regulations without changing the nature of the work itself." If a university should wish to ban classified research, Defense management was also ready. "In that particular case," Foster remarked, "we might arrange to transfer the activities, say, within the next year, to a nearby installation where the same professors and graduate students could carry on the work."

A Pentagon study entitled Project Hindsight has shaken some of the claims made for basic research by uncovering very little technological payoff from pure research. But the universities do more applied R&D than basic research, so any trend away from funding basic research will not be disastrous. In 1969, Congressional progressives, led by Senator J. W. Fulbright (D–Ark), managed to cut funds for social-science and counter-insurgency research and even for the Research and Development Centers. It is doubtful whether this victory represents a long-term trend. Beyond the foreign ideologies they harbor, the standing of the universities is enormously high in Washington. In the 1960s, they improved their share of the federally sponsored R&D from 6 to 9 percent (excluding another 4 percent invested in the R&D Centers). The Defense Establishment is also pushing Project Themis, a program to extend the "benefits" of military research to more universities. Aside from a desire to create "new centers of excellence," the policy reflects the pressures to spread the R&D pork around.

Clearly, the universities are in the national interest. "We cannot provide for the necessary weapons of defense," Robert C. Seamans, Secretary of the Air Force and a Harvard Overseer, has concluded, "without the help of university research laboratories, as well as the production facilities of industry." Dr. Foster, formerly Director of the Lawrence Radiation Laboratory managed by the University of California, admonished U.S. Senators not to be "misled by those who suggest that DoD's academic research represents a sort of 'sandbox for scholars.' . . . The facts are quite different and the historical record shows how authentically important academic research has been in serving national security."

III. URBAN EXPANSION

In the postwar era, the conglomerate university has assumed new functions and acquired new social roles. Since student enrollments have tripled in this period, the university has also had to expand its traditional capabilities by adding to its faculty, dormitories, and classroom and office space. These mutually reinforcing trends of new roles and more students have created—in the words of Logan Wilson, President of the American Council on Education—the "need for elbow room and a more healthful campus environment." Since many of the leading institutions of higher education are urban universities located in the decaying center city occupied by racial minorities, institutional expansion has raised that other great social question of the day: racism.

The question of elbow room and a healthful environment for the university is one of those knotty problems that urban-affairs institutes have been created to solve. The university requires *lebensraum* for its physical facilities. University personnel, especially faculty, require an environment that is not grossly offensive to their finely tooled sensibilities. This means an environment that has good schools, shaded lanes, and a low crime rate. In a ghetto area these objectives in some degree require moving out low-income and dark-skinned people. In an article entitled "Ground Space for the University," Julian H. Levi, as a corporation lawyer associated with the University of Chicago, observed, "This means that he [the faculty member] must have the kind of community where a significant number of youngsters from the community at large are similarly motivated and, if you please, similarly 'advantaged.' It is an unfortunate fact that the high school which is composed primarily of deprived youngsters, whose attendance is limited to the days that they legally must attend, is not the kind of situation in which adequate pre-college training can be undertaken. Thus, a community within which faculty will be prepared to live is a community which is college-oriented." [50] Levi further commented, "As a political scientist, I think we sow the seeds of the dissolution of democracy itself if we wall off disadvantaged families into the central city, and if we say that families who have the freedom of choice are to reside only outside the city." [51]

In order to implement this novel conception of social justice—call it reverse integration—universities have established aggressive real-estate offices and, as in the case of Columbia and Morningside Heights, Inc., real-estate corporations and consortiums. This apparatus devotes itself to buying up prop-

[50] Julian H. Levi, "Ground Space for the University," in Charles G. Dobbins, ed., *The University, the City, and Urban Renewal* (Washington, D.C., 1965), p. 11.
[51] Levi, p. 12.

erties and, in the case of residential properties, moving the undesirables and unreliables out by whatever means necessary. By itself, however, this procedure is inadequate to the task of assembling major holdings for expansion. Word of university objectives generally leaks out; real-estate prices skyrocket; and community resistance begins to form. The presence of local merchants and center-city landlords (who specialize in slumification through illegal conversions and exorbitant rents) are special obstacles to university objectives. They are a strong match for the university in commercial acumen and tactical skill, if not always in gross assets. To master these difficulties, universities have required political leverage.

The major instrument of public power employed by private and state universities has been the urban-renewal program. Urban renewal has the necessary authority to remove obstacles to university objectives: eminent domain. As Commissioner of the Urban Renewal Administration during the Kennedy administration, William Slayton, now President of Urban America Inc., explained, "While some of our growth industries have turned to the countryside for development of their plants, universities have, by and large, elected to keep their roots in the cities. To provide both expansion space and a compatible environment, they have understandably turned to urban renewal for help." [52] The problem, Slayton further commented, is that "our urban universities are landlocked. While they have been making great efforts to acquire land on the open market, this is at best very difficult. The universities realize that they must call upon public powers in urban renewal to assemble land needed for university expansion." [53] The universities are able to employ the urban-renewal program in two respects. As an institution which may help finance an urban-renewal project, the university can call upon municipal authorities to undertake a federally assisted

[52] William L. Slayton, "The University, the City, and Urban Renewal," in Dobbins, p. 2.
[53] Slayton, p. 4.

renewal project in an area near the university community which is judged blighted. As a potential user and re-developer of project land, the university may also qualify to purchase or lease property, once cleared, at a very substantial "write-down" in price. This possibility is highly facilitated by Section 112 of the Housing Act of 1949, as amended in 1959 (about which more later).

Gaylord P. Harnwell, former President of the University of Pennsylvania, has classed urban renewal as yet another example of that "excellent partnership" which has been formed between "the economic, the political, and the educational leaders." As President of the West Philadelphia Corporation, Harnwell led in the creation in 1959 of the "University City" urban-renewal project, which was formed by the University of Pennsylvania, Temple University, the Drexel Institute for Technology, and the Jefferson Medical School, among other institutions. The University City Science Center was also a creation of that program. It is common practice to make the expansion of university facilities the occasion for a grand scheme for a technology complex. "We in this commonwealth have accepted the decline of the coal industry," Senator Joseph Clark of Pennsylvania explained to a regional conference on urban renewal and universities. "We have seen the decline of the railroads. We have seen textiles move south. The answer to these problems lies with brains—university brains. We need those brains to carry out the research and development that give rise to the satellite industries which research and development bring with them." [54]

Urban renewal, then, serves a general purpose which goes beyond "expansion space" and a "compatible environment." This purpose is economic development. It is economic development and economic growth which create the community of interests which unites federal administrators, municipal politicians, and university officials in a common effort. "We

[54] Senator Joseph S. Clark, "The Task of the Urban University," in Dobbins, p. 44.

began by realizing that we had to help institutions, that our future depended upon their existence and continued growth," an official of the Philadelphia Redevelopment Authority explained to this same regional conference of university administrators and interested parties. "We became aware of their need for expansion and for our assistance in acquiring land for this purpose." The university provided "trained personnel" for the city and "new program approaches." He continued: "Not only is a university a leaven in the community —a source of new ideas and trained personnel—it is big business for the community. One person has called the higher education establishment the biggest growth industry in Philadelphia." [55]

For the university, urban renewal is something more than the power of eminent domain to expedite land acquisition; it is a direct subsidy of substantial proportions to finance university construction of new operations. Urban-renewal money finances the cost of demolition and clearing of land by a "Local Planning Agency" dominated by city government, which may then sell or lease land to the university at a writedown of as much as two thirds of the original value of the property. Since land is one of the largest costs in new construction, this subsidy has great consequences. It contributed, for instance, to the financing of the campuses of the University of Illinois and the Illinois Institute for Technology in the South Side ghetto of Chicago. The city of Philadelphia has channeled tens of millions in urban-renewal money to institutions participating in the University City project in the West Philadelphia ghetto area. Urban universities have not fully appreciated the contribution of the black masses, who, by "blighting" an area and lowering property values, have made low-cost university expansion possible.

Penn's Gaylord Harnwell and the University City Science Center later achieved fame in the campaign to eliminate

[55] Francis J. Lammer, "Municipal Concern for Campus Development," in Dobbins, pp. 22–3.

chemical-biological warfare (CBW) from the campus of the University of Pennsylvania. After disclosures by faculty members of CBW research at Penn in 1965, Harnwell first denied the charge, then proposed a prohibition on contracts whose results were not freely publishable. When the prohibition was shown to be only hortatory, Harnwell proposed the abolition of the Institute of Cooperative Research, which was the CBW center, and the establishment of a presidentially appointed review board. When it proved that CBW contracts were still in effect, Harnwell proposed to eliminate the research and transfer it to a non-profit institution (known as the University City Science Center). When it proved that the university had a controlling interest in University City, students sat in at Harnwell's office and the trustees intervened to cancel CBW research.

This process consumed two years. It took this much time for students and faculty, not to overrun the university administration, but to penetrate the skirmish lines to the point where they might glimpse the grandeur of the fortified position. The federal government subsidizes university expansion not only for its direct contribution to economic growth but also for its capability in research and development, which may turn out to be CBW or some other boon to mankind. This is all in the "public interest." The identification of private objectives with the public interest (and the public subsidization of private profit) is A-OK as long as it contributes to economic growth. The argument is that economic growth benefits almost everyone and economic recession hurts almost everyone; and that is that.

MIT, the University of Chicago, the University Circle group including Western Reserve in Cleveland, and various other institutions of higher learning have employed the urban-renewal program to good effect. The University of California at Berkeley and Columbia's Morningside Heights Inc. have tried, but have had rotten luck with their community relations. For the black poor, these efforts have had the usual

benefits of urban-renewal programs. The perfunctory relocation provisions of urban renewal (known in the ghetto as
"Negro Removal") do not adequately protect former residents against higher rents and extended dislocations. Since
urban renewal has demolished much more residential housing than it has built, the nature of the program is to aggravate
a tight housing market. Because of the realities of construction costs, urban renewal has built mainly luxury housing and
new facilities for inner-city institutions. The universities favor
legislative provisions, such as the 221(d)3 program, for
middle-income housing because their people—students and
faculty—cannot afford luxury housing either. These expedi-
ents are often passed off as programs for the poor, which they
are not. They do provide the basis for integration in the center city among the Negro and white middle classes. The genius of this reverse integration under university sponsorship is
that it can claim to demolish the walls of prejudice while
bulldozing the black poor, who are forced into ever more
dense, ever more expensive, and ever more exploited enclaves.

The University of Chicago led the way in the opening up
of this new frontier by blazing a trail through the Chicago
South Side. The hero of this saga was Julian Levi, who must
stand as a model of the innovating executive of the conglomerate university. Before 1952, the University of Chicago had
pursued an essentially passive policy: Chancellor Robert
Hutchins made statements in favor of racial justice while the
university's business office enforced racially restrictive housing covenants through the Hyde Park Planning Association.
This practice was insufficient to prevent the "deterioration"
of the university community—Hyde Park–Kenwood—and a
resulting migration of faculty members. After some incidents
of crime in 1952, a community meeting was held by the university, and the South East Chicago Commission was formed
under the leadership of university officials. Julian Levi, a corporation lawyer whose brother was dean of the law school,
was appointed executive director of this commission. Like

other education managers (such as Clark Kerr), Levi was trained in industrial management.

The strength of the corporate innovator is that, where the original captains of industry were only two-fisted, he is multi-fisted. Levi's policy was essentially reverse integration: barriers against, and the removal of, the black poor and their replacement with the middle classes, including some Negroes. Through the university's connection with banks, insurance companies, and the press, Levi proceeded to put pressure on real-estate speculators, who had an interest in converting the area into a profitable slum. If prospective slumlords did not sell to the university, Levi would report their housing practices to the police, the press, and municipal authorities. He would also put pressure on banks and insurance companies, particularly those which did university business, to declare the speculators *persona non grata*. While the university acquired properties, the commission set up a screening system for prospective tenants in the area through friendly realtors who were members of the commission. The effect of the screening system was to restrict the entrance of blacks into the area.

But these practices are in the realm of the routine. Levi's innovation was in his use of the Neighborhood Redevelopment Corporation Act of Illinois. The device allowed a private corporation to employ public power—eminent domain —to redevelop a slum area if the corporation's redevelopment plan was acceptable to a municipal commission and if the firm owned 60 percent of the land in a neighborhood. Levi took his campaign to the legislature in 1953 and had the act amended to allow eminent domain for the purpose of neighborhood conservation, as well as redevelopment, under the provision of the *consent*, rather than ownership, of 60 percent of the property in an area. Having honed his instrument, Levi was able to form the South West Hyde Park Redevelopment Corporation, and the predominantly white property-owners in the area proceeded to sign consents for the use of eminent domain to eliminate housing inhabited mainly by black people. St. Clair Drake, black author of *Black Metropolis*, led a resistance to the redevelopment corporation, which ultimately failed when the constitutionality of the corporation act was upheld. "What is the *real* thing the University and the others have against us?" Drake later asked. "Is it our buildings aren't kept up, is it our selection of tenants, is it our behavior, or is it because we are black—period?" [56]

Meanwhile, the South East Chicago Commission also commandeered a federal urban-renewal program. The results were in the same spirit as the commission's other efforts. The black poor were moved out of Hyde Park–Kenwood and onto a tight housing market, driving rents still higher. There was the usual lack of adequate relocation procedures, while the rents of apartments constructed in the area were prohibitive for low-income blacks. But Levi, the commission, and the University of Chicago were supported in their policy by the Hyde Park–Kenwood Community Conference, which included liberal faculty members and middle-class Negroes, and which rallied to the cry: "An interracial community of high standards."

Inspired by the university's success in obtaining favorable legislation from the Illinois legislature, Lawrence Kimpton, University Chancellor, wrote in February 1957 to the Presidents of Harvard, Yale, MIT, Columbia, and the University of Pennsylvania: "I believe that we agree that a healthy university cannot exist in a slum, and I believe that all of us are threatened in this regard. . . . We might obtain some value in exchanging experiences. I rather suspect too that there is some federal legislation that we might ponder with the idea of seeing if we could not get forward on some cooperative program." [57] In April, representatives of these universities met

[56] Quoted in Peter H. Rossi and Robert A. Dentler, *The Politics of Urban Renewal* (Glencoe, Ill., 1961), p. 184. See this book for an account of urban renewal in Hyde Park–Kenwood.

[57] Quoted in Julian H. Levi, "Expanding the University of Chicago," in John B. Rork and Leslie F. Robbins, eds., *Casebook on Campus Planning and Institutional Development* (U.S. Dept. of Health, Education and Welfare, 1962), p. 123. See this article for an account of the development of Section 112.

and decided to refer the question to the American Association of Universities (AAU). To a summer 1958 meeting attended by the urban universities above, plus George Washington University, Brown, Johns Hopkins, Tulane, New York University, a personal representative of David Rockefeller, and representatives of the U.S. Department of Health, Education and Welfare and the Urban Renewal Administration, the AAU recommended a national survey by the Planning Unit of the University of Chicago. In this survey, urban universities most often listed slum conditions and deteriorating housing as their chief neighborhood problem, while two universities listed the influx of "undesirable population" as the main difficulty.

In early 1959, representatives of NYU, Baylor, Penn, the University of Louisville, and the South East Chicago Commission appeared before the Banking and Currency committees of the U.S. Congress to argue for an amendment to the Housing Act of 1959. Under the leadership of two liberal Senators, Joseph Clark (D–Pennsylvania) and Paul Douglas (D–Illinois), the issue was carried by voice vote, and Section 112 was added to the urban-renewal laws.

Before Section 112, the problem of the urban universities was that they had difficulty getting urban-renewal money because their expansion also meant the expansion of tax-exempt property. This erosion of the tax base was against the interests of the city government, which was reluctant to support urban renewal for universities. Section 112 provides that any direct cost to a university of acquiring property in the open market, and any costs incurred in clearing the land and relocating inhabitants, may be credited to the local share of the costs in financing an urban-renewal project not only in a university community but anywhere in the city. Normally, the cities pay one third of the cost of urban renewal and the federal government pays two thirds. If the university has been aggressive in the real-estate market, the localities may be relieved of paying for any share of a project, and thus favorably inclined to urban renewal in a university community.

Section 112 has ushered in the golden age of university expansion. Since universities are also exempt under Section 112 from the requirement that cleared land be put to predominantly (70 percent) residential purposes, universities have been able to pursue their designs for science and technology complexes and utopian middle-class communities without restriction. Within five years of its passage in 1959, 75 universities employed the urban-renewal program to finance university expansion.

While urban-renewal funds have financed land clearance and purchase, other federal programs have subsidized the actual construction of university buildings. By the middle '60s the Community Facilities Administration had already approved over $2 billion in federal loans for such purposes at interest rates below market rates. Federal subsidy was crucial to the construction program of higher educational institutions, estimated to amount to some $15 billion in the past decade, and to approach $4 billion a year in the early 1970s.

As a result of his contribution to the urban expansion of universities at the expense of racial minorities, Julian Levi has achieved considerable renown in the field. He is now a professor of "urban affairs" at the University of Chicago, of which his brother, Edward Levi, is Chancellor. In an interview with *The New York Times*, Julian Levi commented that "our experience is that urban renewal is like lifting a watermelon. It's not hard once you get your arms around it." [58]

Rossi and Dentler observed that Morningside Heights Inc. failed in its earlier efforts at community development because it rationalized its policy in terms only of its own interests: expansion space and personnel housing. No doubt Columbia will in the future adopt the policy of the University of Chicago: the identification of the public interest with its private

[58] Quoted in J. Martin Klotsche, *The Urban University* (New York, 1966), p. 72.

interests. The deterioration of the total environment and the erosion of the economic base will be emphasized. The university will present itself as a public-service institution with a plan to solve these problems, which it probably will for the upper- and middle-class people associated with the institution. In a pamphlet for the University of Chicago, Muriel Beadle (wife of George W. Beadle, who succeeded Lawrence Kimpton as Chancellor) expounded the basic principles of university expansion. The university community, Mrs. Beadle noted, had to "accept the fact that the stated objectives of conservation and renewal could not be obtained unless (1) the community accepted integration; (2) treated integration as a class problem; and (3) discriminated against lower-income families and individuals." [59]

"In our minds," an officer of the West Philadelphia Corporation noted, "the institutions *have* to expand and develop if they are to discharge the public responsibility given to them—often by the very people who are in the path of this expansion." [60] The corollary of the public-interest posture is a good program for community participation, which will serve to neutralize community opposition to the university's march. The linchpin to a community-relations program is an integrated-housing program on a middle-income base, which will co-opt the Negro middle classes while it jackhammers the poor.

IV. THE EDUCATIONAL CONSEQUENCES

The inner-city poor are expected not only to accept the advance of the urban universities, but actively to identify with it. For, as Julian Levi asserts, "The peculiar genius of

[59] Muriel Beadle, *The Hyde Park–Kenwood Urban Renewal Years* (Chicago, 1967), p. 17.
[60] Leo Molinaro, "The Union of the University and Community Resources to Serve Philadelphia," in Dobbins.

American higher education has been its ability, in satisfaction of its own philosophy, to shatter class distinctions." [61] The university, with its cast-iron gates and reinforced security guard, is a symbol of hope. Someday they—blacks, chicanos, Puerto Ricans—or their children may inhabit the new high-rise dormitories and faculty apartments being erected over the ruins of their miserable tenements. In modern society, the university spokesmen point out, education is the royal road to social mobility and higher income. What is good for City University is good for the slum.

The evidence does not particularly support this conclusion. Higher education has not, in the years since the beginning of the civil-rights movement, worked great wonders in accommodating the poor of the racial minorities. In the South most black students continue to attend Negro institutions. The state universities, which are the leading public institutions, now accommodate black students as no more than 2 to 3 percent of their enrollments. The total percentage in higher education is somewhat better, but no more than half the percentage of black people in the general population. Equal educational opportunity for the poor is, moreover, a myth within a myth. There has been no change in the last several decades in the correlation between education and social mobility, education and income, and education and occupational status. [62] The obvious change is only in the general level of educational attainment, which is way up. But various forms of stratification—between private school and public school, between wealthy suburban schools and poor city schools: in short, the unequal distribution of educational resources—has neutralized any effect on educational equality.

There is, of course, some correlation between education and income, even if there has been no recent change in the closeness of the correlation. A college-educated black man can ex-

[61] Levi, "Ground Space for the University," p. 15.
[62] Cf. "Social Stratification and Mass Higher Education," Chapter III in Christopher Jencks and David Riesman, *The Academic Revolution* (New York, 1968).

pect to make more money than a secondary-school-educated black man, although this is only as much as a high-school-educated *white* man earns. So the black poor may regard the university, if they wish, as a hope that is better than no hope. But even for the successful entrants the process of adjustment to a white upper-middle-class culture is excruciating. Successful adjustment is obviously easier for middle-class blacks, with consequences for the character of black-student enrollment.

In the judgment of Jencks and Riesman, this result cannot be laid to the higher educational system alone. They argue that educational inequality is the result not so much of the maldistribution of educational financing as of the cultural corollaries of social stratification. Upper-class and upper-middle-class children grow up in families that offer literary and educational materials and stress the goal of higher education as an expectation. If these children do not successfully complete a higher educational course, they risk declassing themselves. Social inertia favors a college education. Lower-class and working-class children grow up in families where literary materials are less available and where, even if higher education is highly valued for children, it is not necessarily expected for them. If these children enter the higher educational system (or, for that matter, the secondary or elementary systems), they must also adopt the upper-middle-class style and cut themselves off from their origins—a painful experience. Social inertia disfavors college education. Jencks and Riesman conclude that inequality of educational opportunity is a structural result of a social class system, and that it disappears only as social equality—and not only equal-opportunity scholarships and loans—materializes. The effect of educational meritocracy, to the degree that it exists, is to *preserve* a class system for the general population, and to create equal opportunity only for the brightest, most ambitious, and most adjustable members of the lower classes, who must also enter a ferocious competition for the limited openings at the top in a restricted number of chiefly professional and technical fields.

Whether inequality of educational opportunity is mainly a result of social stratification itself or of maldistribution of educational resources, the result is the same: a class-based educational system. In 1966–67, the upper income quarter of the population (family income above $10,000, an average of $16,000) supplied nearly 50 percent of the college student enrollment, and the second quarter (between $6,000 and $10,000, an average of $8,300) another 25 percent or so. The lowest quarter (below $3,000, an average of $2,300) provided only 7 percent of the total enrollment in higher education, and the one above ($3,000 to $6,000, an average of $5,500) 17 percent.[63] The success of "meritocracy" is evident only in the percentages of the brightest fifth of the population which attends college: 91 percent of the brightest quintile of high-school graduates from families in the highest income fifth compared to 69 percent of the brightest quintile among the lowest fifth in family income. The gap is relatively narrow. After the brightest quintile, however, over half of the high-income and upper-middle-income groups, including many of their incompetent members, attend college, while only a quarter of the low-income and lower-middle-income groups, *excluding* over half of their members of bright and above-average talent, go on to higher education.[64] These are gross figures, for high-school graduates only, which ignore differences in *types* of institutions (universities, colleges, junior colleges) and differences in *quality* within the same category. The inequality is worse than it appears.

In his "Bill for the More General Diffusion of Knowledge," establishing the first system of public education in Virginia in 1779, Thomas Jefferson wrote that "experience

[63] Carnegie Commission on Higher Education, *Quality and Equality: New Levels of Responsibility for Higher Education* (New York, 1968), p. 19.
[64] From Project Talent 1960 High School Senior Sample reported in Jencks and Riesman, p. 103.

hath shown, that even under the best forms [of government] those entrusted with power have, in time, and by slow operations, perverted it to tyranny." He prescribed that the "most effectual means of preventing this would be, to illuminate, as far as practicable, the minds of the people at large, and more especially to give them knowledge of those facts, which history exhibeth, that . . . they may be enabled to know ambition under all its shapes and prompt to exert their natural powers to defeat its purposes." [65] This bill was the origin of the concept of education for democracy. Education for democracy required universal education, substantial equality of education, and education in democratic principles. Jefferson's leading premise carries more contemporary relevance than the hopes he had for the implementation of the solution. Although education for democracy has been the traditional rationale for mass education in America, the evidence above does not indicate that *mass* education has meant *democratic* education. But the issue is not hot politics. Only black students and black faculty have raised the larger issue by the demand for admission quotas or "open admissions."

Mass higher education is in the service of another principle: economic growth. While the elite universities serve economic growth as research-and-development centers, mass higher education goes on in numberless state colleges and universities, technical and vocational schools, community colleges, and small-time private colleges. It is put out that these systems of education are designed to provide "equal opportunity." Their main purpose, however, is manpower development. The economists of Brookings, the Committee for Economic Development, and other establishment outlets have rationalized and promoted the earlier intuitions of legislators and corporate executives that improvements in the quality of the work force increase the rate of growth. In practical terms,

[65] Thomas Jefferson, "A Bill for the More General Diffusion of Knowledge," in Gordon C. Lee, ed., *Crusade Against Ignorance: Thomas Jefferson on Education* (New York, 1961), pp. 83–4.

business enterprises which are based on engineering, science, and technology require technically skilled labor forces. Traditional organizations which convert their clerical operations to electronic data-processing require new personnel to operate business machines and computers. Since the growth sectors of an advanced capitalist economy are generally technology-based, trained manpower is the scarce factor of production. "Human capital," the business economists are fond of saying, has replaced the grosser kind in determining the rate of development.

There is a contradiction here between education for democracy and education for economic growth which should not be soon forgotten. The democratic criterion implies education up to the limit of individual talent and to the extent of human demand. Education for economic growth implies education to the limits of the labor market and to the specifications of production. By the latter principle, a failure to produce enough computer programmers and scientific researchers is serious, while a gross overproduction of computer programmers and scientific researchers may be just as serious. The consequence is the need for a national manpower policy. Under state capitalism, it is necessary to organize the labor market as rationally as any other. The shape of the education system must not, especially in an advanced economy, depart radically from the manpower projections for various occupational categories. It is necessary to restrict choice, structure opportunities, and channel manpower. Under the terms of the California Master Plan, for instance, enrollment in the university system and the state-college system, after a period of growth, has been limited, while the community-college system absorbs rising enrollments. The rise of regional coordination, statewide systems, and especially new community-college systems is, in part, a result of the necessity for manpower planning. Community colleges, with their technical emphasis and limited opportunities, are the chief device for meeting these requirements and for siphoning off the popular desire for education and upward social mobility. Higher education is being organized as a high-level track system. The high social priority of mass higher education reflects the intense concern of the corporate state with "human capital."

The professional faculty rarely considers these matters. The requirements of education for democracy are sufficiently met, in the professors' judgment, if the flower of Educational Testing Service makes its way into higher education. As it happens, 90 percent of the upper 5 percent in ability (by the lights of the standardized tests) do enter college. Any suggestion that this limited meritocracy is not educational democracy arouses in the faculty the specter of the Red Guard—the threat to "standards" and "quality." Faculty members have their own priority value: education for culture. But there is also a contradiction between education for economic growth and education for culture. Since the former criterion is a utilitarian conception of knowledge and the latter a conception of knowledge for its own sake, the economic criterion undermines education for culture in the ways that have already been explained.

In this process, however, the professional faculty is the executioner as well as the victim. Education for culture requires a commitment to the transmission, as well as production, of culture. But as professionals, faculty members are driven to avoid undergraduate teaching because their professional standing in a national market depends upon research output. If their stock is up in this market, scholars use their leverage to bid down their teaching responsibilities. Liberal education declines with the neglect of undergraduate teaching; liberal education requires a particularly large investment of teaching hours, and a curriculum with a generalist orientation. But the members of the professional faculty are neither teachers nor generalists. Faculty members often fall back on graduate education as the model for liberal education in order to sever this Gordian knot. Since graduate education, which is the certification of professionals and therefore the preservation of the species, is a priority concern of faculty members, they are inclined to argue that graduate education which instructs in the methodology of inquiry is a fitting model for education. There is something to this argument. But a curriculum of grand surveys and specialized courses set by the current research priorities of the faculty may succeed only in boring students with arcane subjects, teaching specialized techniques prematurely, and opening up large conceptual gaps. On the side of research itself, it is questionable whether what a professionalized faculty produces is culture. Culture implies a dimension of ethical point and aesthetic form which is not only lacking in most scholarly and scientific research but which is considered dangerously unprofessional. Research production or knowledge output might be better descriptions for faculty activity.

As it happens, there is a nice fit between the goals of a professionalized faculty and the corporate state's objectives for nationalized higher education. The *specialized* talents of the professionals and the funding sources' *instrumental* view of education are complementary. While faculty specialization undermines undergraduate teaching and liberal education in the service of basic research and graduate education, the education managers are intent upon fulfilling manpower needs that are only marginally related to liberal education. Technical and vocational objectives rule the general system of higher education, while early specialization begins to undermine liberal education even in the elite universities. Accordingly, the states fund track systems in higher education, while the federal government underwrites science and engineering in the elite universities and starves the liberal-arts colleges. As the void in teaching opens larger, corporations appear to fill it with teaching machines and other educational technologies. In 1969, the various educational interests organized a united front to lobby Congress for appropriations. The corporations marketing educational technology (teaching machines, visual aids, etc.) offered to fund this effort, but several of the educational associations vetoed the proposal on the grounds that it would damage their image.

The highest priority of the scholarly and scientific professionals is productive research. This suits the state and corporate apparatus, which funds science and engineering for their contribution to military technology and economic development and which also funds the social sciences for their applications in social management. The result has been an enormous imbalance in the allocation of resources between the sciences and the humanities. The imbalance is repeated within the disciplines, where the utilitarian and quantitative aspects of learning receive priority over the theoretical and potentially iconoclastic dimensions.[66] Since the federal government has matching and cost-sharing requirements for most of its aid, its support has pervasive effects on the allocation of the university's own resources. The academic departments also misallocate resources by bidding for graduate students and faculty members with large fellowships, salaries, and emoluments and by over-investing in graduate education and research facilities.

The corporate state in the last decades has created whole new categories of learning to serve its needs: area studies, foreign-policy research, and urban affairs among them. The scope and funding for education for its own sake and for intellectual investigation which is not prestructured by the policy goals of state capitalism declines year by year. "Policy studies," particularly in international fields, has tended to supplant an actually impartial—that is, "academic"—investigation of problems in the fields of the social sciences. The primary impetus for these policy-oriented programs was the emergence of the United States as the world's leading power

66 For discussions of the imbalances created by federal aid, see Harold Orlans, *The Effects of Federal Programs on Higher Education* (The Brookings Institution, Washington, D.C., 1962); and U.S. House of Representatives, Committee on Government Operations, *Conflicts Between the Federal Research Programs and the Nation's Goals for Higher Education* (Washington, D.C., 1965).

after World War II. In a 1960 report for the U.S. Department of State, entitled *The University and World Affairs,* a committee of the Ford Foundation observed, "To a greater degree than ever before, world affairs are American affairs and American affairs are those of the world." [67]

In this spirit, universities have instituted "critical language" programs, funded by the National Defense Education Act, in foreign-language fields where there is a scarcity of trained linguists. They have also undertaken cultural-exchange programs in cooperation with the State Department under the Mutual Educational and Cultural Exchange Act, and technical-assistance programs in cooperation with the Agency for International Development under Mutual Security legislation. The efforts of AID in the late '50s and early '60s to subordinate university operatives to its policy objectives eventually precipitated a crisis that John Gardner attempted to cool in another commission report, *AID and the Universities.* The enlistment of social scientists by the military agencies precipitated an international incident in the case of the "Project Camelot" affair in Latin America, where "value-neutral" social science was too grossly counter-revolutionary in intent. Policy research has marched on, however, and in 1966 Congress passed the International Education Act, which provided for general funding for "world affairs" programs. Although it still lacks funding because of war and inflation, this legislation indicates future directions. A number of universities, such as Princeton, Columbia, Tufts, and Johns Hopkins, already have "schools for public and international affairs." These schools are essentially professional schools in the field of policy management. In 1970, students at Southern Illinois University protested the creation of a center for Vietnamese studies and programs, sponsored by AID.

The education managers are not unaware of these conflicts

[67] The Committee on the University and World Affairs, *The University and World Affairs* (New York, 1960), p. 11.

and misallocations; on the contrary, they profess a quasi-religious faith in "balance." Their solutions amount to more of the same. If the social sciences are not getting sufficient funds, then we must create a national social-sciences foundation. If the humanities are starved, then we must create a national humanities foundation. And so on. These are token efforts by comparison with the natural sciences and engineering, but this result may be just as well. A federal effort to correct imbalances between fields only creates imbalances *within* fields. The federal bias is unfailingly instrumental in making practicality, quantification, and orthodoxy the priorities. Even within the space program, scientists have protested the emphasis on engineering to the detriment of scientific discovery, and in 1969 several scientists of the Lunar Receiving Laboratory resigned over the issue.

Confronted with the results of their labor, the instinct of the education managers is to pour oily rhetoric over unsettled waters. They are promiscuously committed to both "quality" and "equality" in education. John Gardner went so far as to write a book on the subject: *Excellence: Can We Be Equal and Excellent Too?* Various elaborate schemes for equal-opportunity grants and loans have been devised. All they lack so far is funding. Such schemes also run up against the Jencks-Riesman objection that "opportunity" schemes merely mitigate social stratification which ultimately is the cause of educational inequality.

Another article of faith among education managers—particularly those who currently serve in the conglomerate universities—is the value of "autonomy." The power of this tradition is such that various schemes—block institutional grants, loan programs, construction aid—are continually devised to protect university autonomy against "federal control." The logic of these plans is to shift federal aid from specific projects with specific purposes to generalized institutional support which will leave the internal allocation of funds in the hands of the university administrations. The universities also do not wish any more federal funds channeled through the states, since this process transfers significant decisions to the state governments which harbor potentialities for political interference. Since the Nixon administration celebrates "creative federalism"—the functional partnership of the federal and state governments—and since the states are quite well informed on their own interests in federal aid to education, autonomy is impossible.

The quest for institutional and professional autonomy within the corporate state is quixotic for at least three reasons. The government bureaucracies which fund the universities and scientific research run on the principle of *accountability*. They are not charitable endowments; accountability is the defining characteristic of the organizational unity of a government agency, not to mention the chief control on an agency by legislative appropriations committees. Funding recipients may be on a relatively long or short leash, but there can be no question of their being independent. Secondly, the managers of state-and-corporate capitalism conceive of their role as *social innovation*. Social innovation requires that central management retain maximum control over the allocation of resources, over new programs, and over the processes of growth, although many other functions may be delegated. Finally, as we have seen, the educational establishment is increasingly run according to the managerial principle of *return on investment*.

For the problems that are accorded official recognition, the education managers have reform plans, if not federal appropriations, and are working hard to anticipate the problems of balance, autonomy, quality, and equal opportunity for the 1970s and for every decade thereafter. If by chance the education managers should be bloodied in the initial intellectual skirmishing on these questions, they will fall back quickly on their fortified redoubt: social imperatives. There is a technological imperative, which accounts for the university's role as a research and development center. There is also an advanced-economy imperative, which also accounts for R&D, as well as the university's expansion and its role in manpower development. There is the bureaucratic imperative which accounts for the transfer of authority to the center. There are also explosions: the population explosion, which in the case of student enrollments accounts for expansion of the plant and centralization of authority, and the knowledge explosion, which accounts for the specialization of the faculty.

The social-imperatives argument is a logical gambit. The procedure is to enumerate certain very large and very obvious *facts*—technologies, bureaucracies, advanced economies, large populations, and expanding stores of data—which do not stand the slightest chance of evaporating. The term "imperative" is then added as if it were also a fact rather than an explanation of facts. If the explanation and the value judgment are rejected, it is claimed that the facts themselves have been denied, and that, as everyone knows, is absurd. The imperatives gambit is a reductionist form of social analysis. Social organization, class structure, economic systems, historical conditions, political choices, social values are somehow mere epiphenomena of the functional realities expressed by the imperatives. These superstructures do not affect the fundamental operations of "industrial society" or "post-industrial society."

These same arguments are applied to the transformation of higher education. The university is supposed to have undertaken research and development as a result of the development of an advanced economy. But research and development have taken a particular form: substantial militarization, which in turn reflects a historical form of American society. The university is supposed to have been delivered into the hands of its bureaucracy because of the growth of student enrollments; but this bureaucratization has taken a particular political *form* in which the administrative apparatus is answerable to governing boards and funding sources, but not to the university community. Such antiseptic and denatured analysis of the university is only a reflection of the dominant styles in social analysis. Of social and cultural analysis in his day, Thorstein Veblen commented that "vulgar sentiment will tolerate a sceptical or non-committal attitude toward vulgar convictions only as regards the decorative furnishings, not as regards the substance of the views arrived at. Some slight play of hazardous phrases about the fringe of the institutional fabric may be tolerated by the popular taste, as an element of spice, and as indicating a generous and unbiased mind; but in such cases the conclusive test of scientific competency and leadership, in the popular apprehension, is a serene and magniloquent return to the orthodox commonplaces, after all such playful excursions." [68] Social-imperatives analysis is just this sort of enterprise. It is a vulgar determinism—at its worst exclusively technological or exclusively economic; at its best a combination of the two cast in the form of a historical narrative with occasional references which indicate a concern for civil liberties. As a determinist analysis, it collapses historical possibilities, forecloses social freedom, and trivializes political choice. As a reductionist analysis, it rationalizes state capitalism. Once this base is secured, it is possible to twit the conventional wisdom and make forays into reform politics.

As matters stand, the university system and higher education in general in the United States formally serve three functions: education for democracy, education for culture, and education for economic growth. All of these are valid purposes. But education for democracy, the criterion which rationalizes the educational system for the general population, is not a functioning reality. At best, there is a limited meritocracy which, in addition, does not extend to the non-white poor. The result is that the democratic rationale now serves chiefly an ideological function. The second criterion—culture—has always been the special property of the professionalized faculty. By becoming professionalized and responding to the cues of the national market for academic labor, by

68 Veblen, pp. 132–3.

allowing research priorities to be set by funding sources, and by enforcing specialization in their disciplines, the faculty has ceased to serve the first principle of high culture: the advancement of knowledge for its own sake. Neither does the faculty conserve and transmit ethical and esthetic values, which constitute the second aspect of its cultural responsibility. Culture is the ghost in the machine.

This leaves the rationale of economic growth, which in its various aspects—research and development, manpower development, expansion of the plant and the payroll—dominates the university. The official idea of the university is a pseudo-aristocratic culture suspended within a growth industry with a democratic public-relations front.

4 THE BLACK RESISTANCE

IN MARCH 1967 students of the Black Power Committee at Howard University demonstrated against General Lewis B. Hershey, Director of the Selective Service System. As he attempted to deliver a speech, they jumped onto the stage, shouting, "America is the black man's battleground!" When the university attempted to hold administrative hearings to discipline students for the incident, the proceedings were disrupted. When it went ahead with disciplinary action against four of the Hershey demonstrators, several thousand undergraduates boycotted classes for a day. Meanwhile, student rallies and faculty forums took up the questions of due process in discipline, authoritarianism in administration, and the possibilities for a "militant black university." Finally, at the end of the spring term and the commencement of the summer break, the Howard administration summarily expelled 16 students and dismissed without customary notice five faculty members closely identified with the faculty forums, student protests, and the Black Power Committee. The reason given for the expulsions and dismissals was that the offenders' "general conduct" was detrimental to the university's "fundamental mission."

The 1967 Howard protest was the first major black student rebellion of the decade directed specifically against a university administration. It inaugurated a series of black student protests against the administrations of both black and white institutions of higher education, protests which gathered increasing momentum in 1968–69 and were generally built around the demand for "black studies" programs. The Howard student movement was not, however, the first black-student rebellion ever. Forty years before, in the 1920s, there were major student "strikes" (class boycotts) at Hampton Institute, Shaw University, Florida A&I, Fisk University, Lincoln University in Missouri, and Howard.

The Hampton case is illustrative. In October 1927 students caused a disturbance at a Saturday-evening movie on campus when the authorities attempted to keep the lights on through the showing to ensure that the mixed audience of men and women maintained proper decorum. On the following Sunday evening, students refused to participate in a tradition of the college—the singing of plantation songs—and at a protest meeting elected a student protest committee to direct a boycott of classes. The committee pressed a list of grievances which included requests for the improvement of educational quality, particularly of faculty personnel, but were directed primarily at the paternalism of the administration. Students took particular offense at the close and humiliating administrative regulation of personal and social life—such as a rule requiring that students bathe twice a week—which was designed to indoctrinate the freedmen in the mores of white bourgeois culture.

Although students campaigned only for the recognition and consideration of their grievances, Principal James D.

Gregg, a white New Englander, refused to consider the matter unless the boycott were ended. When this demand was met, Gregg placed all the striking students on probation; as a result, the boycott was resumed. Nonetheless, Gregg was able to break the boycott. Four members of the Student Protest Committee were expelled; others were suspended, while one member, apparently an informer, escaped punishment entirely. Returning students were required to sign an oath of loyalty to the school: "I hereby promise to do my part to carry on the work of the Institute in loyalty, obedience, and cooperation." [1]

In a letter, George Foster Peabody, a white trustee and philanthropist of Negro education, concluded that the Hampton protest was the work of outside agitators and that "our friend Du Bois is at the bottom of this thing." Peabody was figuratively correct. W. E. B. Du Bois, a founder of the NAACP, a pioneer in sociology, and a radical black intellectual, was a symbol and leader of the "New Negro" movement of the 1920s. The principles of this movement—political assertion and a celebration of negritude—naturally had special influence among students and intellectuals. Its currents provided the political impetus and the educational content for the demands of student rebels at such colleges as Howard, Fisk, and Hampton. At the turn of the century, Du Bois had argued for a "classical education" for blacks—similar to that of white liberal-arts colleges—in his dispute with Booker T. Washington's conception of "industrial education"; but by the late 1920s he favored black education with a special emphasis on Afro-American culture, the problems of black America, and strategies for racial equality. In his 1933 commencement address at Fisk University, "The Field and Function of the American Negro College," Du Bois defended his position against the claim that he implicitly condoned segre-

[1] For an account of the Hampton protest, see Edward K. Graham, "The Hampton Institute Strike of 1927," *The American Scholar*, Fall 1969, pp. 668–83.

gation: "We do not advocate segregation by race, [we] simply accept the bald fact that we are segregated, apart, hammered into a separate unity by spiritual intolerance and legal sanction backed by mob law, and that this separation is growing in strength and fixation; that it is worse today than half a century ago and that no character, address, culture, or desert is going to change it, in our day or for centuries to come." [2]

Du Bois and the other "race radicals" argued that a color caste system was a social fact whose pervasive effects could not simply be wished away in the effort to achieve racial equality, while the goal of racial equality itself did not mean the obliteration of the Negro subculture. Rather than modeling Negro colleges on the leading white institutions as if racial justice, social equality, and cultural uniformity were realities, it was necessary, they asserted, to build Negro education on the real virtues of negritude and the real facts of social oppression. This effort would not be politically quietist but the basis for the development of accurate analyses and practical strategies for social change. The alternatives were the fantasies of educational equality as a possibility apart from social equality, and of the cultural identity of the Afro-American subculture with the dominant Anglo-Saxon culture. These fantasies would result in an objectively inferior educational imitation which was also culturally alien to its students. In *The Mis-Education of the Negro*, Carter Woodson, a pioneer in the historical study of the Negro, noted: " 'Highly educated' Negroes denounce persons who advocate for the Negro a sort of education different in some respect from that now given the white man. Negroes who have been so long inconvenienced and denied opportunity for development are naturally afraid of anything that sounds like discrimination. They are anxious to have everything the white man has even if it is harmful. The possibility of originality in the Negro, therefore, is discounted one hundred percent to maintain a

[2] Cited in Buell G. Gallagher, *American Caste and the Negro College* (New York, 1966), p. 246.

nominal equality." [3]

A number of New Negro intellectuals proposed an alternative to imitative and assimilationist colleges; their model was, in effect, a militant Negro university. Horace Mann Bond, a leading black scholar of Negro education, asserted that the "contemporary liberal arts college for Negroes needs to align itself with social forces and derive its mission from them, if it is to make a notable contribution." [4] Although Dean of the College of Arts and Sciences of Howard University, Kelly Miller supported this conception of the role of the Negro college. Miller argued that Negro colleges could not possibly equal the financial resources of the leading white universities and should therefore not duplicate their programs at a lower level. He advocated the development of a unique role for Negro colleges—on the model of the experiences of other institutions for ethnic groups—which white institutions could by their very nature not equal, much less improve on. This unique role was the development of the special cultural attributes, and a consideration of the special problems, of the race. "But for the Negro college," Miller noted, "Negro scholarship would decay, and Negro leadership would be wanting in effectiveness and zeal. The Negro college must furnish stimulus to hesitant Negro scholarship, garner treasure and nourish group tradition, enlighten both races with a sense of the cultural worth and achievement of the constituency it represents, and supply the cultural guidance of the race." [5]

Even James Weldon Johnson, an executive secretary of the NAACP in the 1920s and an opponent of Du Bois' evolving separatism, supported the concept of a special function for Negro higher education: ". . . the teaching of history to

[3] Carter G. Woodson, *The Mis-Education of The Negro* (Washington, D.C., 1932), pp. xi–xii.

[4] Cited in Gallagher, p. 250.

[5] Kelly Miller, "Howard: The National Negro University," in Alain Locke, ed., *The New Negro* (New York: Atheneum, 1968), p. 321.

Negro youth should not confine itself to the experiences of the race in America, but should explore the achievements that lie in the African background. A study of the African cultural background will give our youth a new and higher sense of racial self-respect, and will disprove entirely the theory of innate race inferiority. . . ." A major literary figure of the Harlem Renaissance, Johnson noted the importance of the social sciences and liberal arts, as well as African history and culture, to the concept of a Negro university: "It is something pretty close to a waste of time for Negro students to study the laws of economics without being given an interpretation of the effects of those laws on the economic and industrial plight of Negro Americans. In teaching the science of government, what is purely academic should be supplemented by inferences drawn from government as it is constituted, maintained, and enforced in the United States and the various states, and from its operation on Negro Americans as a group."

Johnson also addressed himself to the great fear of professional scholars—the possibility of political education shading into political indoctrination, of practical considerations eroding academic freedom. "I do not in the least advocate," Johnson remarked, "that our colleges become any part of political machinery or touched by partisan politics, but I firmly believe that special political education of Negro youth is a proper and necessary function for them. The political history of the race should be reviewed; independent political thinking should be inculcated; political rights and responsibilities should be explained, and preparation for exercising those rights and assuming those responsibilities should be given." [6]

That the programs of race radicals of the 1920s and '30s are among the gut issues of the contemporary black student movement testifies to the failure of these race radicals to achieve their ends. The New Negro movement was mainly a

[6] James Weldon Johnson, *Negro Americans, What Now?* (New York, 1938), pp. 48-9.

cultural renaissance led by artists, scholars, and intellectuals; it was a climate of thought rather than a social movement. It could not mobilize by itself the social forces necessary to effect political ends, particularly those affecting the whole structure of Negro higher education. There were many currents of thought within the movement and no agreement on any particular social program or agenda for educational reform. Although the movement had a constituency in the race-conscious wing of the middle class and the educational communities, it did not have an organizational vehicle or a political strategy with which to assume leadership. The National Association for the Advancement of Colored People was the leading Negro organization of the time, and as the editor of its organ, *The Crisis*, Du Bois was a central figure in the association. But, then as now, the NAACP employed tactics of public relations, legal action, and legislative lobbying, not mass political action. It was, moreover, an interracial organization in which liberal whites were co-equal, if not dominant, partners; it was not likely to assume leadership of a New Negro program for black education. For this and other reasons, Du Bois and other Negro intellectuals broke with the NAACP in the late '20s and early '30s, and moved to the left.

The student rebellions of the 1920s were spontaneous affairs, partaking of the spirit of the times but unable to establish a substantial program or sustain a student movement. The rebellions faded when the stock-market crash and the Great Depression undermined the Harlem Renaissance and the New Negro movement, which had depended upon prosperity and, to a degree, on white sponsorship for support of cultural activities. The crushing destitution of the Depression years broke the force of the first great wave of race consciousness which had followed World War I.

It was the war that generated the Great Migration around 1915, which pulled half a million black people into Northern cities to fill jobs being created by war industries at the same time that agricultural depression in the South encouraged them to leave. Urbanization freed the migrants from the more egregious forms of social oppression practiced in the South, while it generated a new social consciousness in the high-powered life of the industrial cities. At the same time, 400,000 black men were pulled out of the ruts of social habit and racial accommodation, and drafted into the U.S. Army to fight in Europe. The tests of war and the relative liberality of France placed the discriminatory practices of the U.S. Army and the racism of the social order in the United States into clear perspective for black soldiers. Meanwhile, their relatives and friends at home were flooded with propaganda which assured them that the war was being fought to "make the world safe for democracy." Black people drew the conclusions, and expected a postwar campaign for racial justice on the order of the postwar reconstruction half a century earlier. Instead, there was the "Red Summer" of 1919, when 25 cities, including major ports of entry for the Northern migration, such as Chicago and Washington, D.C., were struck by race riots set off by acts of racial aggression by whites.

While these social forces inspired political reaction among whites, they had the opposite effect in black society. Migration and urbanization, war and the draft, democratic propaganda and race riots were powerful solvents for racial accommodation and political quietism, which had prevailed since Reconstruction even under the provocations of disenfranchisement and segregationist reaction. The crucibles of war and urbanization counteracted the customary subservience that had been inculcated in the South by a tenant system amounting to serfdom, by political disenfranchisement, by vigilante terror, and by rural inertia.

Out of the new circumstances emerged a new consciousness. It was a *cause célèbre* when blacks fought the white mobs which invaded the black neighborhoods with murderous intent during the Red Summer. In New York, Marcus Garvey, a West Indian immigrant, founded a black nationalist movement which advocated "Back to Africa" principles and in the postwar decade enlisted 500,000 members among the black lower-class masses. The same circumstances inspired the New Negro movement and the Harlem Renaissance, which arose out of the Negro middle classes. The Garveyist and New Negro movements were antagonistic, however, reflecting the traditionally severe class divisions within black society. The Negro intellectuals considered Garvey a crackpot, while Garvey habitually referred to the NAACP as the "National Association for the Advancement of (Certain) Colored People."

Although Garvey's Universal Negro Improvement Association collapsed after his imprisonment and deportation on the charge of using the mails to defraud, the new militant mood persisted until 1929 and, at a lower level, through the Depression. Continued urbanization fueled this mood in the '20s and into the '30s. The drastic restriction of foreign immigration by the war, and by legislation after the war, maintained a heavy demand for black labor to replace cheap immigrant labor in the "New Era" of prosperity. During the 1920s, another 800,000 black Americans migrated to Northern cities.

In these times, the Negro colleges were not entirely resistant to changes, although they were hardly receptive to the program offered by the race radicals. Fundamentally secondary schools rather than colleges, the Negro institutions began to convert themselves in the 1920s into genuine institutions of higher education. The New Negro movement was also not without its minor successes. Carter Woodson, a founding member in 1905 of the Niagara Movement, which was the predecessor of the NAACP, gained acceptance for a "Negro History Week" within the educational establishment. But the major innovation of the time was the installation of black men in the chief administrative offices and, to a lesser degree, in faculty positions of the colleges. Principal Gregg at Hampton Institute was considered a progressive because he moved the school from high-school to college status and installed

Negroes in teaching posts for advanced courses, which had formerly been handled entirely by whites. In 1926, Howard University got its first Negro president; and Atlanta University was established during the decade with a black president.

I. THE BOURGEOISIE MANQUÉ

The installation of a Negro officialdom counted for a great deal in an educational establishment with a missionary tradition. The sources of the paternalism against which black students have revolted since World War I lie in this tradition. Virtually all of the Negro colleges were founded in Reconstruction by earnest egalitarians from the North. In its brief existence, the U.S. Government's Freedmen's Bureau assisted in the establishment of various colleges in cooperation with Protestant church organizations of the North. The major work of the Bureau was Howard University, named after General O. O. Howard, Director of the Bureau. The church denominations founded Shaw University, Morehouse, Morgan, Claflin, Clark, Lincoln University, and St. Augustine's, among others. The denominations, particularly the Congregationalists, often worked through the American Missionary Association, which, with the Freedmen's Bureau, was probably the most important instrument in the construction of Negro higher education. Among other schools, the Association founded Hampton Institute, Fisk University, and Talladega and Tougaloo colleges. The Negro church denominations also played a role in this development, establishing Wilberforce, Morris Brown, and others. But the Negro denominations did not have the financial resources to compete on a large scale with the white organizations. The key roles were undertaken by the federal government through its Freedmen's Bureau and by the northern missionaries, often through the emblematic American Missionary Association.

Whatever their good intentions, these private colleges

could hardly escape paternalism. Their administrative staffs and faculties were white, while their students were black and victims of a slave system (although some students were from the free Negro community). Most of these educators were, no doubt, committed to the idea of racial equality, but their conception of their educational mission involved imitation of the liberal-arts models of the North, with corollary assumptions of Anglo-Saxon culture. Education based on cultural assimilation did not promise to liberate the freedmen from the dominant assumptions of black inferiority. Its effect was to reinforce these assumptions in the deeper reaches of black consciousness, while erasing their superficial manifestations in manners and morals. This result was doubly assured by the fact of white authorities dispensing the educational and cultural blessings to untutored black students. A permanent arrangement of this kind was likely to perpetuate a psychological bondage that would inhibit the formation of political forces within black society which could cope with continuing social oppression. Yet these paternalist arrangements endured in Negro higher education past World War I, and in many institutions past World War II.

If anything, the first generation of white educators was the least overbearing, since it was moved to act by profound commitments to racial equality. The second generation was more likely to accept its dominance as routine. The alternatives to missionary education were no better. Public institutions of higher education for Negroes were generally founded in the South through federal subsidy provided by 1890 amendments to the Morrill Act of 1862. Since these institutions were responsible to the white Southern boards of education, they established new standards of condescension and authoritarianism which not even the privately controlled colleges could match. The state boards normally relied on the Negro president as their agent, and invested him with plenary power, the better to maintain close control. The colleges established by Negro church organizations were interlocked with the authoritarian church hierarchies and infused with top-down traditions. They represented a gain in cultural autonomy, but were no less authoritarian.

While most of the new colleges were modeled on the classical education of the North, Hampton Institute represented an important departure from the norm. Although it was founded in 1867 by the American Missionary Association and the Freedmen's Bureau, Hampton's educational program was given a unique character by its principal, General Samuel Chapman Armstrong. While most of the educators in the other Negro schools were New Englanders who modeled their institutions on New England colleges, Armstrong had observed the educational work of the Labor School for the Hawaiian Islanders. From this experience, his inclinations were no less missionary than those of his cohorts elsewhere, but he gave his program a more practical, occupational, and character-building bent.

One of Armstrong's students was Booker T. Washington, who went on to found Tuskegee Institute. Washington's influence was not only decisive for Negro higher education, but also emblematic of the entire development of the Negro middle class in the United States. The modern black student movement cannot be understood without reference to the Negro middle class, its educational system, and Washington's influence upon them both. Washington's rise to power corresponded with a new era in American history and a new development in Negro higher education. Within the political economy of the United States, the post-Civil War era was characterized by a revolutionary expansion of industrial capitalism which gathered increasing momentum as the nation moved into the twentieth century. During the same time, Washington propagated the concept of "industrial education" as President of Tuskegee and the leading Negro educator in the country. There was obviously a nice fit between Washington's educational theories and the fundamental social developments of the period. The two were happily united by the active philanthropic support of Negro higher education by leading capitalist entrepreneurs.

The first philanthropic effort along this line was the Peabody Fund, established in 1867 through the gift of a wealthy banker, George Peabody (not to be confused with George Foster Peabody). In 1871, at a time when Negro and white teachers received equal salaries, the administrators of this fund allocated only two thirds as much for this purpose to black schools as to white schools of the same size, on the grounds that "it costs less to maintain schools for the colored than for the white children." Two years later, the trustees of the fund again distinguished themselves by opposing the Civil Rights Bill of 1873, arguing that equal educational facilities would naturally result from segregated education in the South. (In 1880, however, the Peabody Fund supported federal appropriations for Negro education.) In 1882, John F. Slater, a Connecticut textile industrialist, established the John F. Slater Fund with a gift of $1 million, the same amount as that which established the Peabody Fund. The general agent of both these funds was Jabez L. M. Curry, a former Alabama legislator and white Confederate veteran and a close associate and friend of Booker T. Washington, who by this time had founded Tuskegee Normal School. Curry's policy was to give special support to industrial education.

In 1903, John D. Rockefeller of the oil trust founded the General Education Board as the instrument for his philanthropic contributions to Negro education. Before this time, the Rockefeller family had already contributed substantial sums to the support of Morehouse College and Spelman Seminary (then, as now, favored objects of their philanthropy), often through the American Baptist Home Mission Association. In 1905, Anna T. Jeanes, heiress to the fortune of a Philadelphia merchant, contributed $200,000 to the General Education Board at the solicitation of George Foster Peabody, a board member. Miss Jeanes specified that the

Principal of the Hampton Institute and Booker T. Washington, Principal of the Tuskegee Institute, be consulted in the disposition of the funds to rural schools. After a visit to Tuskegee in 1911, Julius Rosenwald, a founder of Sears, Roebuck, was induced to contribute a substantial sum to the Institute; he also set up the Julius Rosenwald Fund, which distributed funds both to higher education and to elementary and secondary education in the rural South, where educational facilities for the black population were generally lacking.[7]

The sums expended by these philanthropic foundations were fundamental to the development of Negro higher education. By the late 1920s, the Rockefeller-sponsored General Education Board had expended over $29 million on Negro higher education. The significance of these sums is best understood in the light of the fact that in 1925 the 79 Negro colleges had a combined annual income of only $9 million plus. Their total combined endowment amounted to $20 million plus, of which two institutions, Hampton and Tuskegee, represented two thirds. This distribution indicates that the work of the philanthropies was not purely altruistic. "There can be little doubt," the historian John Hope Franklin writes, "that the interests of the Northern business men in the South were correlated with their efforts to improve Southern citizenry, both black and white." [8] The largest investments were in railroads, textiles, and steel. Their support of industrial education—essentially a form of vocational education—was related to the expectation that improvements in the black Southern labor force would have an industrial payoff.

Direct interests, however, cannot explain in full the sup-

[7] For an account of the philanthropic support of Negro higher education, see Horace Mann Bond, *The Education of the Negro in the American Social Order* (New York, 1966), pp. 127–51. See also Dwight O. W. Holmes, *The Evolution of the Negro College* (New York, 1934).

[8] John Hope Franklin, *From Slavery to Freedom* (New York, 1967), p. 386.

port of Booker T. Washington and his educational doctrines by Northern capitalists, especially since their expectations for improvements in the industrial labor force, which remained overwhelmingly white, were not necessarily realized by the support of Negro education. They were motivated primarily by the cultural and ideological corollaries of their economic interests. Booker T. Washington was a philosopher of "self-help" by which he meant the earnest pursuit of "education, industry, and property" without the undue agitation of social questions. "I believe it is the duty of the Negro—as the greater part of the race is already doing," Washington wrote, "to comport himself modestly in regard to political claims, depending upon the slow, but sure influences that proceed from the possession of property, intelligence, and high character for the full recognition of his political rights." [9] Washington opposed the imposition of education and property tests to restrict the voting franchise only if they discriminated against blacks over against poor whites. Otherwise, he believed the "peculiar conditions" of the South justified disenfranchisement, which was proceeding apace at the time, as long as it was undertaken as a form of class, rather than racial, oppression. In an era of labor violence, Northern industrialists approved of these sober attitudes, based on the character-building virtues of property and hard work.

At the turn of the century, W. E. B. DuBois and other race radicals attacked Washington's "gospel of Work and Money" as a disastrous social strategy in a period in which Southern reactionaries were rolling back the civil and political rights of the black race to pre-Reconstruction standards. They also pointed out that, without the political power afforded by an organized voting bloc, the economic, educational, and social objectives Washington favored would never come to pass. While Washington's concept of industrial education and the concept of liberal-arts education favored by

[9] Booker T. Washington, *Up from Slavery* (New York: Bantam, 1969), p. 166.

the race radicals were not incompatible, and both were necessary for the political and economic development of black men, the race radicals justly complained that the "Tuskegee Machine" channeled available funds from white sources into its own projects. "The tendency is here," Du Bois observed, "born of slavery and quickened to renewed life by the crazy imperialism of the day, to regard human beings as among the material resources of a land to be trained with an eye single to future dividends." [10]

But, as Kelly Miller remarked in comparing Tuskegee's founder to the black abolitionist Frederick Douglass, the spirit of the time favored Washington: "The two men are in part products of their times, but also natural antipodes. Douglass lived in the day of the moral giants; Washington lives in the era of merchant princes. The contemporaries of Douglass emphasized the rights of man; those of Washington, his productive capacity. The age of Douglass acknowledged the sanction of the Golden Rule; that of Washington worships the Rule of Gold." [11] The same spirit dominated developments in the realm of public higher education. Although some Negro colleges had already received federal land-grant funds after the Civil War, publicly supported institutions for Negro higher education were established on a large scale for the first time under the provisions of an amendment to the Morrill Act in 1890. Since land-grant colleges were established for the purpose of encouraging agricultural and industrial training, public higher education went the same route as private education.

If the thrust of Negro higher education had achieved its objective in this period, the result might have been a black industrial working class. This development might well have had unintended political consequences. The irony is that, for all the talk of industrial education and all the funds expended

[10] W. E. B. Du Bois, *The Souls of Black Folk* (New York: Signet, 1969), p. 126.
[11] Cited in E. Franklin Frazier, *The Negro in the United States* (New York, 1957), p. 545.

on such projects, the result was not industrial education, but teacher education. At best, graduates of these programs became teachers of industrial education, or teachers of business, or teachers of education—not workers or managers. There arose a Negro middle class, based in an educational system, which imagined itself entrepreneurial. This professional class embraced, to an unusual degree, the doctrines of classic bourgeois ideology. Washington himself was confused in his objectives. He advocated practical education, but extolled the virtues of rural existence when occupational opportunities were developing in urban centers. He taught his students crafts and artisanal skills which were irrelevant to the occupational requirements of capitalist enterprise developing in the South. While Washington advertised the benefits of industrial education, black men were excluded from jobs in the textile mills. Even if the black masses had gained a position in industrial labor, it is not clear that Washington would have favored a black labor movement. In his "Atlanta Compromise" address, delivered at the Atlanta Exposition of 1895, Washington told a commercial audience: "Cast down your bucket among these people who have, without strikes and labor wars, tilled your fields, cleared your forests, builded your railroads and cities . . . ," etc.[12]

It is not difficult, then, to understand why, whatever Washington may have lacked as an economic analyst, Northern entrepreneurs should have admired him as a moral philosopher. Andrew Carnegie, founder of U.S. Steel, was a close associate of Washington's, and contributed $750,000 to Tuskegee and almost a million to Hampton through the Carnegie Corporation. Carnegie was a cracker-barrel philosopher in his own right, and perhaps the leading exponent of the "Gospel of Wealth," a dominant doctrine of the day. "Thus is the problem of the Rich and the Poor to be solved," Carnegie concluded in a famous essay on the subject. "The laws of accumulation will be left free; the laws of distribution free.

[12] Washington, p. 155.

Individualism will continue, but the millionaire will be but a trustee for the poor; intrusted for a season with a great part of the increased wealth of the community, but administering it for the community far better than it could or would have done for itself." [13]

Collis P. Huntington, a leading railroad magnate, contributed substantially to Tuskegee, and was rewarded with "Collis P. Huntington Hall." John D. Rockefeller, creator of the Standard Oil monopoly, gave generously, and received "Rockefeller Hall." "The more I come into contact with rich people," Washington wrote, "the more I believe that they are growing in the direction of looking upon their money simply as an instrument which God has placed in their hand for doing good with. I never go into the office of Mr. John D. Rockefeller, who more than once has been generous to Tuskegee, without being reminded of this." [14] These connections supplemented and overlapped the fulcrum position of Washington and Tuskegee/Hampton in the distribution of the funds of the major philanthropic foundations for Negro education—the General Education Board, the Rosenwald Fund, the John F. Slater Fund. "My experience in getting money for Tuskegee," Washington concluded, "has taught me to have no patience with those people who are always condemning the rich because they are rich, and because they do not give more to the objects of charity. In the first place, those who are guilty of such sweeping criticisms do not know how much suffering would result, if wealthy people were to part all at once with any large proportion of their wealth in a way to disorganize and cripple great business enterprises." [15]

Washington's acceptance of social inequality as a necessity for economic development was the authentic echo—if an echo can be authentic—of the capitalist ideology of the period. Given these social opinions, it is not surprising that he

[13] Andrew Carnegie, "Wealth," in Gail Kennedy, ed., *Democracy and the Gospel of Wealth* (Boston, 1949), p. 8.
[14] Washington, p. 210.
[15] Washington, p. 128.

should hit upon the idea of autonomous capitalist development as the solution to the economic impoverishment of the black population. To this end, Washington was instrumental in founding the National Negro Business League in 1900, which brought together some 100 Negro merchants, proprietors, and professional men to formulate a strategy for business development. Most of the convention's work was merely hortatory, however, and developed the theme of Washington's opening address; "Fortunately, human selfishness, the desire of every man to get all he can with the least effort or money, has banished all prejudice." [16] A successful taxpayer, Washington argued, would be respected by the white race.

Washington was elected president of the Business League at its founding convention, and regularly re-elected for the remainder of his life. The business ideology caught on in black society, and by 1905 there were 300 chapters of the League. In 1907 Washington published *The Negro in Business*, which compiled Horatio Alger—or, rather, Booker T. Washington—stories of poor black boys who through intelligence, high character, and capital accumulation had made good and earned the respect of white society. In his memorable address to the League in 1910, Washington delivered a "Business Sermon," taken from the Biblical text "To him that hath shall be given." He admonished his commercial congregation to go forth "determined that each individual shall be a missionary in his community—a missionary in teaching the masses to get property, to be more thrifty, more economical, and resolve to establish an industrial enterprise wherever a possibility presents itself." [17]

Responding to the missionary call, the National Negro Business League spent several decades distributing these opiates and waiting for an opportunity to present itself, before it got around to coping with the lack of capital, technical exper-

[16] Cited in E. Franklin Frazier, *Black Bourgeoisie* (New York, 1957), p. 156.
[17] Frazier, pp. 158–9.

tise, and distribution systems which obstructed the development of Negro business. In 1928 it established the Colored Merchants Association, which was to wholesale products for its member retail grocery stores. After a few years, however, CMA failed.

The Business League was supported primarily by Negro professionals, rather than businessmen, of whom there were few in the black community. In this respect, it was entirely typical of the tradition of Negro capitalism which has served as an integrating myth of the Negro bourgeoisie, then and now primarily a professional class. Two years before the founding of the League, "intelligent self-help" was endorsed by the Fourth Atlanta University Conference, devoted to "The Negro in Business." Self-help was even embraced for a time by Du Bois, who edited the proceedings of the Atlanta Conference. After the failure of the Colored Merchants Association, the torch was carried into the Depression years by a "Don't Buy Where You Can't Work Campaign," widely supported in major cities by black political groups and professional associations. The boycott campaign was justified not only as a means to force changes in discriminatory employment practices, but as a means of building black business through racial solidarity. The unstated premise was that black wage-earners, already an exploited consumer group, would bear the costs of higher prices and lower wages which support of business development involved.

In its most recent incarnation, the myth of Negro business is known as "black capitalism," a slogan used by Richard M. Nixon during the 1968 Presidential campaign. The new wrinkle in black capitalism is the possibility of federal subsidy, which has already been provided in small amounts through programs of the Small Business Administration and the Economic Development Administration of the U.S. Department of Commerce. Black capitalism sometimes shades into experiments in co-operative economic enterprise. During a utopian socialist phase, Du Bois advocated producers' cooperation in the early years of the century; more recently "community-development corporations," based on co-op principles, have developed the prospect of subsidy from Congress, which understands them as experiments in capitalist self-help. In their own variety of black nationalism, business economists sometimes compare the black population of the United States to an "underdeveloped country" requiring American subsidy to organize an entrepreneurial class that can develop its nation. Extending the analogy, black capitalism has small prospects of surviving the competition of U.S. corporations, except in the area of marginal business.[18]

The essential class formation of the Negro middle class has endured up to the present time. It is a professional class, based in the education system, the church, and the traditional professions, which has been expanding into the government bureaucracy and, to a much lesser degree, the corporate bureaucracies. The upper reaches of the class, which are comparable to the upper middle class in white society, function as an "upper class." The lower reaches of the class are white-collar workers and, in some instances, skilled blue-collar workers, who are comparable to the lower middle class in white society, but attempt to appropriate full middle-class status. The self-image of the various levels of the Negro middle class reflects its real position in relation to the black population alone, but is seriously skewed in relation to American social structure in general, where each status group in black society ranks significantly lower. This is the social paradox imposed by a color caste system. The paradox is accentuated by the efforts of the various levels of the Negro middle class to appropriate the cultural style and standard of living of social classes in white society whose economic means they cannot match. This enterprise accounts for the conspicuous consumption and social pretensions of the Negro middle

[18] For discussions of business and the Negro middle class, see Frazier, "Negro Business: A Social Myth," Chapter 16 in *Black Bourgeoisie*, and St. Clair Drake and Horace Cayton, "Negro Business: Myth and Fact," Chapter 7 in *Black Metropolis*, vol. II (New York, 1962).

class, which have been described by various social commentators. This pathology is reflected in the efforts of the upper regions of the class to establish a "society" world with debutante balls, Greek-letter fraternities, and exclusive men's clubs.

The effect of a caste system is to establish a double class system for its black population and thus to generate eternal confusion about social roles. The effort to penetrate the veil has led the Negro middle class to become what Gunnar Myrdal called "exaggerated Americans." The corollary of these social aspirations has been a commitment to cultural assimilation. This commitment is not a *direct* desire to integrate and to miscegenate. "Upper-class Negroes," Drake and Cayton comment, "are not, as some superficial observers imagine, pining to be white, or to associate with whites socially. They are almost completely absorbed in the social ritual and in the struggle to 'get ahead.'" [19] Nonetheless, this "almost complete absorption" in social ritual and getting ahead represents a formidable internalization of the culture and values of the dominant social order—culture and values which have not been designed for the benefit of the non-white or the poor. Since it has both direct economic interests in segregation and continuing racial resentments because of white oppression, the Negro middle class tends less to favor large-scale integration than a parallel and equal bourgeois social order. And since the United States is a business "civilization," this aspiration involves a commitment to black capitalism even though the middle class has few roots in business beyond marginal retail enterprise, insurance companies, some successful publishing ventures, and the rackets. This phenomenon led Frazier to refer to the "black bourgeoisie." The Negro middle class is, more precisely, a bourgeoisie manqué that sets standards for an oppressed minority within American society. "Bronzeville from top to bottom," Drake and Cayton remark, "sees its salvation bound up with the devel-

[19] Drake and Cayton, I, p. 557.

opment of Bigger and Better Negro Business." [20]

The linchpin to this class is the educational system because, as a professional class, the Negro middle class requires educational credentials. The system of Negro higher education, like the church, is a stronghold of the black bourgeoisie. Northern migration and urbanization have resulted in an increasing assumption of the instruction of black students by the white system of higher education, but the Negro colleges continue to educate 50 percent of black college students. In its centennial celebration in 1967, Howard University, one of the few Negro institutions with graduate and professional programs, could claim to have graduated one half of the Negro professionals in the United States.

This system has continued to reflect its historical origins. Although the missionaries themselves have increasingly left the scene, the Negroes who have replaced them have carried on the missionary tradition of authoritarianism and cultural paternalism. In the private missionary institutions, authority was concentrated in the white officials—trustees, president, and deans—who ran these institutions, while the faculties, whether white or black, were invested with little authority or independence. Since the rise of a Negro officialdom (excluding the trustees, who are the ultimate authority), these arrangements have not changed. Normally, the deans control appointments and promotions personally or through department "heads" whom they appoint. It is rare for the faculty in a Negro college to have significant independent power in appointments. "When Negro administrators succeeded the white heads," Frazier writes, "they carried on the tradition of paternalism. In the state schools and those conducted by the Negro church organizations, this paternalism has often assumed the character of an autocracy. As a consequence, the administration of nearly all Negro institutions of higher education is not only autocratic but the administration has become the most important element in the organization of

[20] Drake and Cayton, I, p. 726.

these schools." [21] As Frazier points out, the administrations have also maintained control of educational policy. For their part, the faculties have often defined their own success in administrative terms—as a rise in the college bureaucracy—rather than as accomplishment in teaching or scholarship, the values that normally sustain faculties as independent entities. In a society in which the educational establishment is one of the few channels of upward social mobility for Negroes, competition for high position and tenacity in retaining position once gained are fierce. It is not uncommon for deans and presidents to hold court for 25 years or more. As Frazier also points out, these conditions are accentuated in the public institutions, responsible to Southern boards of education which are the custodians of the local racist order, and in the Negro church colleges, which reflect the hierarchical traditions of the denominations.

The transfer of power from white to Negro authorities, limited though its implications are, is itself incomplete. While virtually all Negro colleges now have Negro presidents, the boards of governance of almost all of them, including the best, continued to be white-controlled. Two thirds of the trustees of Morehouse College are white. According to a study by the Southern Fellowships Fund, almost 60 percent of the trustees of the 50 *private* Negro colleges are white.[22] If the colleges controlled by black church denominations were not included in this survey, the percentage would be even higher. The financial sources are also necessarily white, a condition that establishes parameters to the evolution of these institutions. The public institutions, of course, continue to be controlled by white boards of education and Southern state legislatures. The result is a transition from a system analogous to colonial control to modern arrangements that are more nearly neo-colonial—defined by the principle of "indirect

21 Frazier, *The Negro in the United States*, p. 478.
22 Samuel Nabrit and Julius Scott, *An Inventory of Academic Leadership* (Southern Fellowships Fund, 1970).

rule." "The autocratic power wielded by the president," Frazier comments, "is generally derived from the fact that the president is appointed by whites or represents the choice of the white community. The wishes of the faculty in even purely educational matters are generally subject to the arbitrary rule of the president." [23]

This system has decisive consequences for the development of the Negro middle class. Although lawyers, doctors, and churchmen are relatively independent, other elements of this class—educators, government bureaucrats, and corporate employees—are intermediaries in a system of indirect rule. When the entire class is, moreover, educated in white institutions or schools indirectly controlled by whites, the mentality of a comprador class is a result. The question, as Carter Woodson remarked, is "whether these 'educated' persons are actually equipped to face the ordeal before them or unconsciously contribute to their own undoing by perpetuating the regime of the oppressor." [24]

Acquiescence in a system of indirect rule is facilitated by the authoritarian structure of the colleges. As Jencks and Riesman observe of Negro colleges of the 1950s, "The authoritarian atmosphere of the typical Negro college, with its intervening trustees, its domineering but frightened president, its faculty tyrannized by the president and in turn tyrannizing the students, and the tendency of the persecuted at all levels to identify with their persecutors (and in due course to take their place), all harked back to an earlier period of white academic history." [25] An educational system in which there is a "tendency of the persecuted at all levels to identify with their persecutors" obviously resists social change. As "these colleges have for several generations been the major agency for selecting and socializing the prospective members of the black bourgeoisie," the social result will be

[23] Frazier, *The Negro in the United States,* pp. 478–9.
[24] Woodson, p. xi.
[25] Christopher Jencks and David Riesman, *The Academic Revolution* (New York, 1968), p. 425.

political quietism if not active collaboration in the maintenance of the *status quo*. In 1934, Horace Mann Bond observed: "It is an interesting fact that Negro college graduates and students are probably the most conservative representatives of their type in America, where economic, political, and religious issues are concerned." [26] Jencks and Riesman find no reason to alter this conclusion in 1968: "Those who have joined the Negro middle class have been extremely conservative on all issues other than racial equality, and sometimes even on that."

The curriculum and program of Negro colleges reinforce these effects, since they are designed to reproduce the curricula and standards of white universities. Justified on the grounds of racial equality, these educational programs also hold their students in continuing awe of Anglo-Saxon culture. "The same educational process," Carter Woodson noted, "which inspires and stimulates the oppressor with the thought that he is everything worthwhile, depresses and crushes at the same time the spark of genius in the Negro by making him feel that his race does not amount to much and never will measure up to the standards of other peoples. The Negro thus educated is a hopeless liability to the race." [27] Although there are standards of quality and criteria of intellectual merit which are independent of culture and cannot be waived, any curriculum has an implicit cultural emphasis. In their pursuit of "excellence," the Negro colleges either make little concession to this dimension, or stress the traditional curricular priorities of the Negro middle class: business and teacher education. The cultural character of the curriculum is meanwhile paralleled by cultural paternalism in the administrative regulation of dress, social life, and personal conduct. "So instead of trying to promote a distinctive set of habits and values in their students," Jencks and Riesman conclude, "the Negro colleges became purveyors of super-American,

26 Bond, p. 148.
27 Woodson, p. xiii.

ultra-bourgeois prejudices and aspirations. Far from fighting to preserve a separate subculture, as other ethnic groups did, the Negro colleges were militantly opposed to almost everything that made Negroes different from whites, on the grounds that it was 'lower class.' " [28]

II. THE BLACK STUDENT MOVEMENT

The contemporary black student left is opposed to the system of the black bourgeoisie. The logic of the situation has favored the evolution of the student movement, the renegade left wing of the middle class, toward a total opposition to the nexus of social relationships which Negro higher education represents. The immediate issues on the campus level—cultural paternalism, administrative authoritarianism, and imitative curricula—naturally call into question their larger rationales and political sanctions: cultural imitation, political accommodation, and indenture to white authorities. Behind these stands the symbiotic relationship of Negro higher education and the Negro middle class, which embraces a business ideology and functions as a bourgeoisie manqué. And behind everything looms the question of how to deal with white society, which also happens to be a capitalist democracy and the world's leading military and economic power. Any reform issue, however minor, may trigger reactions which bring larger relationships into play. Even opposition to a women's curfew may call into question the cultural paternalism of the college administration, which in turn raises the issues of administrative power and the ideology of cultural assimilation (or, more properly, cultural imitation). Much more surely, a demand for black studies detonates a series of issues concerning administrative power, cultural commitments, social ideology, and relationship to white authorities. The catalytic effect of reform issues favored a radical evolution of the black stu-

[28] Jencks and Riesman, pp. 424–5.

dent movement in the late 1960s.

But a purely local analysis of this movement will not do. The structure of Negro higher education helps to explain the evolution of the student movement from liberal to radical premises, but it cannot explain why the movement should have emerged in the 1960s when the educational conditions had been basically similar in the 1950s. For the origins of the student movement, it is necessary to examine the larger black social movement of which the student movement is a tributary.

The civil-rights movement—and, accordingly, the student movement—shares a common genealogy with the New Negro movement. World War I and the Great Migration were the watershed for the new race consciousness among black men in this century. World War II continued and intensified the social forces set in motion by those events. Foremost of these forces has been urbanization. The wave of migration from the rural South to the urban North, which was set in motion by agricultural depression and the demand for labor in the war industries, fell off somewhat in the depressed industrial economy of the 1930s, only to be reactivated by World War II. The gross national product quadrupled during the war, and black migration during the 1940s came to almost 1.6 million, double the previous high of the 1920s. The push of agricultural mechanization in the South, subsidized by the agricultural policies of the federal government which have pauperized the black farmer, and the pull of postwar prosperity, based to a considerable degree on Cold War military budgets and limited wars in Korea and Vietnam, have sustained the migration of a million or more blacks out of the South in each of the postwar decades. The result is that the black population is now 70 percent urban, compared to 27 percent in 1910; 45 percent in the North, compared to 9 percent sixty years ago; and within the South itself, 41 percent urban, compared to the 1910 figure of 7 percent. This urbanization has tended to improve the economic position of the Negro because of greater employment opportunities and a less rigorous system of racial discrimination in the North. Before World War II, Negro income ranged from 35 to 40 percent of white income, while it reached 55 percent in the postwar period before leveling off in the 1950s.

The re-emergence of a militant social movement was widely expected after World War II because of the apparent re-creation and intensification of post-World War I circumstances. Higher incomes, improved employment, the greater vitality of urban life—but combined with continuing social oppression—were conditions that favored this possibility. There was a large number of returning black veterans who, once again, had experienced discrimination and segregation in the army after being lifted out of routine existence into dangerous circumstances under a barrage of patriotic propaganda. There was also the possibility of racial violence over jobs and housing with the onset of a postwar recession and the elimination of wartime social restraints. But although there were major riots in Harlem and Detroit in 1943, there was no major postwar recession and no postwar riots. And although the Congress of Racial Equality did experiment with "Freedom Rides" in 1947, there was also no immediate postwar black movement.

What was immediately lacking was a political trigger comparable to the "Red Summer" of 1919. Otherwise, conditions were favorable. The afterglow of New Deal reformism and a domestic attitude encouraged by war against racist Nazi Germany counteracted, to a degree, the political climate created by post-war anti-communism and later McCarthyist reaction. Most importantly, the United States had arrived as the dominant power in the world just as nationalist movements in the Third World were gaining momentum. The federal government was now forced to consider the international climate in its treatment of the race problem, while American blacks were influenced by racial self-assertion in other parts of the world, especially Africa. When political catalysts did arrive in the form of the Supreme Court school desegregation decision of 1954 and the Montgomery bus boycott of 1955–56, conditions within the black population and within the country generally were favorable to the new militancy. Although based in the South, this civil-rights movement had the backing of a black vote enfranchised by virtue of migration to the North, and it had financial support from Northern white and black sources. It also was supported by a new urban black population in the South and, most importantly, by a new urban middle class.

Central to the civil-rights movement was its support by the liberal wing of the new Negro middle class, both North and South. This group had significantly grown as a result of the improvements in Negro income, which had both increased the demand for professional services and provided the means for upward social mobility. Its support also helps to account for the early Southern focus of the civil-rights movement. Since it already maintained a high standard of living, the middle class had a primary interest in removing legal and customary barriers to racial equality, which were also barriers to its expansion as a class. As the main redoubt of a caste system, the South was the natural focus for such a campaign. The South also had an articulated Negro middle class with a strong institutional base in the segregated churches and educational system, while most black college students attended southern Negro colleges. The civil-rights movement was a triumph for the liberal and independent sectors of this class. The bolder elements of the Negro churches, which were substantially independent of white control, were a pivotal force. The Reverend Martin Luther King rose to prominence as a result of the Montgomery boycott, and formed the Southern Christian Leadership Conference (SCLC), a ministerial group, in 1957. Middle-class political organizations, such as CORE and the NAACP, played significant roles in the Freedom Rides, marches, and, in the case of the NAACP, in voter registration and legal support.

It was natural for black students—as the Negro middle class in embryo, a politically sensitive sector of the black population, and a rapidly expanding sector at that—to join this movement, and eventually to form its shock troops. In 1960, four students at North Carolina A&T College took seats at a segregated lunch counter and refused to leave, thus originating the sit-in tactic. Soon after, students from Morehouse, Fisk, and South Carolina State had launched sit-in campaigns in Atlanta, Nashville, and Orangeburg. Within a year 50,000 people, many of them students, had participated in demonstrations, often sit-ins, in 100 cities, resulting in 3,600 arrests. In April 1960 200 student veterans of the sit-ins assembled at Shaw University in Raleigh, North Carolina, at a meeting sponsored by SCLC. In an effort to co-ordinate the spontaneous student sit-in movement, the delegates formed the Student Nonviolent Coordinating Committee, the main organized instrument of the black student movement in its civil-rights phase.

The civil-rights movement activated an associated student movement, but the efforts of students to organize and carry out political campaigns inevitably embroiled them with college administrations. The question of the proper stance and strategy toward the white social order was designed to precipitate, faster than any other issue, fundamental conflict between bourgeois administrations and an incipient student left. Direct action against white authorities also quickly exposed the sensitive question of the indenture of Negro college administrations to white financial sources and political authorities. The administrations of state-supported colleges, directly responsible to Southern legislatures and boards of education, were the most nimble. As the result of sit-ins, 18 student activists at Southern University were suspended, while at Albany State College 40 demonstrators were expelled. The administrations of Alabama State and Florida A&M retaliated in like manner. The private Negro colleges pursued policies that were sometimes more subtle but not necessarily different in kind. Some of the presidents of the Atlanta University system actually supported sit-in actions in public statements, but counseled moderation in private. Spelman College, however, dismissed faculty activists and threatened to retaliate against student militants. In South Carolina, Benedict and Allen, both privately supported colleges, dismissed faculty members and issued warnings to students.[29]

If direct-action politics could precipitate such conflict over civil rights, which the college administrations verbally endorsed, the emergence of black nationalist politics was obviously not calculated to assuage strife. In this area, the student movement again followed the lead of the larger black movement. In 1963, the civil-rights movement crested with the march on Washington, which led the Kennedy administration to submit a civil-rights bill to the Congress. After the assassination of President Kennedy, Lyndon Johnson was able to implement a consensus that resulted in the passage of the Civil Rights Acts of 1964 and 1965. In the period when the civil-rights movement had reached a *cul de sac* as a result of political successes, the black masses announced themselves through a series of urban riots in 1964–68. This series of riots —really "spontaneous rebellions," in Herbert Gans's phrase —began ominously with disturbances in Harlem, Philadelphia, and Rochester in 1964 and then hit with unmistakable force with the Watts rising of 1965. The bloody rebellions in Newark and Detroit in 1967, particularly costly in black lives, carried this form of spontaneous protest as far as it has gone to date. The assassination of Martin Luther King in 1968 and the nationwide rebellions that followed—including an uprising near the White House—formed a definitive and tragic symbol of the close of the earlier phase of the black movement and of the necessity to organize the formless protests in the urban ghettos.

The rising of the black urban masses at a time of strategic

[29] For an account of the sit-ins and responses, see Howard Zinn, *SNCC: The New Abolitionists* (Boston, 1965).

pause in the civil-rights movement amounted, in effect, to a critique-in-action of the latter movement. The spontaneous rebellions revealed, first of all, the chasm between the Negro middle classes with their political objectives, and the black masses with their social needs. Although fundamental to the achievement of racial equality, civil-rights objectives were clearly of practical benefit only to the middle classes, who were economically equipped to take advantage of them. The civil-rights movement lacked an economic program that spoke to the realities of ghetto life, while its tactical emphasis on non-violence had limited appeal in the center cities with their routine violence. Finally, the movement's emphasis on integration seemed to imply cultural assimilation, which was alien to the distinctive subculture of the urban masses and often a bitter cup for the middle class as well.

At this juncture, the other stream of black protest—lower-class-based black nationalism—began to gain its head. The postwar rise in race consciousness, which had gained momentum in the 1950s, had resulted in the growth of nationalist groups as well as the civil-rights movement. Foremost of these was the Nation of Islam. After a wartime crisis when the organization's refusal to recognize draft laws almost resulted in its demise, the Black Muslims made progress with their religious nationalism, particularly in the 1954–60 period. In the 1960s, the organization leveled off with perhaps 50,000 members. The Nation of Islam grew directly out of the Moorish Science Temple, with which the Muslim founders were associated and which was, after the Garvey movement, the largest nationalist group in the 1920s. Malcolm X, minister of the Harlem mosque, was the son of a Garvey organizer. The religious and cultural nationalism of the Muslims spoke to the questions to which the civil-rights movement failed to address itself. While the latter movement tacitly embraced middle-class Anglo-Saxon culture and risked reinforcing notions of racial inferiority, the Muslims celebrated blackness and denounced the "white devils." The Nation of Islam had an implicit economic program in its successful prosecution of various business ventures that provided services for the faithful.

Malcolm X was the pivotal figure in detaching cultural nationalism from a religious setting and making it the basis for an ideology of political action. In the last year of his life, Malcolm broke with the Nation of Islam and attempted to transcend the limiting features of Muslim doctrine and practice. The elaborate religious fantasy of the Muslims actually tended to appeal to recently arrived, uprooted Southern immigrants rather than to the more savvy mainstream of the black masses, while a militant eschatology of apocalyptic destruction of white society covered functional political quietism. While they celebrated blackness, the Muslims also condemned not only the pathologic aspects of the "culture of poverty," but neutral and even positive aspects of the American black subculture (soul food, for instance). In practice, the Nation of Islam often functioned, with its rigorous discipline, its self-denying morality, and its business enterprises, as a means of upward social mobility into the middle class for lower-class blacks. Instead, Malcolm X placed himself in the Pan Africanist tradition of radical black intellectuals, while maintaining, unlike the latter, a mass following, if not a mass organization. His late pronouncements were characteristically radical nationalist, verging on revolutionary socialist. He emphasized the international linkages of black peoples, occasionally attacked capitalism as a system, and sometimes praised socialism. After his trip to the Middle East and Africa, Malcolm founded the abortive Organization of African-American Unity, modeled on the Organization of African Unity of the African states. While his political views and organizational efforts were still evolving, Malcolm was assassinated in early 1965.

The left wing of the civil-rights movement, in its effort to cope with the political crisis of the movement and with the demands posed by the urban rebellions, was strongly influenced by black nationalism, particularly in the late formulations of Malcolm X. This influence was understandable in view of the cultural strengths of nationalism, its actual base in the black masses, and Malcolm X's radical interpretation of it. Many of the younger militants had had their doubts about non-violent direct action on grounds traditional with radical black intellectuals. The student and ex-student cadres of SNCC were the first to formulate a political response to the movement's crisis, which moved in the direction of black nationalism. This was the "Black Power" slogan voiced in the Meredith March in 1966 by Stokely Carmichael, newly elected Chairman of SNCC. CORE soon followed suit in endorsing black power, while SCLC and the traditional civil-rights organizations held back.

Black power was an elastic doctrine that could mean any-thing from black capitalism to a black social revolution. At first, it appeared to mean development of political power on the traditional model of the upwardly mobile ethnic group. The SNCC effort to field an independent black political party in Lowndes County, Mississippi, was in this vein. While CORE stuck with this relatively moderate formula-tion, SNCC steadily evolved toward revolutionary national-ism, based on a principle of Third World solidarity, in a round of incendiary speeches in 1967 by Carmichael and his successor, H. Rap Brown. By this time, SNCC had largely moved out of student politics and was attempting to establish a base in the urban ghetto.

It was at this juncture that the Black Power Committee appeared at Howard. Like SNCC, the black student left at Howard and other Negro colleges evolved under the influ-ence of black nationalism. Many young black radicals have emerged from the centers of social discontent and black na-tionalism: the Northern cities. Like their white counterparts, black students are politically more volatile than the general population. The solidarity of the student subculture and the intellectual orientation of educational communities nurtures revolutionary ideology. A student movement and a renegade intelligentsia have also emerged because the black middle class, like the black masses, suffers racial oppression.

As an organization which identified itself with the evolving black movement, the Black Power Committee endorsed the radical doctrines in advance of any direct engagement with university authorities. In this case, its most important commitment was to the creation of a "militant black university." Like most militant groups at Negro colleges, the Committee was small, including fewer than 50 members in a university of 9,000 students. It first engaged the university administration on the basis of political action directed against off-campus white authorities—in this case, an anti-war demonstration against the director of Selective Service. This demonstration was an expression of a key tenet of the black left—the indivisibility of "Third World struggles" against "white imperialism"—namely, American capitalism. Direct action against a government official also placed the Howard administration in the untenable position of having to choose clearly between racial solidarity—highly valued among all classes in black society—and political loyalty to the national authorities. Although it is technically a private institution, Howard is sometimes considered a "federal" university because it receives one half of its funds from special Congressional appropriations, while the U.S. Secretary of Health, Education and Welfare sits on its board as an *ex officio* member. Inevitably, the administration would have to place its relations with the national government above whatever residual sympathy it might feel for blacks protesting against white authority. During the protests in the spring of 1967, Howard's president, James Nabrit, appearing before the House subcommittee which controlled university appropriations, repudiated the "very small but noisy and active elements" at the university and assured the congressmen that he proposed to "deal with" the demonstrators.[30]

Once the university announced its intention to discipline

30 For accounts of the Howard protest and its issues, see Michael Miles, "Colonialism on the Black Campus," *The New Republic*, August 15, 1967, pp. 15–16, and Keith Lowe, "Towards a Black University," *Liberator*, September 1968, pp. 4–10.

the Hershey demonstrators, the Black Power Committee appropriated the cultural value of racial solidarity for its own in its struggle with the administration. This appropriation was crucially important, since there is no inevitability to student support of the black left. The student culture at Negro colleges is not militant; on the contrary, it is thoroughly Joe College. Elaborate Greek-letter fraternity systems dominate student life, while sports are the chief collective enterprise uniting the various groups in the institution. The fraternities also serve this latter unification function, since college officials —as members of the Negro middle class commonly do—retain their fraternity affiliations into adult life and actively participate in adult branches. The atmosphere of the Negro colleges is, in short, thoroughly bourgeois. In this respect, they are like other state universities, especially Southern examples. By social origins, students at Negro colleges are not, however, overwhelmingly middle-class. Only 25 percent of the students come from families with middle-class incomes by general American standards, although another 25 percent come from lower-middle-class and upper-working-class families which function as a middle class in black society. The remaining 50 percent or so come from families which are distinctly lower-class or working-class.[31] Far from attenuating the middle-class atmosphere of the colleges, this fact requires these institutions to enforce rigorous middle-class values—the better to "socialize" upwardly mobile lower-class students into middle-class culture. This socialization process is not ordinarily difficult, since the Negro middle class constitutes the faculty and administration, while the upper-middle-class students dominate the fraternities and the lower-class students are anxious to master the techniques of upward mobility. In a violent political crisis, however, which some Negro colleges have experienced, these institutions of socialization can lose control

[31] For the social origins of students in Negro colleges, see Earl J. McGrath, *The Pre-Dominantly Negro Colleges and Universities in Transition* (New York, 1965).

of proletarian students. The Negro colleges cannot afford to operate routinely on the permissive principles of liberal white universities whose students are overwhelmingly middle- and upper-class in origin.

Racial solidarity is one appeal, if effectively developed, which can mobilize support for the black left in an otherwise unsympathetic environment. On this basis, perhaps half of the undergraduate body at Howard came to support the Black Power Committee against the administration in the spring of 1967. Civil liberties, second to racial solidarity as a broadly appealing issue, also contributed to this process. Negro college administrations characteristically maintain tight political control of their campuses. Typically, the administration appoints faculty sponsors to supervise student newspapers; regulates the kinds as well as the time and manner of political rallies; charters only those student organizations which are to its political and cultural tastes; makes regulations without the participation of those affected; determines rules violations and penalties without due-process procedures; prohibits campus appearances by militant political figures; and violates the canons of academic freedom in its political supervision of the faculty. A sequence of political events dramatizing these issues built student support at Howard, and a Student Rights Organization joined the Black Power Committee in organizing protest. Students were mobilized by the administration's attempt to hold disciplinary hearings before an administratively controlled body, and by the resulting disruption. In the course of the spring, the Howard administration prohibited the appearance of CORE's Floyd McKissick in order to "insure that a proper balance" be maintained in the political views of speakers. It also announced that the "total corporate interests" of the university required that all public announcements and news releases by students and faculty be cleared in advance through the public-relations office. As a result, by the time of the May 10 boycott (50 percent effective in the undergraduate college), the student government, which had condemned the original Hershey demonstrations, and even the apolitical fraternities were endorsing the boycott.

By the fall term, the Howard administration was thoroughly engaged as the adversary by the student left. As a result of the issues of political rights and civil liberties raised by radical political activity, student activists were pursuing the general issue of university authoritarianism and the particular caste neurosis of their university administrators—an Uncle Tom/Emperor Jones complex—resulting from the arrangements which allowed officials to be Emperor Jones on campus while having to play Uncle Tom to off-campus white authorities. The successors to the Black Power Committee pursued the issue of a militant black university which had arisen the previous year. At the same time that cultural nationalism was influencing the black movement and a black-studies curriculum was arising as an issue, the university had let it be known through its policies and statements that it was interested in pursuing the vision of a "first-rate university." The college-board score for verbal aptitude required for admission to the university was raised to 350. This pursuit of "high standards" would have the effect of excluding lower-class blacks, who were most likely not to meet these standards, while increasing the percentage of whites attending the university. Kenneth B. Clark, a Negro sociologist and a Howard trustee, explained that Howard should become a "national urban university" and that a "predominantly 'Negro' college is an anachronism that is no longer tolerable." Campus rumor had it that the administration was interested in reducing the percentage of black students to 40 percent, and financing its ambitions with the support of Congressmen desirous of creating a federally sponsored "great" national university in Washington.

This policy was anathema to student militants. The *de facto* identification of improvement of standards with integration was particularly offensive to students, who would often cite "Nabrit's Law": "Whenever two or three Negroes are gathered together, the standards must go down." Militants opposed the use of standardized tests as an admission criterion, charging that the tests were culturally biased. To the model of the first-rate university, they counterposed their own idea of a militant black university. The fundamentals of this vision were quite similar to the proposals first made by New Negro intellectuals in the 1920s and '30s. It was proposed that, far from raising admission standards in such a way as to exclude ghetto blacks, the university should identify itself more closely with the "black community," by which was meant the urban ghetto, not the rural South or the "Gold Coast" suburbs of the middle class. It was sometimes suggested that the university launch community-development programs which would be of clear economic and social benefit and based on the principle of community self-determination. Secondly, the black left wanted a racial emphasis in the curriculum. It was often noted that Howard's music department did not teach musical forms, such as jazz and blues, originated by Afro-Americans. The militants demanded black studies in history, literature, art, and sociology, and additional emphasis on African studies and languages.

A black university implied, moreover, a reorganization of the entire curriculum and a redirection of the mission of the university. No longer would the curriculum be a fair reflection of the leading multiversities. Even though the methodologies of academic disciplines were independent of race, it was felt that most fields would benefit by an emphasis of practical value to the race. An economics department might feature the economics of the ghetto and the effect of national economic development on black America; the school of social work might teach a client-oriented practice. The fundamental mission of the university would also change. No longer would Howard operate as the "Black Harvard." Speech courses to refine accents and Freshman Assembly, a required course to introduce students to "culture," would have to go.

Central to the theoretical and actual conflict between the visions of a "militant black" and a "first-rate" university has been another crisis of Negro higher education. An irony of the civil-rights movement was its effect of opening the white educational establishment to black students and faculty and thus draining the Negro institutions of many of their best people. An irony of the black militancy that followed civil rights has been the similar effect of black-studies programs in well-financed white institutions to bid away black faculty members and students from the Negro establishment. In this tightening competitive market, the Negro colleges have meanwhile been passed over by federal subsidy, which goes to the best white institutions and their high-powered research operations. Among other things, the "militant black" university is a proposal to deal with this crisis by developing a distinctive program and mission which, for all their wealth and market power, the white institutions will be unable to duplicate. Even while the best of their number face decline and the worst face extinction, the Negro institutions have redoubled their efforts to achieve first-rate (or, as the case may be, second-rate or third-rate) status. The key to the achievement of competitive parity is large-scale federal subsidy, and, accordingly, Negro educators have become increasingly angry and desperate in their supplications to the U.S. Office of Education. This first-rate objective is, of course, in keeping with the aspirations and character of the Negro middle class from which Negro college officials spring. Any other course would force Negro officialdom—not to mention the faculties and many students—to deny its own history. This is why a Howard faculty member reflected in the spring of 1967 that if the student movement concentrated on limited issues, it might succeed; but if it pursued the program for a black university, there would be a "virtual civil war on campus."

Except for minor incidents, the Howard campus was relatively quiet in the fall of 1967. In March 1968, however, one year after the Hershey demonstrations, students seized the

Administration Building and occupied it for several days. Students were able to negotiate an agreement with the trustees on various "student power" and "black university" issues. In this extended occupation, the first of its kind among the student rebellions in the United States, student leftists were also able to extract an "amnesty" agreement from the administration. This Howard precedent had considerable influence on the course of events at Columbia a month later.

In the fall of 1968, the Student Association sponsored a "Toward a Black University" Conference at Howard. In February and March of 1969, student militancy once again gathered force in a series of demonstrations extending throughout the university and into the graduate and professional schools. On February 2, medical students began a boycott of anatomy classes, protesting inadequate laboratory equipment and the leadership of the department's chairman. A week later, law students launched their own class boycott, and later briefly occupied the Law Building in support of a demand for an equal student vote in all decisions of the Law School. In March, students in the College of Fine Arts followed suit with a boycott and demands for student power within the college. Students in the College of Liberal Arts supported this boycott and later joined in a seizure of the Fine Arts Building, the New Classroom Building, and the office of the university president. The university was able, however, to force the vacation of these buildings by obtaining a temporary restraining order from a Federal District Court. The following month, nevertheless, graduate students in the School of Social Work and students in the Department of Sociology and Anthropology again launched class boycotts and occupations. In early May, these demonstrations developed briefly into a seizure of all buildings on campus by small groups of students, and a series of incidents of hit-and-run violence. On a court order, federal marshals intervened and made 21 arrests.

By the conclusion of the 1968–69 school year, the student left had forced changes in, or reconsideration of, a whole range of policies basic to the character of Howard University. Some of these demands concerned student life, such as women's curfews, the use of alcoholic beverages on campus, and the like. Other demands, of a more politically significant nature, pressed for black studies and African studies, and for student participation in the governance of the university at all levels. Students were successful in winning important political rights: autonomous control of student-government funds, an independently run student newspaper, and the freedom to invite campus speakers of their choice. The university agreed to abolish compulsory ROTC—an important indicator of the traditions of Negro colleges, many of which were founded by Union generals (General O. O. Howard, General Clifton B. Fisk, General Samuel Chapman Armstrong, etc.). The university also agreed to remove the "Department of Business" from the College of Liberal Arts.

Other student demands had less promising implications. There were demands, some of which were successful, for the elimination of various academic requirements and examinations, such as foreign-language and science requirements for graduation. It was apparent, at the end of the school year, that the interpretation of "revolutionary" politics by some student leftists involved *deus ex machina* powers, independent of the level of student support for a political program. This attitude was reflected in the increasing use of low-level terror tactics—arsons, threats, and bombings.

The student left at Howard and other Negro colleges is not much stronger than its counterpart at white institutions. In the absence of indicative surveys, it can be roughly estimated that not more than 1 or 2 percent of the student population are likely to be radical activists, while their loyally radical constituency varies from 5 to 20 percent. Up to half or more of the student body may swing into support of the left, depending on political developments, while the remaining students stay determinedly neutral or, to a lesser extent, support the administration. Accordingly, the success of the left at Howard and other colleges varied widely, according to the nature of the administrative response and the left's own political deftness and sense of justice.

The Howard pattern has been the basic form of student revolt throughout the Negro colleges. The sequence is: political action against the white social order; retaliation by the Negro administration on behalf of the white authorities; mobilization of student resistance to the administration on the basis of racial solidarity and basic political rights; escalation of the conflict between students and administration on the basis of university authority versus student power; first-rate university versus militant black university. This pattern is complicated by the willingness of the Southern state authorities to use massive force to put down black student revolt. This action can lead directly to insurrectionary battles between students and the state authorities. In 1966, in the first incident of this kind, the Texas state police directed massive firepower against a dormitory at Texas Southern, which allegedly harbored a sniper. (During the same term, the Texas Southern administration, responsible to a state board of education, refused to charter a militant political group, Friends of SNCC, and refused to renew the contract of its faculty sponsor.) After a militant speech by Stokely Carmichael in 1967 at Vanderbilt University (an institution attended by Southern white gentry) in Nashville, black students on the other side of town at Fisk and Tennessee A&I univerisites became involved in a riot scene with the police. In Nashville in 1968, after the assassination of Martin Luther King led to a repetition of these events, the Tennessee National Guard launched an invasion of the Tennessee A&I campus with half-tracks and helicopters. The A&I administration later expelled or suspended over 200 students.

Also in 1968, 500 students from South Carolina State, a state institution, and Claflin College, a private college, began a campaign to desegregate the bowling alleys in Orangeburg. This led to 15 arrests and 20 hospitalizations. Ten days later, police and National Guardsmen responded to a report of arsons on the South Carolina State campus, where they fired on unarmed students, killing three and wounding 40, primarily with shots in the back. In this case, the college administration did not intervene. Students began a boycott against downtown business, and eventually the bowling lanes were desegregated. The year before, however, 90 percent of the students had boycotted classes in protest against the administration's refusal to rehire two white graduate students whom it had found politically impalatable. The instructors were Woodrow Wilson Fellows, teaching in a Negro college under a program sponsored by the Woodrow Wilson Foundation, which has had more than one incident of this kind.

The tempo of revolts and the level of violence tended to increase steadily in the late 1960s. Besides the confrontations at Howard, Fisk, and Tennessee A&I, 1967 saw student demonstrations at Southern University, Allen College, South Carolina State, and Jackson State. In 1968 there were again incidents at Howard, South Carolina State, and Tennessee A&I, and also at Virginia State and even at Tuskegee Institute. At Tuskegee, students held the trustees hostage in support of their demands for African studies and the abolition of compulsory ROTC, until the National Guard arrived. Fifty-four students were expelled, but after they obtained a federal court injunction ordering a hearing, they were readmitted on probation.

In 1969, there were no less than 17 major protests at Negro colleges.[32] By this time, the lines of opposition between the student left and the administrations and state authorities were clearly drawn, so that the patterns of revolt changed somewhat. There were more incidents of violent student (or

[32] There is minimal reporting of student protest in Negro colleges. One source is *The New South*, in its political surveys of the Southern states. The Urban Research Corporation, in *Student Protest 1969* (Chicago, 1970), surveys student protest in Negro institutions.

presumed student) protest. During a radical campaign at Lane College in Tennessee, the science building was burned down, following the appearance of a militant East St. Louis group known as the Black Egyptians. At the Baton Rouge and New Orleans campuses of Southern University, there were a series of violent and potentially violent confrontations between student demonstrators and the state police and National Guard.

Actual violence occurred more often at schools with lower-class students than in the "Negro Ivy League." It was also more frequent by this time for student protest to begin immediately with an anti-administration program, such as a demand for black studies, relaxation of social regulations, and student power. This was the case at Lane and Southern. The "black university" program often drew an ambivalent or even hostile response from many students, who conceived their values and commitments in solid black-bourgeois terms. The "cultural civil war," which is fundamental to the conflict between student militants and accommodationist administrations, extends into the student body if basic questions are pressed. When students demonstrated in support of the wage demands of maintenance workers at North Carolina College, the hard-line speech of the college president received a standing ovation at a special convocation of students. At the Atlanta University Center in 1968, there was wide student support for a relaxation of social and academic regulations. But when student militants took the trustees hostage at Morehouse College in 1969, 500 student counter-demonstrators opposed the militant demand for a black-controlled board of trustees.

The 1969 student protests at North Carolina A&T have special significance since they involved protests, at various times, by black students, white students, junior faculty members, black high-school students, militant political organizers, and black workers. Like Howard University, where Stokely Carmichael was once active in the Nonviolent Action Group and the law school has turned out leading civil-rights lawyers, North Carolina A&T has been involved in the black social movement since its inception. A&T students invented the sit-in and thus inaugurated the black student movement. In December 1968, Stokely Carmichael delivered a militant speech at the college, after which the president of the student body announced a two-day class boycott in support of student grievances against administrative regulations. In March, students again boycotted classes, this time in support of the wage demands of striking cafeteria workers. The cafeteria workers at A&T were following the example of striking cafeteria workers at the University of North Carolina at Chapel Hill. At UNC, a coalition of black students (called the "Black Student Movement"), white student leftists, and junior faculty members (especially teaching assistants) supported the strike and picketing of the dining hall, which led to intervention by state troopers, but eventually to a favorable wage settlement.

Meanwhile, at Duke University in Durham, black students seized a building and demanded an Afro-American-studies program. This action was supported by a white leftist Student Liberation Front, which was able to mobilize several hundred students in support. After a series of student rallies, demonstrations, and a class boycott, student support grew to upwards of 1,000 students and the university apparently agreed to black student demands. It later turned out that participation of black students in the determination of the program was not part of the administration's package, which led to the efforts of black students and local organizers to create Malcolm X Liberation University. This enterprise may become the first actual embodiment of the "black university."

Later in the spring, there were more political incidents at North Carolina A&T in Greensboro. The principal of Dudley High School invalidated the election of a student militant as president of the student body, while the city board of education obtained a court injunction to prevent A&T students from joining in demonstrations at the high school. Later, sniper fire was reported on the A&T campus and the National Guard conducted a sweep of the campus with armored personnel carriers. A student was killed in the confrontation and 200 students were arrested, some of them from Scott Hall, where the sniper fire was reported to originate. The guard had been ordered out by Governor Robert Scott, son of former Governor W. Kerr Scott, after whom the building had been named.

The black student demonstrations at Duke and UNC were a part of the black-studies movement throughout the country. In 1969, there were no less than 85 black student protests in white institutions of higher education. Although these protests received the greater publicity, they were not necessarily as significant as the revolts in the Negro colleges; the importance of a black student revolt is often in inverse ratio to its coverage in the white press.

Coverage centered on protests at major universities, such as Brandeis and Cornell, whose most trivial doings are reported —with some reason—as if they were grist for society columns. This is not to say that there were not real causes for protest. The leading universities were generally as lacking in programs for the study of Afro-American history and culture and in facilities for a normal social existence for black students as any Southern Baptist church school. Black students received a superficial embrace from these schools, while they had to cope with local housing discrimination, the scarcity of students with a similar cultural and racial background, a fugitive social life, and even discriminatory fraternity systems. At Cornell, the hostility between black students and the right-wing fraternities culminated, incredibly, in a cross-burning in front of the black women's dorm. The militancy of black students at these institutions was also a function of an awareness of their privilege in relation to the black masses, and a resulting collective guilt.

The wage demands and strikes by cafeteria and maintenance workers at some schools sometimes offered the opportunity for a real unity between these students and average black men and women. More often, black students would demand programs for ghetto development which would enable them to establish a real relation with their impoverished fellows. Sometimes these programs were feasible, especially in urban universities, but at times they were ersatz. Black students at elite universities were also given to posing as ghetto soul brothers, although their actual background was often impeccably suburban-middle-class. White members of the university community often accepted this image out of their ignorance of black society. These liberal university communities evinced a slightly intimidated sympathy for the newly arrived Afro-Americans, who they were sure were potentially violent black proletarians. For this reason, even a small number of organized black students could usually count on a gun-shy administration and the automatic support of the liberal wing of the community. The political result was occasionally an absurdist drama in which the black students had most of the fun.

The cutting edge of the black student movement in white institutions was generally further down, in the city universities, the state college systems, and the community colleges. In these cases, it was less a question of middle-class students attempting to "identify" with their black brothers than it was a substantive matter of whom these institutions were, in the final analysis, to serve. These movements were in the mainstream of the black social movement, and the issues which they pressed were continuous with racial issues in other sectors of society.

Fundamentally, these issues came down to the basic matter of racial inequality. Only 6 percent of the students in the higher educational system in the United States are black, while blacks constitute 12 percent of the population. Since half of these black students are actually educated in segregated Negro institutions, only slightly over 3 percent of the students in the white educational establishment are black, and in half of the white colleges the black students compose less than 2 percent of the student body. Despite the flutter of special recruitment efforts in the late '6os, the effect was as much a redistribution of black students among institutions as it was an actual increase in the total number of black students attending college.[33] From these facts of admission followed most of the other demands of the black student movement on the campuses: more black faculty members to serve more black students, different programs to serve different students, new kinds of personnel services for new kinds of students, and new programs for an emergent community.

At the City College of the City University of New York, for instance, 13 percent of a full-time day student body of 12,000 were black or Puerto Rican. In New York City's high-school system, which the City University ostensibly served, 50 percent of the students were black or Puerto Rican. Accordingly, minority-group students at City College, in an organization called the "Black and Puerto Rican Community," demanded an equivalent enrollment in the college of black and Puerto Rican students. The students, many of whom were enrolled in a special admissions program for minority students known as SEEK, also demanded power in the policy determinations and hiring practices of the program, and the institution of special studies in black and Puerto Rican culture. They also campaigned for Spanish-language requirements for students majoring in education who were likely to teach in *el barrio*, the Puerto Rican ghetto. With this program, the Black and Puerto Rican Community was able to establish real links between its members and their less privileged counterparts in the high schools. This coalition was reflected in a series of demonstrations, disruptions, and occupations which were supported by local high-school students as

33 Alexander W. Astin, "Racial Considerations in Admissions," in American Council on Education, *The Campus and the Racial Crisis*, 1969.

well as by white leftists and sympathizers. Eventually, 200 junior faculty members also swung into support of a student boycott.

One feature of the City College campaign, which has been even more prevalent at institutions of higher education with a working-class constituency, was a physical clash between white and black students over the political and racial issues. This polarization of the student body was complicated by the rise of "black anti-Semitism" as an issue in New York City. City College traditionally served a highly motivated Jewish constituency, while various Jewish intellectuals and academicians looked back on City College as their vehicle of upward social mobility. Black anti-Semitism is meanwhile a real phenomenon resulting from hostility between blacks and Jewish ghetto merchants, and from the availability of Jews as a scapegoat for social oppression. Despite these complications, the student movement at City College succeeded in realizing most of its demands and in accelerating a program of "open admissions" in the City University system.

For a variety of reasons, the most notable of the black student rebellions of 1968–69 was the San Francisco State College strike. As in the case of CCNY, only 10 percent of the student population at the college was from San Francisco's various non-white minorities, although 40 percent of the city's population and 54 percent of its high-school enrollment was composed of these minorities. The percentage of black students at the school had actually declined from more than 10 percent in the late 1950s to around 4 percent in 1969. This was a result of the complex workings of California's Master Plan for Higher Education, which had established a three-level track system that tended to work against the non-white poor. The Master Plan established admission standards which allowed only the top third of the high-school graduating class to enter the state college system, and only the top eighth to enter the university system, while the bulk of the population was provided for by a community-college system.

The result of these standards was a clear class bias in which two thirds of the students in the university system came from families making $10,000 plus, while only one half of the students in the state college system and one third in the community colleges were from families with incomes of that level. Families making less than $10,000 meantime paid half of California's state taxes and composed 70 percent of the population, while non-white ethnic groups—blacks, Orientals, and Mexican Americans—amounted to 25 percent of the state's population.

In these circumstances, the Black Student Union, chicanos, and Oriental students formed the Third World Liberation Front (TWLF) in the fall of 1968. Many of these students were enrolled in the Equal Opportunity Program, a special admission program for the "disadvantaged" which comprised 300 students and had been established partially because of radical pressure the year before. As was the case in many white institutions, the special admission program did not relieve political pressure, but intensified it by enrolling a larger number of non-white students, who at the same time were susceptible to guilt over their privilege in relation to their fellows. The class boycott was touched off in the fall of 1968 by the suspension of a black instructor who was a member of the Black Panther Party. Soon after, the Third World Liberation Front demanded open admissions for minority students and the establishment of an autonomous and degree-granting black-studies department, as well as an autonomous school of ethnic studies. Over the next four months, there were continuous class boycotts, picket lines, and disruptions, not to mention arsons, bombings, and clashes with the Tactical Squad of the San Francisco Police Department. As a result, the school was closed for four months in the most sustained student rebellion in the history of higher education in the United States.

The TWLF was able to enlist a high percentage of white students to support its demands, with 4,000 students, or two thirds of the student body, at one point marching in support of the strike. The American Federation of Teachers local, including mainly graduate assistants and junior faculty members, chose the moment to call a strike of its own in support of the students and for its own wage demands. The AFT strike was endorsed by the San Francisco Labor Council of the AFL-CIO. This endorsement resulted in some unprecedented alliances of student radicals and labor unions which found students welcome on the picket lines of the striking oil, chemical, and atomic workers at the Standard Oil refinery in Richmond, California. In this manner, the San Francisco State strike created almost utopian tactical alliances, if not actual coalitions, among students, blacks, faculty, and labor. By force of example, the TWLF spawned some 60 imitations throughout the country and triggered similarly motivated revolts at other state institutions in California, such as San Jose State, San Fernando Valley State, and the College of San Mateo.[34]

In early 1969, the TWLF signed an agreement which appeared to fulfill their demands, although the state college president, S. I. Hayakawa, later effectively reneged on the agreement. Hayakawa also succeeded in firing Nathan Hare, the TWLF's candidate to direct a school of ethnic studies. A protégé of E. Franklin Frazier, Hare sponsored the Black Power Committee at Howard. In 1970 a U.S. District Court of Appeals ruled in favor of Hare and other faculty members dismissed as a result of the student rebellion there.

The student left at San Francisco State also failed to win autonomy for any prospective ethnic-studies programs. This was typical throughout the country. Almost universally, black student revolts resulted in some manner of black-studies program. There were usually also concessions to the demands for positive community programs and admission reforms, al-

[34] For different views of the strike, see Martin Nicolaus, "S.F. State: History Takes a Leap," *New Left Review*, March-April 1969, pp. 17–33, and John Bunzel, "Black Studies at San Francisco State," *The Public Interest*, Fall 1968, pp. 22–39.

though these, because more difficult to achieve, were more token. In the case of the demand for autonomy, however, there were no major successes, although participation schemes were often devised. The demand for "self-determination" was the sticking point, and on that issue, university administrations did not compromise. The demand itself rested on contradictory premises. Self-determination was a revolutionary demand, but the black student left wanted its revolution on reformist terms—a dependable line of credit from white financial sources. These are the horns of the dilemma of the black left: revolution or reform.

III. PROSPECTS FOR A BLACK LEFT

Traditionally, black political movements have followed dual tracks: an integrationist, sometimes politically militant middle-class movement following one track; a nationalist, often politically quietist lower-class movement following quite another. The politics of the two classes have followed from their racial strategies, assimilation and separatism, which have cut across and often confused strictly political distinctions among left, center, and right. The nationalist movements, although "militant" on racial issues, have not usually been politically radical. The only consistent carriers of radical politics have been middle-class intellectuals, who have been sensitive to the international influence of movements for national self-determination, socialist revolution, or both. These Afro-American intellectuals have sometimes found a home in the middle-class movements, but have often been politically rootless. The nationalist movements proceeded from the Back to Africa movement of the 1920s to the Black Muslims of the 1950s without much support from either the middle class or the intellectuals.

The crisis of the civil-rights movement in the early 1960s precipitated a change in this pattern. The urban rebellions in particular shifted the focus of black politics to the Northern ghettos and the political mood in the direction of cultural nationalism—a typical product of the ghettos. Under the influence of these events, and in keeping with the tradition of radical black intellectuals and the example of successful national liberation movements in the Third World, the left wing of the civil-rights movement, notably SNCC, moved toward revolutionary nationalism. During the same period, Malcolm X, who was also influenced by Third World nationalism, moved lower-class nationalism away from a strictly religious and cultural orientation toward revolutionary socialism and thus influenced students and intellectuals, includding SNCC militants.

A result of this convergence of middle-class radicalism and lower-class nationalism was the Black Panther Party, founded on the West Coast in 1966. By combining black nationalism and revolutionary socialism, this organization attracted not only the traditional nationalist constituency of lower-class youth but also middle-class elements, especially students and intellectuals. Through a series of armed clashes with police and resulting notoriety, the Black Panthers grew in a few years from several ex-students in Oakland, California, into a national organization claiming 35 chapters and 5,000 members (although its original leaders have been killed or driven into jail or exile). The convergence of the left wings of the middle-class and lower-class movements was symbolized by the brief merger of the Panthers and SNCC in 1968—and by Eldridge Cleaver, a former Black Muslim, an ex-convict, and, like Malcolm X, a self-made intellectual.

In the 1960s, the nationalist mood not only transformed black cultural styles but influenced all political persuasions. Besides a great upsurge of militant (but not necessarily leftist) black nationalist groups, there was a black-power orientation to experiments in producers' cooperation, to demands for community control of schools, police, and municipal agencies, and even to the renewed interest in black capitalism. But despite the vogue of cultural nationalism and its political fallout, the dominant politics of black society remains interracial and liberal. None of the nationalist organizations has anything like the membership, wealth, and influence of the NAACP, which has over 300,000 members. Black liberals have also made successful ventures into electoral politics as congressmen, mayors, and state officials and have become more prominent in federal officialdom and in the councils of party power.

In the formulation of Bayard Rustin, an organizer of the 1963 March on Washington, this liberalism is premised on a move "from protest to politics." This strategy requires a new liberal coalition of the racial minorities, the liberal middle class, and, putatively, organized labor, which will be able either to dominate the Democratic Party or launch a new third party. The appropriation of a major party will be the prelude to the capture of municipal and state governments and, crucially, the federal government. With governmental power in hand, the interracial coalition can proceed with a policy of integration in schools, housing, and employment as an essential condition for racial equality, and with a social program of unprecedented scale in the areas of urban reconstruction, social welfare, education, housing, and redistribution of income—described by Rustin and A. Philip Randolph as a "Freedom Budget."

As grand designs go, this is a plausible program. From this stance of "realism" and "practicality," black liberals criticize the radical nationalists as fantasts and wishful thinkers. It is observed that revolution is an implausible undertaking in the United States and impossible for a minority of 12 percent of the population without wide support within white society— support which will probably never materialize. These critics also observe that the more reformist formulations of black power, as well as the future utopias of the revolutionaries, ignore the economic integration of the black population into the general economy which renders complete autonomy a reactionary fantasy. Finally, the liberal realists note that the fundamental aspirations of the black masses, not to mention the middle class, are for upward social mobility and integration into the larger social order on the basis of equality. Radical nationalism, they conclude, fails both as social vision and as practical politics.

The ideology of radical nationalism seems to concede nothing to the social reality of white society and even to provoke a united white front against the irreconcilable militants. Yet there is something lacking in the liberal realism which assumes that a working majority is available for an aggressive program of racial integration and justice in the United States. It is also questionable whether the black vote, which has so far been picked up in return for token programs and symbolic gestures of solidarity, can command the leverage to force radical changes in the allocation of social resources. Black society could make substantial political gains by its vote only if its support were problematic for the normal run of Democratic Party politicians. Only a high level of political sophistication and a strong network of political and social organization could put this issue in doubt. But poverty, ignorance, and social disorganization are the problems which the liberal strategy was designed to solve in the first place.

In their appreciation of the internal conditions of black society, black nationalists are the greater realists. Unlike liberal politics, nationalism does not beg the question of social disorganization, but confronts it directly. Social and political organization of the black ghetto is generally obstructed by the defeatist psychology of social oppression. In cultural nationalism and the celebration of negritude, the nationalists have a therapeutic program to deal with the problem of cultural identity of an oppressed people. The Garvey movement and the Nation of Islam are the only movements that have had any notable success in organizing the lower-class black masses. While the tacit acceptance of the standards of Anglo-Saxon middle-class culture by the middle-class movements have tended to exacerbate the problem of inferiority feelings among the black masses, the nationalist movements have shored up cultural identity, and in this way dealt with the psychology of inferiority which impedes effective political and social organization.

The nationalist movements have been able to build on a distinctive subculture that has taken root among the Afro-American population in spite of the experience of slavery, which virtually expunged the original West African cultural heritage. The most virulent slave system in recorded history, American slavery treated Negroes as a slave race by nature and consequently accorded them no legal or moral standing whatever. Black men were regarded simply as a form of capital investment in a system of agricultural production for commercial export. This plantation system organized its black population like factory gangs, and broke up all forms of social organization, including the family. As a result, the original African culture was broken down and almost eliminated except for some surviving Africanisms, particularly in language. This African culture was not uniform, since the slaves originated in differing African cultural groups. For these reasons, Martin Delaney, a nineteenth-century black abolitionist and early black nationalist, regarded Afro-Americans as a "broken nation."

Nonetheless, American blacks do maintain a distinctive cultural formation. This culture is not the "national culture" that nationalists believe is a basis for a national political entity. It is a *subculture* which took form in the South after the Civil War and Emancipation, when American blacks were able to reconstruct a family organization and establish their own church denominations (under slavery, independent religious observance, not to mention reading and writing, was disallowed). Taking its character from the life style of a rural peasantry and from whatever cultural tradition could survive a slave system, the Negro folk culture was often able to fashion cultural and aesthetic products out of the facts of oppression itself, but it always had to exist within the limits of general Anglo-Saxon social and cultural dominance. Urbanization disorganized this rural folk culture and seriously weakened family organization and the cultural relevance of the church, while permeating the community with the electronically communicated culture of the Anglo-Saxon middle class. As a result of such factors, Glazer and Moynihan have argued that the "Negro is only an American and nothing else."

Although this conclusion may justly apply to the Negro middle class, which has largely repudiated its cultural distinctiveness, it cannot be applied to the black masses. These continue to maintain a distinctive subculture, which shares common features with the general culture, but diverges in other respects. It is a hybrid culture. This is why Richard Wright characterized the Afro-American as the existential "outsider" and W. E. B. Du Bois emphasized the "double consciousness" of a black man in a caste system. The distinctiveness of the subculture develops out of several elements: the remnants of the African heritage, surviving folk culture from the old rural peasant existence, a history of racial and social oppression, and, most important, the "culture of poverty" of the urban ghetto. Although this subculture has demonstrated a rare creative power, particularly in its development of new musical forms such as jazz and the urban variants of the blues, it is also, as Oscar Lewis says of the culture of poverty, a "relatively thin culture" in practical terms. As a product of poverty and oppression, it fails to satisfy many of the elemental psychological and social needs of black people. In short, this subculture tends to reinforce, as well as to compensate for, the dominant culture's message of black inferiority.

Any black social movement must, however, build on this subculture in order to reach the black working and lower classes. To choose the dominant white middle-class culture would be simultaneously to admit cultural inferiority and to erect cultural barriers to mass politics. To embrace the sub-culture unambiguously, however, is also to embrace the social defeatism on which the culture is partially based. Both alternatives in this case seem to carry the same message of white superiority. The paradox of cultural nationalism is that an unqualified acceptance of the Negro subculture can lead directly to political apathy and establish severe limits to the possible social accomplishments of a nationalist movement. The Black Panther Party resolves this dilemma by attacking cultural nationalism as politically defeatist and insisting on the necessity for a "revolutionary culture." This alternative resolves the cultural dilemma to the extent that the revolutionary movement is politically viable. In practice, most cultural nationalists have not wholly accepted the real Afro-American subculture, but have created an idealized, fictional version that contains a tacit critique of the *status quo* subculture. This was true of both Garvey's UNIA and the Nation of Islam. Both also accepted enough of the dominant bourgeois culture to advocate their own variety of black capitalism and upward social mobility and thus to end as politically quietist.

Another aspect of the political realism of the radical nationalists is their frank recognition of the class divisions of black society, which are more severe than in white society. In terms of income, the Negro middle class actually controls a larger share of the total income going to the black population than its white counterparts control of total income going to whites. The upper-income fifth among blacks receives almost 45 percent of total black income, compared to a white figure closer to 40 percent. The second fifth receives 24 percent of total income among blacks, also higher than the second fifth among whites.

The civil-rights movement of the 1950s and 1960s reinforced this economic superiority by opening the general economy to the middle-class elements who are equipped to exploit it. The income gap has not actually been opened wider be-

cause the black working classes and lower classes have bene-
fited from an inflationary Vietnam War economy, which
since 1965 has reduced unemployment rates in the black
community. During this period, the black population has
made relative income gains on the white population for the
first time since the early 1950s. The median family income
has risen from 54 percent of the income of whites to 60 percent.[35] This is traditional for the black masses, who historically have made relative economic gains only during periods
of war. Since they also lose ground proportionately faster in
recession, the deflationary policies of the Nixon administration will wipe out at least some of these relative gains, if not
all of them. The Negro middle class will, of course, be better
secured against losses than the lower classes.

Superimposed on these income differences in black society
are color and cultural distinctions. The Negro middle class
tends toward the mulatto racially, while the lower classes
tend toward full-blooded negritude or "blackness." The
middle class also normally embraces the standard bourgeois
culture of the United States, while the distinctive Afro-
American subculture is actually the property of the lower
classes. The total result of these factors is less a class division
than a class chasm that makes political organization across
these lines extraordinarily difficult. The black left, however,
employs a political strategy designed to mitigate these differences and to facilitate political organization. The left inverts
the value of light skin so that it ceases to be a mark of superiority and a cause for aloofness. It also embraces the black
subculture with a nationalist ideology. Since political radicalism originates with the left wing of the middle class, the students and intellectuals, these nationalist doctrines are
designed to create closer ties between the middle-class radicals and the black masses. The real differences in income and

[35] Cf. "Recent Trends in Social and Economic Conditions of Negroes in the United States," *Current Population Reports* (Bureau of
Labor Statistics), July 1969.

opportunity are less subject to ideological modification, but the black student movement—middle-class either by origin or by prospects—has campaigned for open admissions and community development to make the general advance of their ghetto brothers a condition for their own social advance.

The revolutionary nationalism of former SNCC militants and the Black Panther Party is now the dominant ideology on the black left and therefore highly influential with the black student left. Revolutionary nationalism appropriates the advantages of black nationalism, but in its commitment to "revolutionary culture" it avoids the cultural trap of having to embrace the political defeatism of the black subculture or of having to design elaborate religious and cultural fantasies to compensate for this defeatism. Everything therefore depends on the viability of the revolutionary ideology. Current revolutionary doctrine is essentially a species of left-wing communism, drawing on the experience of successful communist nationalism in China and Cuba. Competing for doctrinal influence with the explicit communism (though in a Third World nationalist mutation) of Mao and Castro is the noncommunist but still Marxist-Leninist revolutionary socialism of the left wing of the Algerian Revolution through the writings of Frantz Fanon. The black left of revolutionary nationalist persuasion seeks to apply to the case of blacks in the United States a "colonization" analysis based on this Third World variety of Marxism-Leninism. It is argued that the black population in the United States constitutes a "black colony" which is exploited by American capitalism in its imperialist stage in ways that are essentially similar to the colonial exploitation of Africa, Asia, and Latin America by Western imperialism. The strategy of revolutionary nationalism follows from the analysis. Since Castro and Guevara were able to prosecute a revolution in Cuba by guerrilla warfare and the Chinese and North Vietnamese Communists by waging a "People's War," it follows that American blacks must wage a similar "war of national liberation" against the

U.S. government. It is granted that, given the balance of forces, national liberation could succeed only if a social revolution simultaneously occurred among the white population. For this reason, the Black Panther Party is willing to make tactical alliances with the white left.

Colonization is a relevant analogy, but not an analysis. The black population in the United States is not a "nation" and therefore not a "colony" either. In its cultural analysis, the black left generally follows Martin Delaney, who regarded American blacks as a "nation within a nation." Unlike the American Indians, however, Afro-Americans have no consciousness of a territorial claim, since they were imported as slave labor into a social system already established. Under colonialism, non-white peoples with an independent culture were subjugated by European or American imperialism. Although the colonial system involved cultural domination as well as economic exploitation, the subjugated people had a clear claim to its own territory and a collective consciousness of that fact—underscored by its vast numerical superiority to the foreigners. Although the slave system and the subsequent forms of oppression of black men in America created analogous systems of economic exploitation, cultural domination, and "indirect rule," Afro-Americans could never establish a national territorial claim and regard whites as "foreign invaders" while taking courage from numerical superiority. The characteristic forms of economic exploitation have also been different. Colonialism involved the export of the raw materials of the colony to the industrial mother country in exchange for finished products. American blocks were imported as slave labor, but under the modern conditions of industrial capitalism they may "export" their labor from the ghetto to white society, but also suffer from the dispensability of unskilled labor to the economic system. What is left of the colonization thesis is simply the substitution of the word "colonization" wherever the word "oppression" or "exploitation" might be appropriate, and hence another radical contribution to the vulgarization of the political vocabulary.

If there is no colonized nation, there is also no political logic to a war of national liberation. Without a latent national consciousness, Afro-Americans cannot be expected to rise up against the foreign invader. They also cannot be expected to defeat the foreign invader if he constitutes 85 percent of a population which is overwhelmingly loyal to the existing order and commands the world's most formidable military machine. The revolutionary nationalist analysis also tends to amalgamate two distinct Marxist-Leninist analyses: proletarian revolution cutting across racial lines and war of national liberation cutting across class lines. Accordingly, there is an ambiguity concerning whether the Negro middle class is to be won over through racial appeals at the expense of the white allies, or white youth and workers are to be won over through class appeals at the expense of black bourgeois allies. The same ambiguity recurs concerning ultimate ends. It is not clear whether the objective is a united socialist society which accommodates both races or an independent black nation midwifed with the aid of white allies. In a 1969 article in a radical journal, *The Black Scholar*, Stokely Carmichael actually revived the idea of "black zionism" or a return to a homeland in Africa.

Since the level of economic development of the black population in the United States is much higher than that of Third World countries, there is also no rationale for corollary doctrines of left-wing communism. Maoist doctrines of agrarian populism assume a relatively undifferentiated peasant population, abject poverty, and the vanguard role of a small elite of radical intellectuals. In the United States, the black labor force is moving rapidly into white-collar and blue-collar occupations and moving out of the typically lower-class position of service jobs, farm labor, and unemployment. Blacks cannot be regarded simply as lower-class masses. Nonetheless, the Black Panthers have adopted the Maoist formula of populist mysticism ("Power to the People") and elite organization ("Panther Power to the Vanguard"). It is questionable whether white-collar workers and industrial workers, much less middle-class students, can be counted on to accept the organizational reality of this formula, even if the latter can be persuaded to shout the slogans.

In spite of the foreign analysis and strategy of the black left, social conditions in the United States should continue to generate black rebellion and offer political opportunities for the black left. In the nineteenth century in the South, the "forced dependency" resulting from tight systems of social control such as the slave system and its successor tenant system inhibited the development of rebellion. Escape from this system through migration to Northern cities began to undermine the controls which prevented the natural response of rebellion against the real facts of social oppression. Since World War I and the Great Migration, there has been a continuous movement of protest against these conditions. The middle-class and lower-class nationalist streams of this protest movement began in the 1960s to unite, while social reform has failed to materialize and race consciousness continues to rise on the basis of urbanization and modern communication systems. In a number of cases, black students in the colleges and high schools have coordinated a common political campaign. These general conditions should continue to sustain a black student movement into the 1970s.

It would, finally, be a mistake to overestimate the extent to which the black left is committed to a "war of national liberation," or to any particular ideology. Richard Wright wrote: "Even when embracing Communism or Western Democracy, [the Negro] is not supporting ideologies; he is seeking to use *instruments* . . . for his own ends. He stands outside of those instruments and ideologies; he has to do so, for he is not allowed to blend with them in a natural, organic, and healthy manner." [36] The fundamental commitment of the

[36] Richard Wright in Foreword to George Padmore, *Pan Africanism or Communism?* (London, 1956), p. 13.

black left is to black self-determination, while ideologies and strategies are devices to serve that fundamental objective. When black students demand an *autonomous* program of black studies, they are registering their commitment to this goal.

The identification with Third World revolutionary movements—of Ghana, China, Cuba, Algeria, or the Al Fatah in the case of the Black Panthers—is not so much with ideological doctrines, which vary in any case, as with successful struggles for self-determination by "people of color" against white Western colonial or neo-colonial domination. The success of these nationalist movements in the Third World since World War II is a unique factor that makes for a heightened racial militancy in the United States by constant force of international example.

For Afro-Americans, Africa is decisive. The development of African nationalism represents a special opening for the black left because it was the Afro-American W. E. B. Du Bois and the West Indians Marcus Garvey and George Padmore who founded Pan Africanism, the distinctive ideology of the African independence movements. Du Bois organized the first international Pan African conferences in the decade after World War I and participated in the 1945 gathering along with many future nationalist leaders. One of these was Kwame Nkrumah, who later in Ghana led the first successful independence movement in Africa; Stokely Carmichael is now a protégé of Nkrumah, who is in exile in Guinea.

Pan Africanism shares the central principles of the black liberation movement in the United States: self-determination, cultural renaissance, repudiation of white domination, and the international solidarity of people of color. The Pan African left also advocates principles which would take the black left in America beyond left-wing communism: nonalignment in foreign policy and thus a rejection of simplistic two-camp theories (capitalist/communist) of international politics, "African Socialism," which involves not only a social-ized economy but democratic forms of control; and "positive action," or mass political action as a chief tactical weapon in lieu of guerrilla warfare. The adoption of Pan African prin-ciples by the black left in America involves only an accept-ance of its own tradition. A Pan African strategy in the United States, however, would require an appreciation of the special American reality in which the black population is an *op-pressed minority* with a distinctive subculture and not a black colony with a national culture. It would also require a unique objective: a socialist democracy which was culturally pluralis-tic on terms of equality, rather than an independent black nation or a culturally homogeneous society. Solidarity of Af-rica, finally, could hardly consist in a plan for political unifica-tion but only in effective opposition within the United States to the Western neo-colonialism which stands as a major ob-stacle to the creation of a United States of Africa.

5   PROSPECTS FOR A NEW LEFT

ON APRIL 30, 1970, President Richard Nixon ordered U.S. troops into Cambodia; a few days later, four students were shot and killed by Ohio National Guardsmen during a protest demonstration at Kent State University. The result was the first sustained national student strike in the history of American higher education. The strike shut down a total of 450 colleges and universities (a number of which, however, were closed pre-emptively by state and university authorities). The Kent State incident and the later killing of two black students at Jackson State in Mississippi were the bloodiest incidents of violent repression of the spring, but 12 students were wounded by shotgun fire at the University of New York at Buffalo and nine students bayoneted at the University of New Mexico. For their part, students initiated violence against property: students at the University of Iowa, Ohio University, Colorado College, the University of

Nevada, and the University of Alabama, among other schools, burned ROTC buildings. Civil war in the United States was no longer strictly a metaphor.

The national strike was a rude refutation of the widely expounded thesis that the student movement was in decline. This impression gained currency because the national antiwar moratoriums of fall 1969 had drawn student protest off-campus, while there was also a tendency toward political exhaustion at the elite universities after the explosive spring of 1969. Actually, the pattern of student protest in 1969–70, even before the national strike, was one of expansion, not demobilization. In a survey of 195 institutions from September 1969 through February 1970, the American Council on Education found that 84 schools, or over 40 percent of the sample, experienced protests directed against university policies, while 141 schools, or over 70 percent of the sample, had protests relating to the October Moratorium and November Mobilization against the Indo-China War. Similarly, the Urban Research Corporation discovered a 23 percent national incidence of protest at colleges and universities during the first three months of 1970, compared to a 20 percent incidence in the first months of 1969. These protests were not significantly less violent or significantly less popular than the 1969 protests. A key difference was the declining level of national press coverage.[1]

Over half of these protests, according to the Urban Research Corporation survey, occurred at schools which had not previously had major demonstrations. In 1969–70, the student movement tended to expand into new institutions, particularly state universities, and into virgin regions, such as the Midwest, South, and Southwest. There were demonstrations

[1] American Council on Education survey—interim results reported in Alexander Astin, "Campus Activism 1970: Trends and Their Implications," paper presented to American Personnel and Guidance Association. For the Urban Research Corporation survey, see *Student Protest, Part II: Continuing Revolt on Campus* (Chicago, 1970) and the report of *Chronicle of Higher Education,* April 6, 1970.

in the Midwest at such schools as Ohio State, Southern Illinois, and the University of Iowa; in the Southwest at the University of Nevada and the University of New Mexico; and in the Southern and border states at Washington University, the University of Kentucky, the University of South Carolina, and West Virginia University, among other schools. In the face of increasingly severe repression, political rights were often an issue, and in this area national student support was rendered to the Black Panther Party and to the Chicago 7, who were tried and convicted in 1969–70 of conspiracy to incite riot at the 1968 Democratic Convention. Ecology and anti-pollution were new issues. In an effort to forge an alliance between students and labor, the student left opposed on-campus recruitment by General Electric, which was implementing its union-busting strategy of "Boulwarism" against the electrical unions in a long strike. But the staple issues of 1969–70 remained racial justice, the Indo-China War and militarism, and student power, with an increasing emphasis on educational content.

The expansion of the student movement in 1969–70 was evidence against the elite-manipulation explanation of the dynamics of student rebellion. After the SDS convention in the summer of 1969, the student left was badly splintered. Trends in left analysis encouraged radicals to regard the student movement as trivial and to move off-campus in an unsuccessful search for new constituencies. Under these conditions, the student movement should have declined, according to the propositions of "hard core" theory, and indeed it was this inference which led many observers to proclaim the end of the student movement. Although the opposite occurred, the disarray of the New Left (the "Movement") did have serious consequences for the student movement. In the absence of coherent radical leadership, there was a tendency for the student movement to move simultaneously into liberal orbits, such as ecology, and toward spontaneous and violent uprisings, such as the burning of a branch of the Bank of

America near the University of California at Santa Barbara. Some left militants meanwhile occupied themselves with terror bombings. In the spring of 1970, 30 ROTC installations were objects of arson; yet the major political result of the national strike was the liberal Movement for a New Congress, originating at Princeton University. The natural successor to the 1968 movement to nominate Eugene McCarthy for President, this effort received an impetus from federal legislation lowering the voting age to eighteen.

The failing grip of the New Left on the student movement is the logical result of the left's recent history. The Movement in the United States, like its counterparts in other Western countries, has manifested a steady drift toward left-wing communism, which has led it away from the student movement and has been a cause for some satisfaction among the analysts of "neo-totalitarianism" who had predicted it all along.

The neo-totalitarian conception does not quite apply, however, since left-wing communism is defined by a repudiation of Stalinism and of the bureaucratic sclerosis and nationalistic indifference to world revolution manifested by Stalin's heirs. Left-wing communism is an effort to outflank Soviet Communism on the left in revolutionary militancy, particularly in the Third World, and in commitment to the social visions of utopian communism. But the doctrine remains within the orbit of Marxism-Leninism. The trick of combining Leninism with anti-Stalinism is accomplished by detaching post-revolutionary Soviet history from the revolutionary practice of Lenin and Trotsky. Great emphasis is laid on the social backwardness of Russia in 1917 and the active hostility of the Western capitalist democracies which, it is argued, necessitated "forced march" industrialization, bureaucratization, and militarization of Soviet society. Any gap between cause and effect is bridged by reference to the villain in the piece—Joseph Stalin.

Social revolution in the West, left-wing communists argue,

need not result in a brutalized socialism because the level of economic development is so much higher in the industrial countries of the contemporary era. If revolution can be managed in the United States, moreover, the main counter-revolutionary obstacle to socialist revolution everywhere will be removed. Finally, the promising experience of China and Cuba indicates that there is no inevitability to Stalinism in a socialist state. From a "world historical" perspective, the argument runs, the cases of China, Cuba, and Vietnam also demonstrate that the history of communism is on balance positive, particularly in industrializing countries. These considerations militate for a "New Left" which is neo-Bolshevist and pro-communist. Although some young enthusiasts may look to the Third World examples of Castro and Mao for their theory and practice, sophisticated left-wing communists regard Lenin and Trotsky as making more important contributions to the understanding of revolutionary action in the developed world. As the major revolutionary opponent of Stalin, Trotsky is an especially important symbolic figure.

Historically, the New Left emerged in Europe as a leftist repudiation of Soviet Communism after the repression of the Hungarian Revolution in 1956 and Khrushchev's revelations of the crimes of Stalin in 1955. In the United States, however, the New Left appeared in the early 1960s as an aggressively non-ideological movement rather than as a variety of left-wing communism. In its pragmatism and activist emphasis, it was typically American. But left politics abhors an ideological vacuum, and direct action requires strategic guidance on how to proceed. As the best-articulated systematic alternative to liberal social analysis, the Marxist tradition increasingly supplied the analysis necessary for strategic decision. The inadequacy of pragmatic activism was especially evident as the United States government began to prosecute the Vietnam War in earnest after 1965. The organization of an anti-war opposition and the systematic critique of war policy (and, by extension, American foreign policy) did not lend themselves

to the widely advertised virtues of "community organizing."
Here again, the Leninist tradition was available with its theory of economic imperialism. The left wing of the civil-rights movement had meanwhile split off to launch the black-power and later the black-liberation movement. As the black left evolved toward revolutionary nationalism, it was increasingly influenced by its more successful nationalist counterparts in the Third World, which usually endorsed some variety of Marxism. Accordingly, the black left in the United States took over a Marxist perspective and communicated it to the white left, which was very much concerned to maintain its standing with a black left that somehow seemed more "real." In some quarters, this deference to the black left degenerated into White Pantherism (not a parody, since such groups existed).

The convergence of race and war has made for a trend toward Marxism-Leninism in the New Left movement in the United States. This evolution has also been facilitated by the re-emergence of the remnants of the old left, who are more intellectually sophisticated than the young left. Repressed during the McCarthyist reaction of the early '50s and inhibited by the Cold War scare of impending Soviet supremacy created by Sputnik I in 1957, high Soviet growth rates, and the "missile gap" in the late 1950s, the Marxist-Leninist sects began a successful re-entry into American politics after the Cuban missile crisis of 1962 dispelled some of the fear of Soviet power. The old left maintained considerable prestige with the young left in the 1960s, based on its superior intellectual tradition and its avoidance of the delegitimation suffered by American liberalism through its implication in the Vietnam War. The influence of the old left in the United States is also founded on its martydom during McCarthyist repression and thus on its failure, while in Western Europe the old left formations have been discredited by their "success" as loyal oppositions within a larger state-capitalist framework. In France, for example, the student left generally despises the Communist Party for obstructing the May Rebellion in 1968 and for pursuing a social democratic policy under the cover of a revolutionary rhetoric.

Inertial forces have also contributed to the evolution of the New Left in the direction of left-wing communism. The history of the "Movement" is a history of movement leftward. Its main contribution to American politics has been the opening up of the left side of the foreshortened political spectrum. Again and again, this movement has explored the limits of permissible action and broken the bounds of respectable thought. Although it has contributed little in the way of durable analysis and scored no permanent organizing successes, the New Left has been vindicated intellectually by a social order which fairly begs for radical critique and politically by the follow-up of its initiatives by other political groups in the society. The Movement has functioned as a "vanguard" force whose exploratory probes have revealed social oppressions and activated social forces. Its success, however, was largely guaranteed by the facts of social oppression themselves and by the unnatural absence of an organized left. By the late 1960s, the momentum of the New Left had carried it to the end of the political spectrum: left-wing communism.

As the quality necessary to make the Movement move and therefore the highest activist virtue, militancy was central to this process of movement leftward. In the early 1960s, militancy was expressed as moral fervor; politics and society were explained in moral categories. Although the overt moralism of the early civil-rights movement later gave way to an exclusively "political" view of society, a precipitate of moralism remained. The assumption of all Movement political analysis was that the key determinant of social change was the Movement itself, and therefore that social change could be effected through a collective act of will. A revolution was "made" by revolutionaries. If radical results did not follow from radical actions, the conclusion drawn was that the political will was defective. The response had to be to raise the level of militancy. While the turnover of social analyses, radical constituencies, and revolutionary classes in New Left thinking was rapid, the emphasis on subjective commitment was constant. The change was that political will supplanted moral commitment.

One result of this subjective politics was terrorism. The bombing incidents of 1969 and 1970 were a logical development of a cult of militancy. Terrorism was a form of political magic, since the search for a radical constituency was given up almost entirely and political will and the technical means served as magical substitutes. Without a social program, revolutionary or otherwise, directed to specific constituencies, terrorist acts were essentially protests of wayward moralists.

The leftward momentum of the Movement has been guaranteed by another crucial fact: the New Left is a bourgeois left. Since leftists do not think well of bourgeois types, it is a dilemma of some import that leftists are themselves bourgeois. To remove the burden of guilt, the left characteristically endeavors in various ways to declass itself. This enterprise may be carried out in theory: the left may declare itself a part of the working class. It may be carried out in practice: leftists may renounce the norms of bourgeois respectability and thus convert themselves into a lumpen-bourgeoisie despised impartially by upper and lower classes alike.

The bourgeois left's quest for radical certification reinforces the psychology of radical one-upmanship which prevails within radical movements. *Nouveau* radicals are anxious about their radical credentials and psychologically vulnerable to outflanking on the left, much as newly arrived liberals in government are anxious about their "realism" and eager to prove their fundamental conservatism. Within the left, the posture of more-radical-than-thou is an effective device for psychological manipulation. There is also a permanent tension between truth criteria and activist imperatives, between the intellectuals and the activists in radical movements.

The result of this history has not been a "new" left. Increasingly, the characteristic doctrines of the New Left movement have gravitated toward a neo-Leninist neo-orthodoxy which is given a certain pop flavor through the misapplication to the United States of Marxist revisions developed for wildly different conditions. In its most egregious form, this ideological exoticism may actually involve the import of Maoist "people's war" and Castroist "guerrilla warfare" as revolutionary strategies for the United States. The populism of these doctrines, justified in China and Cuba by the predominance of the peasant masses, is grotesquely inadequate to the facts of the highly differentiated labor force of advanced industrial societies.

This fascination with revolutionary movements in the Third World betrays the ultimately populist and anarchist, rather than Marxist, bent of the New Left in the United States. In spite of a Marxist vocabulary, New Left analysis, like populist and anarchist thought, normally reduces the "ruling class" to the scale of ruling cliques and magnifies the "working class" into all classes outside the ruling class. Unlike Marxism, this populist mode regards society as simply a structure of privilege, and has no comprehension of capitalism as a functional system of production. New Left analysis also rarely relates cultural, ethnic, national, racial, and generational factors to its class analysis, which is crude to begin with. The main accomplishments of the New Left in America in the realm of Marxist theory have concerned the taking up of historical vulgarizations of Marxist analysis: the "social fascism" slogan applied by Communist parties to social democrats in the 1920s and '30s is the prototype of New Left characterizations of liberalism; a contempt for "bourgeois democracy" may be the pretext for a contempt for democratic process and civil liberties in general. The anarchist inclination of the Movement is reflected in the oscillation between utopian experiment and terrorist action, to the neglect of mass action and competent analysis.

An authentically Marxist, usually Trotskyist formulation of left-wing communism is more relevant to industrial capitalist societies. But the effort to relieve Bolshevism of the responsibility for subsequent Soviet history is disingenuous. Although economic backwardness, counter-revolution, and the personality of Stalin were important factors in the miscarriage of socialism in Russia, Leninist theory and practice were also crucial to this process from the beginning. Lenin's organizational weapon, the vanguard party, was fundamentally authoritarian in its implications not only for society but also for the industrial working class, and not only for this class but also for the left political formations and for the Communist Party itself. The "dictatorship of the proletariat" theoretically meant the dominance of the industrial working class in society, but democratic politics within the dominant class. Historically, the class dictatorship soon degenerated into party dictatorship and eventually into a personal dictatorship. During Lenin's own tenure, other left parties were suppressed; the workers' soviets lost authority; and Trotsky, hero of the anti-Stalinist left, suppressed the workers' soviet at Kronstadt. Leninism represents a blind alley for the left in the West, although Marxism as such remains a vital political and intellectual tradition.

A separate current within the radical movement is the Pop Left. A mutation resulting from the overlap of the New Left and youth-culture movements, the Pop Left dedicates itself to cultural radicalism and regards the development of new forms of community as part of a general transformation of life styles, values, and sexuality—as part of a "cultural revolution." Following Marcuse's formulation in *Eros and Civilization*, the cultural revolution generally turns out to depend upon "automation" and economic advance. Since cultural repression and sexual repression depend upon the necessity for work and the organization of production, automation leads to the cultural revolution by routinizing production and removing the necessity for work. This viewpoint is a variety of "technological anarchism."

It is far from clear, however, that the necessity for work has been removed, except for a narrow stratum of the upper and upper middle classes. Even among these groups, the exemption from work is largely the temporary prerogative of upper-class youth. Although economic advance may eventually have revolutionary effects on the work ethic and thus on culture itself, this prospect is still remote. The actual rate of increase in productivity per man hour—"automation"—is only 3.2 percent per year. This rate is not higher than the rates of other periods of industrialization. Automation does not represent a rise in the rate of technological change so much as an increase of productivity in new fields outside heavy industry. The impact of technology on culture is less the result of high growth rates, much less a "quickening rate of social change" (the United States excels in neither department), than it is the result of industrial change taking place *within* the field of culture itself.

The cultural-revolution posture also assumes that the level of economic development of the United States depends mainly upon technological innovation. The technological anarchists ignore the economic relationship between the United States and the rest of the world and the effect this relationship may have upon their own claim to represent a new, higher civilization. In his study of the nineteenth-century British Empire, J. A. Hobson observed that the English were becoming a parasitic nation of *rentiers*, dependent upon the income from imperial investments. In the same vein, Lenin postulated that the upper levels of the working class in Britain were a "labor aristocracy" whose high wages were derived from imperial super profits. The Pop Left endorses the economic-imperialism thesis without understanding that it implies that the cultural revolution is a phenomenon of imperialist parasitism. By the middle of the 1960s, the gross output of American direct investment abroad amounted to over $100 billion, a sum larger than the GNP's of all nations except the Soviet Union and the domestic U.S.[2] It is not clear that the U.S. economy is based on foreign investment, according to the classic formulation of the economic-imperialism thesis by Hobson and Lenin, much less that it is mainly supported by direct investment in backward countries: most capital export is to the developed world of Europe and the British Dominions. But the economic integration of a world market under the dominance of American capital is a leading characteristic of the postwar era.

Cultural revolution is an integrating myth of the youth subculture. Its effort to achieve "instinctual liberation" signifies not a transformation of the dominant culture but the traditional concern of youth culture, bureaucratically managed and trapped into prolonged adolescence, with self-realization and expressive values. The longing to escape instinctual "repression" in the Freudian sense and to move into the instinctual beyond of "de-sublimation" reflects the actual sexual regulation to which youth are subject and their passive dependence in the face of impersonal regulation by educational and military bureaucracies. The youth culture is not alone, of course, in suffering bureaucratic regulation of its life, and to this degree the enterprises of the youth culture have universal significance. But the emphasis on sensual expression and personal identity has special relevance for a transitional stage of life in which personality and sexuality are in the process of formation.

Since the cultural transformation that the Pop Left advertises has only a limited basis in social reality, its "cultural revolution" is at best a cultural rebellion. The Pop Left has attempted to create the social preconditions for its cultural transformation in the form of "communes," but these are usually ephemeral and dependent upon the spare change of the dominant economic order. Since the youth subculture is

[2] See Leo Model, "The Politics of Private Foreign Investment," *Foreign Affairs*, July 1967. For a defense of the economic-imperialism thesis against the standard objections raised against it, see Harry Magdoff, *The Age of Imperialism* (New York, 1969).

enclosed by the dominant culture, the cultural rebellion tends to parody the dominant order as it repudiates it. Thus the faddism, the banality, the breathless superficiality of so much of the cultural effusion of the underground. The capitalist dynamics of mass consumption and popular culture not only result in the exploitation of cultural rebellion for the "youth market," but conditions the essence of the cultural movement which tends toward the pop and two-dimensional. In its tacit assumption of the intrinsically liberating potential of technology, the Pop Left mirrors the dominant order's confidence in "automation" and "technology," even as it disassociates itself from them in rural communes.

The cultural left's ideology is a form of Pop Marxism, since a change in the mode of production is thought to usher in cultural revolution and utopian communism. But Pop Marxism, like the technocratic doctrines, is reductionist because the social transformation is semi-automatic without a political struggle for control of the forces of production. The main condition for automated utopian society, according to this attitude, is really a "spiritual revolution" which will be embodied in a cultural movement. This is a form of political magic. Inded, the technological anarchists are interested in magic of all kinds: astrology, witchcraft, and ersatz religion.

Here again, they share the presumption of the dominant order that transcendence has been banished from historical time and can be validly sought only outside the historical world. This mode is not an alternative to bureaucratic capitalism, but a symptom of it. The nature of a bureaucratic order is to reduce human subjects to natural objects and human experience to quantifiable data. In the flattened world of bureaucratic rationality, politics is a category of administration. But when human transcendence is expelled from the natural and historical orders, it returns in pseudo forms. Max Weber observed that bureaucratic orders tended to throw up "charisma" as a qualification for bureaucratic leadership—a magical power that political leaders in America have increasingly attempted to appropriate. Probably the foremost of the new magical powers is technology, the all-purpose substitute for rational social theory and organization. Thus Samuel P. Huntington's neo-Stalinist conception of "forced-draft urbanization and modernization" through the terror bombing of rural Vietnam substitutes the application of military technology for social change with a social and political content. Similarly, the popular notion of the "rate of social change" generally means nothing more than changes in the technological environment. Technological determinism is the approved magic of official liberalism.

Cultural rebellion has been fertile enough to produce its own cultural expressions—most notably, rock music. In other areas, such as theater, these artistic efforts have been reductive. In its efforts to celebrate "life," the cultural left has, often enough, abolished the distinction between art and non-art and therefore made only a theoretical statement rather than an artistic point. The cultural left also follows the underground tradition of parody and reduction of classical forms, a technique which has begun to pall after a century of practice. The paradox of this mode is that it reduces art to formal aesthetics instead of increasing its vitality. In many ways, the cultural left has simply recapitulated the history of modern art, much as the New Left has recapitulated the modern history of political ideology. Although both are highly distinctive as social phenomena, they have been culturally and ideologically imitative.

The recent evolution of the Movement in its several varieties of anarchism, populism, and left-wing communism does not augur well for its future. The left-wing communists have the most political impact. But their neo-Leninism has a fatal effect on the organizational style of the radical left, since the construction of a vanguard party will serve to delegitimate the left with its only mass constituency: educated youth. The counter-legitimacy of the left has depended on its claim to represent an alternative to an elitist social order.

Educated youth, whether student or non-student, is not likely to follow the lead of a self-appointed vanguard, for the reason that it is conditioned to expect, even if it does not get, control of its own destiny. The contemporary left is uniquely situated in serving an educated constituency. Its response so far has been to develop a growing suspicion of the radical potential of an educated mass, again on the grounds that it is not working-class and therefore not revolutionary. The combination of vanguard ideology and repudiation of its own constituency is an ideal formula for political isolation.

The current lines of development of the radical movement are well established. Within the white movement, the tendency is for radicalism to broaden its generational base while remaining within the same social strata. Thus the radical movement has moved downward into the upper-middle-class suburban high schools and upward into professional associations and teaching faculties. The high-school movement has focused on the bureaucratic regimentation and political and cultural regulation of student life within the secondary educational systems. Dress codes and restrictions on free political expression are typical issues. A survey by the Center for Research and Education in Civil Liberties at Columbia University found that 348 high schools in 38 states had serious disruptions in the winter of 1968–69. A random survey in 1969 by the National Association of Secondary School Principals discovered that 59 percent of all high schools and 56 percent of junior high schools, particularly large urban and suburban institutions, had student protests. Although race was an issue in only 10 percent of these protests, it was usually the occasion for the violent protests. A survey by the U.S. Department of Justice indicated that 75 percent of schools with a black enrollment of more than 10 percent had protests over racial issues.[3]

Within academic professional associations—the American

[3] See the report in *Chronicle of Higher Education*, November 10, 1969.

Psychological Association, the Modern Language Association, the American Sociological Association, and others—black caucuses and white radical caucuses have appeared to challenge the posture of value neutrality affected by the professional disciplines. Radical protests have also been undertaken in non-academic professional associations, including the ultraconservative American Medical Association. Salaried professionals within the federal government have even registered protests against the policies of their bureaucratic superiors. In 1969, civil-rights lawyers in the Justice Department protested the lax enforcement of the civil-rights laws by the Nixon administration, which was pursuing a "southern strategy" of electoral predominance. In 1970, officials of the Department of Health, Education and Welfare were faced with a protest meeting by employees who felt that the social programs of the department were undermined by administration policies and appointments.

The gravitational center of the radical movement within the white middle class remains the college campus. The expansion of the student movement into the larger community colleges is one of the few indications of an extension of the movement into other classes.

The black student movement has occupied itself with the assimilation of its recent gains. Since black-studies programs and special admission policies expand the potential base for the black movement on white campuses, the black left will probably continue to grow. In the 1969–70 school year, black demands were the leading protest issue; there were major strikes at the University of Michigan and the University of New York at Buffalo. The Negro campuses exhibit the same signs of escalation, polarization, and political exhaustion that prevail on elite white campuses. Many administrations of Southern Negro colleges have maintained control of their institutions by ready expulsion of student militants and higher admission and tuition requirements for Northern urban students who are a principal source of militancy. In 1970, the administration of Mississippi Valley State College co-operated with state authorities in arranging the arrest of 889 students, the largest mass arrest ever conducted on an American campus. The occasion for the arrests was a class boycott in support of demands for improvements in academic standards, faculty, and physical plant. The Negro President of the college, Dr. J. H. White, canceled all scholarships and required that returning students sign an agreement promising to participate only in officially sanctioned demonstrations and to refrain from boycotts and other "acts of harassment." In an interview, Dr. White explained that there was a "technique for handling whites that all Southern Negroes must learn. I'm an old bellhop, I've been around white folks all my life." Although the President of the college is responsible to an all-white state board of higher education, the student handbook, *The Informer*, declares that on-campus the President's "decisions and statements are final and represent the attitudes and policies of the college." [4]

There is also a strong high-school movement among black students, but this movement, unlike its white counterpart, is discontinuous with the college movement because of the differing class origins of college students and urban high-school students. The black high-school movement, which protests against the functional and cultural inadequacy of the ghetto educational systems, is led by the militant lower-class youth that spearheaded the urban rebellions. The middle-class college and lower-class high-school movements have nonetheless joined forces on several occasions. One of the most important effects of the black student movement has been to inspire counterparts within other oppressed minorities in the United States, notably Mexican Americans and Puerto Ricans. In a number of cases, all of these minority movements have made common cause in the formation of "Third World Liberation Fronts."

[4] Joseph Lelyveld, "Black Students Challenge the Order at Mississippi Valley State," *The New York Times*, May 25, 1970, p. 29.

I. THE NEW CLASSES

The most profound question concerning the future of the student movement is whether it portends the emergence of a radical movement in other sectors of the population. Potentially and even actually, the student movement represents a mass movement with a potential base outside the upper and upper middle classes. There are more than seven million students in the United States. Of these, three quarters come from families above the median income, so that the higher education system remains predominantly middle-class even on the community-college and junior-college level. Nonetheless, this system represents an institutional channel through which the radical movement might reach the white-collar and blue-collar working classes, of whom there are almost two million representatives in the higher educational system. Many of these are "new working-class" people who are given limited technical and clerical training for future employment in technical and white-collar jobs. A radical student movement that reaches these elements might well be the introductory phase of a new radical labor movement based on the new working class.

It is important not to confuse this new working class, trained for routine clerical and technical tasks, with the new middle class, educated for professional and scientific work, that plays an increasing role in modern production. Besides turning out the cultured rich, managerial cadres, self-employed businessmen and professionals, the elite and middle-level institutions also produce a new class of salaried professionals. While the former groups constitute a privileged class that is generally committed to the *status quo*, salaried professionals and technical experts occupy an ambiguous position between the new working class and the managerial and propertied classes. They are not self-empolyed but bureaucratized; their status depends on educational credentials, not property or business enterprise; they are paid well but not lavishly.

The upper levels of the bureaucratized professionals are upwardly mobile, with a shot at elite status and the emoluments of petty *rentiers*. To the extent that they have a purely technical training and an instrumental mentality, technical and professional personnel are a docile work force that does not question the fundamental rationales of the organizations in which it works. This is notoriously true of applied scientists and engineers, of which American industry employs no less than 400,000. A sign of the times, however, came in 1970 when the Cooper-Church amendment to limit American operations in Cambodia received the organized support of 200 industrial scientists from Eastman-Kodak, General Electric, RCA, Bell Telephone, Union Carbide, and especially IBM.

The simple necessity for massive inputs of informational and educational services, technical expertise, and research and development for modern production spells middle-level status (or less) for most of the new middle class. Very few of the 500,000 college teachers in the United States can expect to become tenured professors at elite institutions, much less Presidential advisors. Teachers in the secondary and elementary schools are meanwhile reduced to new working-class status, however much they may cling to a professional ideology and a middle-class self-image. There are two million teachers in the United States, constituting the largest single occupational grouping. The rise of the American Federation of Teachers, a teachers' union that employs collective bargaining and strike techniques, to challenge the National Education Association, a pseudo-professional association, is an indicator of the loss of status and income expectations among teachers in primary and secondary schools. The massed ranks of professional and technical workers cannot expect elite status; more importantly, the rapid expansion of the stratum tends to reduce the possibilities for the fulfillment of more modest status expectations.

Although the "professional, technical, and kindred" occupational category is not a precise indicator of the new middle class, the fact that this category is the fastest-growing occupational category is an important index of the expansion of the class of bureaucratic professionals and technical personnel. Having already doubled as a percentage of the labor force in the postwar period, this occupational category will have increased by 4.6 million members from 1964 to 1975—a growth rate of 50 percent, the largest increase of any occupational category both absolutely and proportionately.

A large part of the expansion of this category reflects the general growth of the "service sector" of the economy. While farm employment continues to decline precipitously and employment in the goods-producing sector of the economy—mining, manufacturing, and construction—grows moderately, employment grows twice as fast in the service sector of the economy: government, transportation, public utilities, wholesale and retail trade, finance, and services. Thus, farm employment will have declined from 14 percent of all employment after World War II to 3.9 percent by 1975, while blue-collar occupations will have declined from 40.7 percent in 1947 to an estimated 33.7 percent. On the other hand, white-collar workers (including professional and technical workers), who were 34.9 percent of the total labor force in 1947, are expected to constitute 48.3 percent of the total by 1975.[5]

Any social movement that mounts a serious radical challenge to the existing social order must organize the growth sectors of the labor force. Within the general category of white-collar workers, the growing components are profes-

[5] For statistical evidence on occupational structure, see *The Manpower Report of the President* (Washington, D.C., 1969). For a study of the relationship between technological change and the occupational structure, see the report of the National Commission on Technology, Automation, and Economic Progress, *Technology and the American Economy* (Washington, D.C., 1966).

sional and technical workers and "clerical and kindred" workers, while sales workers and "managers, officials, and proprietors" remain stable as a percentage of the labor force. Professional, technical, and clerical workers will constitute 30 percent of the labor force by 1975. These are the sectors of the population—the new middle class and the new working class—which are experiencing the full force of the processes of industrialization at its current stage, and which are therefore most affected by its social dislocations and the shock of a new industrial discipline. These are also the groups—particularly the new working class, such as clerical workers—which are the least organized and thus most subject to political and economic exploitation. In these fields, the writ of the conservative trade-union bureaucracies carries the least distance.

Within the service sector of the economy, the fastest-growing employer is government, especially state and local government, which assumes most of the burden of administration of federal programs. This growth reflects the tendency of the modern state to supply not only welfare services and police and military protection, but the infrastructure of capitalist development. Unorganized and exploited by inflation and high taxation, public employees have demonstrated a new labor militancy in the past decade by asserting their right to strike for reasonable wages; witness the massive postal strike of 1970. Education is another example of a government-related field which has experienced labor unrest in the form of teachers' strikes. Another potential arena of labor strife in the public sector is medical care, which has grown very rapidly in the postwar period and has come to employ vast numbers of service, clerical, technical, and professional personnel.

The "knowledge industry," the 30 percent of the economy that has been mentioned before in this essay, is concentrated in the service sector. A rapidly industrializing field which is growing at twice the rate of the remainder of the economy, the knowledge industry employs large numbers of unorganized clerical and technical workers, as well as salaried professionals. In the manufacturing sector, the industries which have large components of research and development and other knowledge factors have also been the major growth industries. Instrumentation, chemical products, and electrical equipment are representative. A common characteristic of science-based manufacturing and the service sector of the knowledge industry is their employment of increasing numbers of educated white-collar workers.

The educational system is critical to the knowledge industry and the service economy. It is a significant component of the knowledge industry, and therefore an important factor in its own right for a radical movement. Even more important, the educational system supplies the knowledge industry with its educated labor force, pre-eminently professional and technical personnel but also managerial cadres and educated clerical workers. By 1975 two thirds of the total labor force in the United States will have a high-school education, compared to under half in the late 1950s. Over 26 percent will have at least one year of college and almost 15 percent will have college degrees, compared to something over 18 percent and 9 percent with similar levels of education in the late 1950s. The high educational level of the American work force indicates the political significance of a radical student movement in the high schools and colleges. A radical movement which develops its full potential within the educational system will simultaneously effect changes in the political consciousness of the young high-school and college students who will later become white-collar workers and salaried professionals. Radical politics in the schools, together with later exploitation in the dynamic sectors of industrial capitalism, establishes some of the necessary preconditions for the emergence of a radical movement among the new working and new middle classes.

Within the new working class in the United States, there have been considerable signs of labor unrest. But it will be very difficult for a radical movement to reach this class. Within the educational system, working-class students are characteristically oriented toward upward social mobility and vocational ends. They resent radicals of higher classes who interfere with their effort to "get an education." Technical and vocational schools, community colleges, and junior colleges are generally commuter schools which lack any educational community or sense of student solidarity. The new working class does not consume high culture and thus is not affected by the radical messages communicated through this high culture. Radicalization of its members depends upon the exposure of the false expectations of upward social mobility that they entertain on the basis of their limited technical training, and upon the revelation of the class bias of the educational system. The regimentation of students in these systems is another issue of radical potential. These factors are reflected in the high incidence of student protest within the very large community colleges.

Working-class students will also be affected by the political climate among white-collar and technical workers generally. Since the white-collar force maintains a middle-class self-image and has dreams of upward mobility, it is notoriously difficult to organize. But there are cultural and generational factors affecting the labor force which offer opportunities for its radicalization. The black labor force is increasing at a rate one third higher than the white, and three times higher in professional and clerical occupations. Many of these Afro-Americans are upwardly mobile and acquire middle-class status in black society in these occupations. But they still suffer from the pervasive racism in the United States.

Another cultural factor is the entry into the white-collar labor force of large numbers of women who are routinely relegated to the least attractive work and are discriminated against in promotion. The female labor force in the 1955–65 period grew at twice the rate of the labor force as a whole, while the rate for *young* women was three times the general rate. From 1965 to 1975, young women in the labor force will have increased twice as fast as the general force and women as a whole will have grown one third faster. In general, the rate of increase of young workers, male and female, is higher than the rate of growth for the labor force as a whole: almost three times as high in the decade ending in 1965 and twice as high in the decade ending in 1975. Youth of all classes have manifested views in the opinion polls which are politically to the left of the older generations. This is a reflection of a historical experience conditioned by the political ferment of the 1960s, rather than by the national integration of the wartime and Cold War years.

The influx of youth may also have a radicalizing effect on the blue-collar industrial class, particularly since younger workers are more likely to have technical skills that qualify them as new working class. The technically skilled blue-collar workers in the science-based growth industries might become the base for labor militancy which will go beyond income issues toward autonomy and meaning in work.[6] It is also of great significance that the black blue-collar labor force is growing at three times the rate of the white force. Blue-collar workers now constitute 30 percent of the black labor force as a whole. In the League of Revolutionary Black Workers in the automobile industry, there is already evidence of militant labor action among blacks.

Because of the Indo-China War, moreover, inflation and taxation have resulted in declines in the real disposable income of various elements of the industrial working class for the first time since before World War II. This development has already had effects on labor militancy, but these trends do not spell an automatic turn to the left. Blue-collar workers might just as well respond to ultra-conservative claims that new social programs are the source of high taxation and the inflation is best controlled through sound fiscal policies, as to a left analysis in terms of military spending and an unprogressive tax structure. For reasons of nationalism, racism, and cul-

[6] See Serge Mallet, *La Nouvelle Classe Ouvrière* (Paris, 1963) for a discussion of this point.

tural orthodoxy, blue-collar workers have no intrinsic love for the left. Finally, a *status quo* trade-union bureaucracy is entrenched within the industrial working class. The reactionary potential of unionized blue-collar workers was demonstrated in the "hard hat" attacks on peace demonstrators in 1970.

Unlike the new working class, the new middle class, particularly in its student embryo, has already been receptive to the influence of the radical movement. It is the support given radicalism by this group, more than the radicalism of alienated intellectuals, upper-class renegades, and the underground, that constitutes the significant political potential of the Movement. Probably the most politically sensitive sector of the population, the liberal-arts students who support the left are highly intelligent, advanced in political awareness, and accustomed to dealing with concepts—thus susceptible to ideological appeals. In their student days they are relatively free-floating, without many inhibiting institutional and personal commitments. There are limits, however, to the success of the radical movement within this group. The main limit is not the division between the humanities and the sciences but that between the generalists and the specialists, the theoretically and technically oriented students, which cuts across the "two cultures." Theoretical scientists and science students are educated to question fundamental rationales and often come to support radicalism. Applied scientists support radical politics less often, while higher technical workers, such as engineers, almost never endorse radicalism. Within the humanities and social sciences, similarly, the technically oriented students are generally immune to radical appeals.

This technical orientation constitutes a barrier to the growth of the student movement and, by extension, to the possibilities for a radical movement among salaried professionals and technical workers generally. Technical orientation is generally accompanied by bureaucratic organization, a result not only of the technical requirements themselves but also of the management controls to which the technical output is subject, and the standardization of product which management encourages. Although the professionals and technicians are relatively willing organization men by habit and training, there are limits to their identification with top management. The concern of progressive management for new organizational forms which maximize the conditions of "autonomy" for its advanced labor force reflects this fact. The inherent character of even the most technical forms of brain work requires an independent intelligence to carry them out. It is not possible to reduce this kind of work to automatic responses and thus to impose an industrial discipline that propagates stupefaction and docility. Efficiency itself requires a transcending consciousness among the brain workers.

This situation creates a political problem for management, since the effort to maintain managerial controls may conflict with the requirements for mental work as the technicians see it. We have seen how Defense management solves this problem for its basic and applied research in universities by creating semi-autonomous research institutes which allow the R&D workers to escape the standard impositions on employees within the governmental bureaucracy. But the increasing inputs of educated labor required for modern production preclude similarly privileged arrangements for millions of mental workers. Such a procedure would not be cost-efficient or profitable. Educated labor means alienated labor. Impatient though they are with general theory or political argument, the technicians will be forced to consider the causes for declining autonomy and increasing regimentation in their work. They will be forced to consider the effects on technical rationality of management decisions based on profitability. The political organization of the economy will forcibly limit the horizons of their work. Thus it happens in the United States that a Pentagon cost-analyst can discover a $2 billion cost overrun on a transport-plane contract, and be fired; that an air controller in the Midwest who criticizes an inefficient system of air-traffic control will be removed; that space scientists who want a space exploration program oriented to scientific discovery will be forced out.

Scientists have already begun to exhibit a new political consciousness. The major examples have been the massive lobby against the deployment of the anti-ballistic missile organized by the Scientists and Engineers for Social and Political Action and the "research stoppage" of March 4, 1969, against the Vietnam War and the militarization of science led by the Science Action Coordinating Committee of MIT.

The acquiescence of the salaried professionals will also depend on high remuneration and opportunities for upward mobility. It is also true that higher management in government and industry has come to recruit more of its number from its professional and technical cadres since science, technology, and specialized knowledge occupy an increasingly important role in its operations. In the higher circles of power there are many "new men" from the scientific and professional cadres. In this limited sense, the scientists, engineers, and salaried professionals have been a rising stratum. "Technocracy" is typically an ideology of a rising group in laying claim to ultimate power.

It is not, however, *as* scientists and professionals that these new men exercise power, but as managers and politicians in the fields of knowledge and technology. Although they also fulfill important staff functions in research and planning for the decision-makers, these roles confer an ethereal "influence" on the technical advisors which tends to filter out through the decision-makers' selection of advisors of congenial viewpoint. It is highly doubtful that these advisors determine management decisions beyond structuring them within rational limits. Although the salaried technocrats place great faith in the schema of co-management and new forms of managerial autonomy, there is not much possibility of these panning out within the corporate and governmental bureaucracies. The actual trend is to centralize policy decision while decentralizing administration and, with it, the illusion of control. Collectively, this group is not winning new authority. And as the class continues to expand, this fact will become more evident. With the expansion of the class, the prospects for individual solutions will also decline and the necessity for collective power increase. As a system of illusion, technocratic ideology will remain important in obstructing these realizations with fantasies of power.

The expansion of the new middle class will also pose material questions of status and income. These will be matters of "relative deprivation," since salaried professional status generally confers economic benefits above the national median. The problem for the authorities consists in maintaining the relative economic and social status of professionals and technical personnel while the class increases rapidly as a percentage of the labor force. Since the percentage of professional and technical workers is not increasing within the occupational structure at the expense of "managers, officials, and proprietors" but at the expense of working-class categories, this accommodation would seem to require a redistribution of income. There has been no significant trend in the redistribution of income since World War II. While the status of this class depends upon its educational credentials, the correlations between education and income, and education and social mobility, though definitely positive, have likewise not improved in the postwar era.

II. TECHNOCRACY AND THE INTELLECTUALS

The bureaucratization of the brain workers distinguishes them from an ideologically oriented intelligentsia. They are not free-floating intellectuals who are structurally irresponsible toward the social order and interested in ideological systems for their own sake. At the same time, however, they constitute a growing *public* for the intellectuals. The expansion of the class of bureaucratic professionals and technical experts does not signify the decline of the intellectuals, supposedly driven out of business by specialists. The intellectuals, relatively few in number in any age, are essentially independent craftsmen who produce for a market; it is the state of the market, not bureaucratic trends, which determines their destiny as a group. The market for higher culture and ideas has been increasing, by the evidence of the sales of quality paperbacks, the circulation of quality magazines, the audience for avant-garde movies, the prosperity of the underground, the patronage of art museums and culture centers, and the sales of records, art prints, and Victorian pornography. A typically modern figure like Norman Mailer has to be seen as an intellectual entrepreneur skilled in the arts of self-promotion, public relations, and sales strategy. Since the bureaucratic experts confine themselves to manageable problems, technical dilemmas, and policy questions, the market for values, meanings, and systematic theory remains open to the traditional figure of the intellectual.[7] These matters are his "specialty."

The "technocrats"—the true believers in technology—are not necessarily specialists; they are themselves often intellectuals who from their staging areas in the academic bureaucracies make forays into the larger marketplace of ideas. They have developed a characteristic sales formula in which a "hard-nosed" realism bordering on reaction is combined with sudden displays of reformist zeal. Both of these tactics are shocking and contribute to notoriety and sales. The postwar success of the technocratic intellectuals is related to the rise of the professional and technical workers and the self-image entertained by that class. The technocratic intellectuals have filled a potentially dangerous ideological vacuum, since the "experts" are necessarily preoccupied in their serious work

[7] See "The Sociology of the Intellectual," Section 2 of Chapter XIII in Joseph Schumpeter, *Capitalism, Socialism, and Democracy* (New York, 1962), pp. 145–55.

with logistical matters that make dull reading for the lay audience. The market supremacy of the technocratic intellectuals is now threatened by the increasing discontinuity between the future they predict for technocrats and the banal reality, illustrated by the glut on the market of academic Ph.D.'s. The "action intellectuals" have been challenged in the 1960s by re-emergent left-wing intellectuals for shares of the market and the ideological leadership of the new middle class. This left-wing and literary intelligentsia has been immeasurably strengthened by the political disasters suffered by the American establishment, while they have also generated considerable momentum by virtue of their better literary style, their concern with "culture" and "values," and their breezier treatment of the "whither America?" questions.

This competition between the technocrats and the intellectuals is ultimately a deadly serious business, indicators of which are their theoretical postulation of each other's liquidation as a stratum and their infighting in the public prints, intellectual communities, and academic bureaucracies. The technocratic viewpoint prevails in the academic, governmental, and corporate bureaucracies. This is not surprising, since the ideology serves to integrate the technical workers into the operation and provides an elaborate rationalization of bureaucratic functioning. While this technocratic domination of the bureaucracies is remarkably complete, the paradox is that those bureaucracies which require large numbers of brain workers tend to generate oppositional communities. While the academic bureaucracies are managed by neutral experts, university communities are congenial environments for radical ideology. While governmental bureaucracies are invincibly conservative, the local communities they generate in capital cities are fairly liberal in viewpoint. This phenomenon is related to the habits of consumption in culture and ideas among the highly educated class; it is also a result of the influence of democratic liberalism and the left.

Organized by the market mechanisms and distributive outlets of culture, a community grows up that is vaguely hostile to the bureaucracy, even though depending on it for existence. While the industrialization of culture serves in its popular forms as a primary instrument of mass stupefaction and control, it paradoxically has a subversive effect on the highly educated consumers of high-brow and middle-brow culture. This comes of the anti-bourgeois tradition of modern culture and the influence that left intellectuals and cultural producers wield in the cultural markets. Radical culture and politics are packaged and disseminated for profit by media and culture corporations; the conservative economist Joseph Schumpeter observed of the intellectuals and the cultural markets that "unlike any other society, capitalism inevitably and by virtue of the very logic of its civilization creates, educates, and subsidizes a vested interest in social un-rest." [8] This is the basis for the conservatives' hatred for the "liberal media." But this leftist subversion of culture results from a larger fact: a cultural vacuum in capitalist society that alienates cultural producers but requires *in extremis* these same anti-capitalist artists to fill the void.

Even the techno-bureaucrats who practice their "discipline" in an orthodox manner may acquire sympathies for subversive causes. The bureaucracy that maintains matchless command-and-control internally may find itself suspended over an abyss of illegitimacy and indifference. While it may count upon the dutiful performance of its specialized functionaries, the bureaucracy may be unable to extract a commitment and loyalty to the rationale of the whole operation. In the case of the university rebellions, and pre-eminently of the May Rebellion in France, there has been a remarkably sudden and complete, though temporary, collapse of the legitimacy of the central bureaucracies. There is a certain analogy between the May Rebellion—and, on a smaller scale, student rebellions—and the revolution of 1848, the "revolution of the intellectuals," which was international in scope and

[8] Schumpeter, p. 146.

temporarily victorious. (In 1848, the old regime collapsed before the advance of the middle class and the working class until it was able to mobilize the peasant masses outside the cities and to deploy the army that was still loyal to the declining aristocracy.)

The signal weakness of the socialist movements of the past was the lack of a class which was actually capable of assimilating socialist ideals and of sustaining a movement based on those principles, while also possessing the technical means of implementing the alternative system. This lack was compensated for by centralized parties controlled by renegade intellectuals or trade-union bureaucrats. Although the professional and technical cadres do not as yet constitute a social class in the traditional sense but rather a component of the middle class, they supply a crucial factor for a socialist democracy: technical competence on a mass basis. The democratization of the social order is a plausible undertaking only on this basis. This stratum could mount a radical challenge only in a general alliance of the new working class, the oppressed minorities, and such progressive elements of the blue-collar working class as may appear.

There is not the slightest possibility of the left organizing these social forces without a systematic alternative vision which first identifies these progressive social forces in its analysis and then appeals to them in its social content. From the analysis of these forces so far, it follows that a new socialist movement must develop popular democratic forms and formulate democratic models for society if it is to organize the new technical, scientific, and professional stratum that is not only capable of implementing these forms but will demand them as a condition of its allegiance. Secondly, a socialist movement cannot afford romantic nostalgia about the radical struggles of the remembered past, but must identify and organize the new sectors of human enterprise which are being subjected to capitalist industrialization. Among these fields are education, science, medicine, and culture. In culture, for instance, this process involves the organization of culture markets, the formation of cultural corporations, the dominance of large capital, movements of consolidation and merger, the replacement of craftsmen by teams of assembly, the standardization of product, the development of elaborate distribution systems, the substitution of technology for human labor, and the subordination of the whole to the criterion of return on investment.[9] Accordingly, the fields of education, culture, and science are serious arenas of political action. "The de-specialization, generalization, and autonomous management of higher education, the de-commercialization of the media and of culture, the de-centralization and multiplication of centers of democratic decision making, the enlargement of local, provincial, and regional autonomies, the multiplication of self-managed cultural centers and installations," the French social analyst Andre Gorz has commented, "are all fundamental demands from now on." [10]

Thirdly, the socialist left must develop counter-models of social organization and resource allocation as essential instruments of political strategy. It is only through the production of counter-models of institutional organization, social planning, national resource allocation, and ultimately through the elaboration of a "global alternative" that the left will be able to escape programming by the logic of an alien system. It is only through the detailed articulation of such counter-models that the left will be able to refute the multiple rationales for official policy at every level, and, more important, to develop a concrete relevance and appeal to the specific worlds of white-collar workers and the new working class. This articulation must begin with the analysis of contemporary class structure and its deformative effects on distributive justice, "equal

---

[9] See Norman Birnbaum's discussion of the industrialization of culture in The Crisis of Industrial Society (New York, 1969); see also "The Bureaucratic Ethos," Chapter 5 in C. Wright Mills, The Sociological Imagination, for a discussion of the bureaucratization of thought in the social sciences.

[10] Andre Gorz, Strategy for Labor (Boston, 1967), p. 131.

opportunity," and the wage structure. It must also speak to the conditions of alienation in labor and the necessity for meaningful and autonomous work if it is to reach the new working classes.

This project means the articulation of a vision of libertarian socialism. Behind it, this project has the historical wreckage of two alternative socialisms in the industrialized world. The first is social democracy, which through the pursuit of socialism by parliamentary means was eventually absorbed as an integrating mechanism into the systems of capitalist democracy in England and Germany. The second is Bolshevism, which has inspired socialist movements in advanced industrial countries with overcentralized strategies suitable to the non-developed world. The failure of social democracy in World War I and the Stalinization of Soviet Communism between the wars created a political impasse on the left after World War II.

In the 1960s, there was an opening to the left. The May Rebellion in France threw into question a historical generalization that had become a metaphysical axiom: that no revolution was possible in a fully industrialized country. The general strikes in Italy in 1969–70 confirmed the impression that a new era of mass action had opened in the West. In Eastern Europe, the evolution of socialism in Yugoslavia and in Czechoslovakia before the 1968 Soviet invasion indicated avenues out of the apparent impasses of socialist planning: bureaucratization, authoritarianism, and the evisceration of political liberties. Implementing new socialist forms after its break with Stalin, the "socialist democracy" in Yugoslavia established "workers' councils" in authority over factories and pointed the way to a democratization of the industrial economy. The powers of the central planning bureaucracy were circumscribed and also subjected to group determination of social priorities. A theory and practice of "market socialism" opened new possibilities for practical limitations on the powers of the state and for the debureaucratization of the society. The country began to articulate a dependable body of law and due-process protection of individual liberty. Although these progressive measures were all implemented within a context of party controls and reform from above, they also were effected within a relatively underdeveloped country industrializing at a rapid rate. When Czechoslovakia, a fully industrialized country, attempted to follow the Titoist suit in 1968, it was invaded by a Soviet Union sensitive to the dangers of "revisionism," capitalist or otherwise, and to its strategic posture in Eastern Europe.

The prospects for a socialist movement in the United States are not assured or even necessarily promising. Ultimately, they will not be determined by anyone's "objective conditions" or by the march of the historical forces celebrated by official liberalism: capitalism, industrialization, science, nationalism, and the militant state. Some of these forces have opened up the possibility of such a movement, but they cannot guarantee it. In practice, the fate of the left movement in the United States will probably be determined by a political choice. If it follows the Leninist route, the left will construct a political apparatus irrelevant to the level of social and economic development in the country and thus to the consciousness of the social forces it must organize; it will be forced into unequal and premature battle with the state on the state's own terrain—internal security and organized violence; it will project a social model unrelated to the condition of society and incapable of realization by a militarized movement. The ultra left in the United States has had no relevant social analysis, and therefore has been unable to become a social movement. Instead, it has been a protest movement specializing in mass demonstrations, of varying levels of militancy, around national politics, the Vietnam War, conscription, and political repression.

The black left may change this situation. Although it has wandered far afield to import socialist ideologies, the black left has a more relevant alternative in its own tradition: Pan

Africanism. If it takes the Pan African way, the black left may perform the service of modernizing the white left, which could learn from the theory of African Socialism and positive action. Otherwise, the prospects for a new left depend upon the educational value of political failures and upon the example of labor militancy among white-collar employees and salaried professionals.

Pre-eminently, the left can learn from the dynamics of student rebellion. As the producer of educated labor and the base of students and intellectuals, the schools will be the cockpit of any new left movement. The center of a left movement must be prepared to suffer the characteristic methods of the world's leading *status quo* power. "If it's going to take a bloodbath," Ronald Reagan said in 1970 of containing the student movement, "let's get it over with." The bloodbath has already arrived: the "Orangeburg Massacre" of three South Carolina State students in 1968, the killing of Berkeley and North Carolina A&T students in 1969, the fatal shooting of four Kent State and two Jackson State students in 1970. And it is not over.

INDEX

Regents, *see* California, University
of—Board of Regents at;
Trustees
Research and development
(R&D), 147–165, 283
background of, 147–158
economic imperialism and,
187–188
extensive federal support for,
152–158
demonstrations at Stanford
against, 48
demonstrations at Wisconsin
against, 61
findings of American Council of
Education on, 100
liberal arts and, 161
separation of university and,
26, 163–165
Reserve Officer Training Corps
(ROTC), 28, 40
arson following Cambodia invasion, 91, 258–259
as source of officer cadres, 160–
161
Howard abolition of, 233
Resistance, The, 13
"Revolution and Counter-Revolution (But Not Necessarily
About Columbia)" (Brze-
zinski), 82
Revolutionary nationalism
ideology of, 252
Pan Africanism and, 256–257
SNCC and, 225
Revolutionary Youth Movement
(RYM II), 13
Ridgeway, James, 125
Riesman, David
on authoritarian atmosphere in
black higher education,
215, 216–217
on the inequality of education
opportunity, 178–179, 186
Riverside Research Institute, 162
Rochester (New York), 222
Rockefeller, David, 174
Rockefeller, John D., 203, 208
Rockefeller, Nelson A., 6, 62
Rosenwald, Julius, 204, 208
Rosenwald Fund, 204
Rossi, Peter H., 175

Rostow, W. W., 80
ROTC, *see* Reserve Officer Train-
ing Corps
Rourke, Francis E., 128, 132, 136
Rudd, Mark, 7, 14
Ruml, Beardsley, 135
Rural commune movement, 102
Rustin, Bayard, 246

St. Augustine College, 200
San Fernando Valley State Col-
lege, 243
San Francisco Labor Council of
the AFL-CIO, 25, 243
San Francisco State College strike
(1968–69)
AFT and, 43
California state authority and,
31
Hayakawa and, 5
history of, 241–243
outcome of, 243–244
use of court injunction at, 27
San Jose State College, 47, 243
San Mateo, College of, 243
Santa Barbara, University of Cali-
fornia at, 93, 261
SAS, *see* Students Afro-American
Society
Savio, Mario, 65–66
Scalapino, Robert A., 66
Science Action Coordinating
Committee (MIT), 284
Science, the Endless Frontier
(Bush), 147
"Scientific management," 113,
127
Scientists and Engineers for So-
cial and Political Action,
234
Schumpeter, Joseph, 288
SCLC, *see* Southern Christian
Leadership Conference
Scott, Joseph, 97
Scott, Robert, 238
SDS, *see* Students for a Demo-
cratic Society
Seamans, Robert C., 165
Section 112, *see* Housing Act
(1959)
SEEK, 240

MICHAEL W. MILES

*Michael W. Miles teaches history and political
science at Goddard College and lives with his
wife in Vermont. Born in Portsmouth, Virginia,
in 1945, he received an A.B. from Princeton
University and is on leave of absence from the
graduate department of history of the University
of California at Berkeley. He has taught at
Tennessee State University and contributes to*
The New Republic *and other publications.*
The Radical Probe *is his first book.*